THEORY AND PRACTICE OF COMPUTATION

PROCEEDINGS OF THE 8TH WORKSHOP ON COMPUTATION: THEORY AND PRACTICE (WCTP 2018), MANILA, THE PHILIPPINES, SEPTEMBER 17–18, 2018

Theory and Practice of Computation

Editors

Shin-ya Nishizaki
Department of Computer Science, Tokyo Institute of Technology, Ookayama, Meguro, Tokyo, Japan

Masayuki Numao
ISIR, Osaka University, Ibaraki, Osaka, Japan

Jaime Caro
Department of Computer Science, University of the Philippines – Diliman, Quezon City, Philippines

Merlin Teodosia Suarez
De La Salle University, Manila, Philippines

CRC Press
Taylor & Francis Group
Boca Raton London New York

CRC Press is an imprint of the
Taylor & Francis Group, an **informa** business

A BALKEMA BOOK

CRC Press
Taylor & Francis Group
6000 Broken Sound Parkway NW, Suite 300
Boca Raton, FL 33487-2742

First issued in paperback 2020

© 2019 by Taylor & Francis Group, LLC
CRC Press is an imprint of Taylor & Francis Group, an Informa business

No claim to original U.S. Government works

ISBN-13: 978-0-367-20417-4 (hbk)
ISBN-13: 978-0-367-77663-3 (pbk)

Visit the Taylor & Francis Web site at
http://www.taylorandfrancis.com

and the CRC Press Web site at
http://www.crcpress.com

Theory and Practice of Computation – Nishizaki et al. (eds)
© 2019 Taylor & Francis Group, London, ISBN 978-0-367-20417-4

Table of contents

Theory and Practice of Computation – Nishizaki et al. (eds)
© 2019 Taylor & Francis Group, London, ISBN 978-0-367-20417-4

Preface

Modern research studies on computation started in the 1930s with the study of computability. At around the same time, computers were developed. In computer science, harmony of theory and practice have been considered important. Researchers in the field should establish a theory to address real world issues. On the other hand, experimentation and simulation are thought to be a trigger for improvement of theories.

WCTP 2018 is the eighth workshop organized by the Tokyo Institute of Technology, The Institute of Scientific and Industrial Research – Osaka University, University of the Philippines – Diliman and De La Salle University-Manila that is devoted to theoretical and practical approaches to computation.

It aims to present the latest developments by computer science researchers in academe and industry working to address computational problems that can directly impact the way we live in society.

Following the success of WCTP 2011–2017, WCTP 2018 was held in University of the Philippines Bonifacio Global City, on September 17 and 18, 2018. This post-proceedings is the collection of the selected papers that were presented at WCTP 2018.

The program of WCTP 2018 consisted of selected research contributions. It included the most recent visions and researches of 5 talks in work-in-progress session and 21 contributions. We collected the original contributions after their presentation at the workshop and began a review procedure that resulted in the selection of the papers in this volume. They appear here in the final form.

April, 2019

Shin-ya Nishizaki
Masayuki Numao
Jaime Caro
Merlin Teodosia Suarez

Theory and Practice of Computation – Nishizaki et al. (eds)
© 2019 Taylor & Francis Group, London, ISBN 978-0-367-20417-4

Scientific committee

Jaime Caro (University of the Philippines – Diliman)
Rommel Feria (University of the Philippines – Diliman)
Henry Adorna (University of the Philippines – Diliman)

John Paul Vergara (Ateneo de Manila University)
Mercedes Rodrigo (Ateneo de Manila University)

Allan A. Sioson (Cobena)

Merlin Suarez (De La Salle University – Manila)
Raymund Sison (De La Salle University – Manila)
Jocelynn Cu (De La Salle University – Manila)
Gregory Cu (De La Salle University – Manila)
Rhia Trogo (De La Salle University – Manila)
Judith Azcarraga (De La Salle University – Manila)
Ethel Ong (De La Salle University – Manila)
Charibeth Cheng (De La Salle University – Manila)
Nelson Marcos (De La Salle University – Manila)
Rafael Cabredo (De La Salle University – Manila)
Joel Ilao (De La Salle University – Manila)

Koichi Moriyama (Nagoya Institute of Technology)

Masayuki Numao (Osaka University)
Ken-ichi Fukui (Osaka University)

Satoshi Kurihara (University Electro-Communications)
Mitsuharau Yamamoto (Chiba University)
Hiroyuki Tominaga (Kagawa Univeristy)

Shin-ya Nishizaki (Tokyo Insitute of Technology)
Takuo Watanabe (Tokyo Institute of Technology)
Masaya Shimakawa (Tokyo Institute of Technology)
Shigeki Hagihara (Tohoku University of Community Service and Science)

Theory and Practice of Computation – Nishizaki et al. (eds)
© 2019 Taylor & Francis Group, London, ISBN 978-0-367-20417-4

Organizing committee

Jaime Caro (University of the Philippines – Diliman)
Rommel Feria (University of the Philippines – Diliman)
Henry Adorna (University of the Philippines – Diliman)

Theory and Practice of Computation – Nishizaki et al. (eds)
© 2019 Taylor & Francis Group, London, ISBN 978-0-367-20417-4

Biographies

Shin-ya Nishizaki is Full Professor at the Global Scientific Information and Computing Center, Tokyo Institute of Technology and Associate Professor, Department of Computer Science, Graduate School of Information Science and Engineering, Tokyo Institute of Technology, Japan. He received a Ph.D. in 1994 from Kyoto University for a thesis entitled "Simply Typed Lambda Calculus with First-class Environments".

Masayuki Numao is professor at the Information and Physical Sciences, Graduate School of Information Science and Technology, Osaka University. He is performing research on the development of computers provided with learning capability and has supported the completion of information environment by sending to the world numerous new technologies, such as high-efficient algorithms, background knowledge acquirement for learning, applications intended for intelligent tutoring systems (ITS).

Merlin Teodosia Suarez is professor at the College of Computer Studies, Software Technology at De La Salle University, where she also earned her PhD in Computer Science in 2008. She worked on automatic analysis of student misconceptions learning object-oriented programming in Java. She proceeded to work on emotion-aware systems focusing on education and health-care applications. She is currently investigating approaches to provide support to individuals diagnosed in the autism spectrum disorder, and stroke patients requiring physical therapy.

Jaime Caro is Professor of Computer Science at the University of the Philippines Diliman and heads its Service Science and Software Engineering Laboratory. Dr. Caro was Assistant Vice President for Development of the University of the Philippines for 14 years. Dr Caro's past positions include President of the of the Computing Society of the Philippines (CSP), President of the Philippine Society of Information Technology Educators (PSITE), Vice President of the Game Developers Association of the Philippines (GDAP), Vice President of the Mathematical Society of the Philippines and Chairman of the CHED Philippines Technical Panel on Information Technology Education. Dr. Caro received the Doctor of Philosophy in Mathematics degree from the University of the Philippines Diliman in 1996. His research interests include Information Systems, Combinatorial Optimization, and Algorithms. Application areas of researches are in Education, Medical Informatics, and Climate Modeling.

Theory and Practice of Computation – Nishizaki et al. (eds)
© 2019 Taylor & Francis Group, London, ISBN 978-0-367-20417-4

An investigation of carefulness among students using an educational game for Physics

M.P. Banawan
Ateneo de Davao University, Davao City, Philippines

M.M.T. Rodrigo
Ateneo de Manila University, Quezon City, Philippines

ABSTRACT: This work is an investigation of the implications of outliers in a student carefulness model. The authors built and empirically validated a model of carefulness among students using the gameplay logs of an educational game for Physics. In their prior work, carefulness was found to exist but there was no relationship found between carefulness and post-test learning gain. In this work, cluster-based outlier analysis is used and found that clusters of outliers existed in the dataset. After qualitative inspection of the clusters formed, we found that outliers existed and some even formed a cluster of outliers. We also found that the learning gains of the outliers and non-outliers were statistically different and the degrees of carefulness between the clusters that existed in the more careful group were also significantly different, i.e. carefulness existed in varying degrees and levels. With the findings of this work, outlier detection and removal resulted to a more robust carefulness model that had significant relationships to learning gain. We recommend that appropriate meta-cognitive interventions and scaffolding in educational software be designed such that students will be more careful and gain more learning.

1   INTRODUCTION

1.1   *Carefulness, defined*

Carefulness is a construct that has been researched in the fields of education and social science as it is deemed to be an important facet in learning. Carefulness means giving cautious attention, being thorough and painstaking in action (Morris 1969). Generally, when a student is more careful, then that student is less likely to commit trivial errors and mistakes. Careful students have been seen to possess more self-discipline than students who are not as careful (Gong et al. 2009) and self-discipline has been found to be a determinant of academic performance (Duckworth & Seligman 2005). When a student is not careful, thereby commits careless mistakes, it can lead to the student's poor academic performance (Duckworth & Seligman 2005; Kirby, Winston & Santieste-ban 2005; Rodriquez-Fornells &Maydeu-Olivares 2000). Social science and education researchers have extensive studies on carefulness. These research have linked carefulness to improved problem-solving skills and higher-order thinking (Whimbey 1980). Carefulness is described as a key to help students become better problem solvers, such that tasks like re-reading the problem carefully or cautiously will result to a better understanding of the problem and help the student proceed correctly (Whimbey & Lochhead 1991).

1.2   *Physics playground*

Physics Playground is a two-dimensional educational game developed to help students to understand qualitative or Newtonian Physics (Shute, Ventura & Kim 2013). The game requires the player to

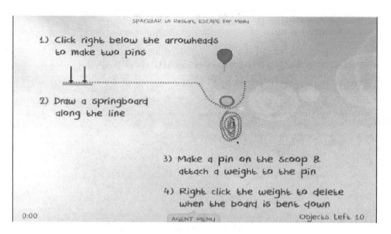

Figure 1.   Screenshot of physics playground (ramp level).

draw the agents: ramp, pendulum, lever or springboard. Physics Playground has been the test bed of a number of prior work that investigates a number of different constructs like student affect, behavior, learning, persistence, wheel-spinning, etc. Physics Playground has adopted the concept of "stealth assessment", i.e. it does not rely on overt tests to approximate student knowledge or interest but instead relies on records of student behavior within the system in a manner that is invisible to the students (Moore & Shute 2016).

1.3   Student carefulness in physics playground

The developers of Physics Playground developed a model of the different competencies that the game measures, i.e. conscientiousness, creativity and the conceptual understanding of Newtonian Physics (Shute, Ventura & Kim 2013). These competencies were mapped to cognitive constructs and their in-game indicators. One such construct is carefulness. According to Physics Playground developers, the following actions of the student while playing the game are indicative of carefulness:

1. number of object limits reached in a problem,
2. average number of objects drawn per level,
3. average time spent drawing per object,
4. average time between actions,
5. average time before making an action on the first attempt

We expanded the carefulness indicators of Physics Playground to include other indicators of carefulness as reflected in social science research and prior work. These indicators are mastery, novelty and creativity. We mapped in-game indicators to these social science constructs and created additional handcrafted/derived features. In our prior work and empirical validation using Philippine sample sets, we found that carefulness exist and can be robustly predicted using the expanded set of indicators. Upon further investigation, we found that the carefulness model did not have any relationship to the post-test learning gains of the students (Banawan, Rodrigo & Andres 2017a; 2017b).

1.4   Research objectives

In this study, we would like to investigate the carefulness model within Physics Playground and consider the possibility that outliers may exist in the dataset. We would like to take a closer look at the characteristics of natural groupings within the dataset and determine any relationship that may exist between carefulness and learning gain within these groupings. We would also like to further understand the characteristics between the more careful students and the less careful students.

2 METHODS

2.1 *Physics playground carefulness in-game indicators*

As, previously mentioned, the developers of Physics Playground identified predictors of carefulness. These features, along with the social science predictors, are defined in this section.

2.1.1 *Object limits*
The number of object limits reached in a problem, also known as object limits, was imposed by the game developers to curtail the students' behavior of "gaming the system". As some students draw unnecessarily many objects that stack one above the other to achieve a solution without using any of the appropriate Physics concepts, the game developers imposed an object limit when a student draws more than ten (10) objects in solving a problem.

2.1.2 *Objects drawn*
The average number of objects drawn per level is the total number of objects drawn relative to the number of attempts.

2.1.3 *Time spent drawing*
The time spent drawing is the average time in seconds spent drawing per level or the average time in seconds spent for events like draw pin, draw rope, draw freeform and other draw event.

2.1.4 *Time between actions*
The average time in seconds between actions is the time difference between the start time of the current event and the end time of the preceding event.

2.1.5 *Time 1st attempt*
The time 1st attempt is the average time in seconds before making an action on the first attempt. This feature refers to the elapsed time from Level Start to the first event.

2.1.6 *Gold badges*
In Physics Playground, a gold badge is earned if the student draws three (or less) objects in coming up with a solution to the problem and eventually solved the problem. This feature is indicative of the mastery of the student.

2.1.7 *Silver badges*
Another feature that is indicative of the student's mastery is the number of silver badges earned. A silver badge is earned if the student draws more than three objects in successfully solving the problem.

2.1.8 *Timediff*
The timediff is the average difference between the time spent on problems and the median time. After inspecting the time-based features of Shute, et al. (2013), it has been observed that the time spent on solving the problem should also be relative to the overall time-based performance on a specific problem – the median time for the problem. The time difference is computed to see if an attempt took longer or lesser than the median time for a specific problem. A high timediff value means that the student is slower than other students and a low timediff value means that the student is faster than the other students for the specific problem. Also, a high timediff value is indicative of less mastery than a lower timediff value.

2.1.9 *Unique solutions*

Since PP is an open-ended learning environment, a student may solve the problems in any order and in any number of times that the student wants. In trying to capture the unique attempts, problems answered for the first time are noted. Also, unique solutions for reattempted problems are counted. For example, using a springboard solution in the next attempt when a pendulum solution was used in a prior attempt. Unique solutions refer to two cases, (1) unique problems attempted and (2) unique solutions used for reattempts. This feature is indicative of the student's creativity and/or novelty.

The nine (9) features presented in this section comprise the full feature set used in this study and in Banawan, Rodrigo & Andres (2017a; 2017b).

2.2 *Data preprocessing*

The dataset used in this study is derived from primary data collected during a deployment in three locations in the Philippines. Physics Playground fine-grained action logs were cleaned, annotated (via consensus by Physics experts/teachers) and aggregated to result to 176 student instances comprising this study's dataset. During the annotation phase, the experts coded an attempt as careful or not using the replay files of actual gameplay. This aggregated dataset was normalized to rescale the attribute values using the statistical normalization $z = (X - \mu)/s$, where the attribute values represented as vector X is subtracted by the mean of the attribute values (represented by μ) then divided by the standard deviation, s.

2.3 *Cluster-based local outlier factor (LOF) outlier detection*

In the field of data mining, outliers are usually removed as they distort the resulting model. Not handling outliers skews the model such that the mean and covariance estimates of the observations do not reflect actual behavior of the data, hence, the need to detect and remove outliers. Outlier detection has been used to find anomalies in datasets to better understand the deviation of observation points to the central tendencies or behavior exhibited by the entire sample. It involves finding patterns like anomalies, discordant observations, faults, defects, or peculiarities in the data that do not conform to expected behavior (Chandola, Banerjee & Kumar, 2009). Other work in outlier detection involves the use of standard deviation as the method to determine if a certain point is an outlier. A set threshold is identified as the criteria, for example – if a certain observation point is three (3) standard deviations from the mean then that point is considered as an outlier. As outliers affect the standard deviation and the mean, the method of using standard deviations to detect outliers may be problematic. Hence, a number of outlier detection work used clustering to detect outliers (Elahi, et al. 2008; Pamula, Deka & Nandi 2011). In Educational Data Mining (EDM), outlier analysis resulted to an understanding of students' behavior and detect students with learning problems (Romero & Ventura 2007). Outlier analysis was used to examine the factors that affect student achievement particularly in over and under-performing schools in the US. Clustering analysis in educational data mining answers research questions pertinent to understanding learners' behavior during their use of educational software or intelligent tutoring systems (Baker & Yacef 2009). In general, it is used to discover natural groupings of data with the goal of achieving homogeneity. For this paper, we used X-means clustering (Pelleg & Moore 2000) as we wanted the algorithm to discover the optimal number of clusters that are naturally formed in the data (Jain 2010). The detection of outliers used the local outlier factors (LOF) where the local density of an object is compared to the local densities of its neighbors (Breunig, et al. 2000). Outliers are the points that have lower density than the densities of their neighboring points.

3 RESULTS AND DISCUSSION

3.1 *Natural groupings between outliers and non-outliers*

Three well-separated clusters were formed after the X-means clustering algorithm was used. Clusters 0, 1 and 2 are presented in Table 1. Cluster 0 had 60 students. Cluster 1 had 3 students. Cluster

Table 1.   Three groups formed after X-means clustering.

	Cluster 0	Cluster 1	Cluster 2
Non-outliers	56	0	105
Outliers	4	3	8
Total	**60**	**3**	**113**

Table 2.   Cluster centroids of non-outlying clusters.

	Cluster 0	Cluster 2
Object Limits	4.83	4.61
Objects Drawn	23.45	32.82
TimeSpentDrawing	3,928.07 sec	5,483.05 sec
TimeBetweenActions	144,520.00 sec	215,882.86 sec
Time1stAttempt	17,873.08 sec	18,778.14 sec
Gold Badges	7.27	5.52
Silver Badges	20.54	15.25
TimeDiff	−12,571.57 sec	64,735.32 sec
Unique Attempts	37.16	24.25
Carefulness Label	2.51	2.36

Table 3.   Cluster centroids of outlying clusters.

	Cluster 0	Cluster 2	Cluster 1
Object Limits	4.00	16.50	46
Objects Drawn	36.25	19.71	75.06
TimeSpentDrawing	5,866.36 sec	2,841.79 sec	10,463.56 sec
TimeBetweenActions	328,000.53 sec	111,316.41 sec	234,177.16 sec
Time1stAttempt	30,247.59 sec	18,654.50 sec	18,248.95 sec
Gold Badges	2.05	7.75	7.67
Silver Badges	11.00	23.25	13.00
TimeDiff	169,533.81 sec	−51,479.06 sec	87,704.57 sec
Unique Attempts	16.50	62.63	26.67
Carefulness Label	2.13	2.32	2.18

3 had 113 students. After forming the clusters, LOF was used in the computation of outlier scores of each student where outliers were separated from the non-outliers. Outliers were found from the three clusters. It is notable that cluster 1 had all points or cluster members computed as outliers, making cluster 1 an outlying cluster. The non-outliers were found only from two clusters, i.e. Cluster 0 and Cluster 2. Tables 2 and 3 present the mean values of the features per cluster for each of the two groups, i.e. outlying and non-outlying groups. Table 4 shows the mean carefulness of the outlying and non-outlying groups, revealing that the outliers tend to be less careful than the non-outliers. Cluster 0 had 56 students in the non-outlier group and 4 students in the outlier group. These students had few Object Limits reached which implies that they were able to solve problems by drawing only the optimal number of objects, attempted fewer problems, were relatively slower than the rest of the students. Cluster 1 had all 3 students in the outlier group. These students had the most number of Object Limits reached, i.e. they have drawn more than the optimal number of objects required for the solution. They also spent a relatively longer time in solving the problems but eventually were able to solve them, Cluster 2 had 105 non-outliers and 8 outliers. This is the

Table 4. Mean values of carefulness in the outlying and non-outlying clusters.

	Carefulness
Non-outliers	2.46
Outliers	2.24

biggest cluster formed. Cluster 2 students were the most careful students based on their mean carefulness value. They worked on the problems faster than the other two clusters and solved the most number of problems. The mean values of carefulness for the two groups, i.e. outliers and non-outliers, reveal that the non-outliers have a relatively higher mean value of carefulness than the mean value of carefulness for the outliers. We, therefore, characterize the non-outlying group as the more careful group. We, also, characterize the outlying group as the less careful group. A closer look at the non-outlier group or the more careful group (table 2) reveal two clusters, cluster 0 and cluster 2. Cluster 0 mean values describe the group of students who have fewer objects drawn in solving the levels, spent fewer time in drawing the objects and between actions. They also have more gold and silver badges, are faster than the other students (as evidenced by the timediff mean value), and have tried more unique problems (or have fewer retries of attempts of the same problem). They also have a slightly higher carefulness mean value. Given these mean values we characterize Cluster 0 of the non-outliers (or more careful group) as those who have more mastery as evidenced by the badges earned, time spent on the problems and the re-attempts. Conversely, Cluster 2 of the non-outliers, while also careful, did not exhibit the same level of mastery as those of the careful students in Cluster 0. Probing further, it can be observed that the non-outliers are characterized by: (1) those who have exhibited mastery (as evidenced by the number of problems solved, time spent in the solutions) and creativity (as evidenced by the number of unique problems attempted or number of unique solutions used); and (2) those who did not know the concepts as much, yet spent more time in solving the problems. In the outlier group or the less careful group (see table 3), we find three sub-groups or clusters (Cluster 0, Cluster 1, and Cluster 2). Characterizing the three clusters based on their mean values, we found that Cluster 0 (4 students) did not show evidence of doing the task at hand, i.e. had the least number of Object Limits, solved the fewest number of levels, attempted the least number of levels, took the more than the usual time spent on the problem by others, and had the lowest carefulness mean value. Cluster 0 students were least careful, did not solve as much number of problems, took the longest time in solving problems, drew the least number of objects (seemingly not engaged with the task at hand). Cluster 2 students were the most careful of the outlier group, solved more problems among all outliers and did their solutions faster than the rest of the outlier group. Cluster 1 students were also not as careful, solved some problems by drawing the most number of objects and had the longest time drawing these objects or trying to solve the problems than the rest of the outliers. 2 of the 3 clusters of outliers were least careful but one cluster was relatively more careful than the other 2 outlying clusters but not as careful as the clusters in the careful group (non-outlying groups). In summary, the outliers are divided into three types of students (1) those who spent the longest time solving problems yet solved the least number of problems; (2) those who were able to solve the problems but solved them too fast; and (3) those who solved the problems in a non-optimal way by drawing the most number of objects.

3.2 Comparison of carefulness means between the outliers, non-outliers and the within-cluster groupings

We performed independent t-tests to verify if there is a significant difference between the carefulness means between the outlying and non-outlying groups. The same tests were also performed for the different clusters for the non-outlying group, as we are particularly interested only on non-outliers and our student carefulness model. The result of the one-tailed distribution for the t-test performed between the carefulness values of the outliers and non-outliers reveal that the difference in their means is not statistically significant ($p > 0.05$). Both groups, i.e. outliers and non-outliers, cannot be differentiated in terms of one group being more careful than the other. Running the same one-tailed distribution for the t-test of the 2 clusters in the non-outliers reveal that there is a significant difference between their mean values ($p < 0.01$). Hence, within the non-outliers, there are 2 significantly different clusters, i.e. one cluster being the more careful cluster than the other.

3.3 *Comparison of the means of post-test learning gains of the groupings*

In a prior work of the authors, carefulness did not have any relationship with post-test learning gains. Post-test learning gains are computed from the pre and post test results taken by the students prior to and after their PP usage. In that prior work, the criteria that was used to identify outliers was only standard deviation and that those points which were two (2) standard deviations away from the mean were removed. Using the LOF algorithm, we compared the learning gains for both the outliers and non-outliers in this study to find out if one group had more learning gain than the other. The result of the t-test did not corroborate the authors' previous finding, as there is a significant difference between the learning gains of the non-outliers from those of the outliers ($p < 0.05$). The t-test results on the two clusters of the non-outlying group revealed that there is no significant difference between the learning gains of the clusters in the non-outlying group ($p = 0.34727$), i.e. the size of the difference between the two clusters that are not outliers is not relative to the variation of their post-learning gains. This shows that the sub-groupings within the careful cluster shows that learning gains among careful groups is not significantly different but the (not careful) outlying and (careful) non-outlying groups have been found to be significantly differentiated relative to the post-learning gains, with the careful group or non-outliers having higher post-learning gains than the outliers.

4   CONCLUSIONS AND FINDINGS

This study corroborates prior work of the authors that carefulness exists within the Philippine sample sets. Outliers have been identified using X-means clustering and the local outlier factor. With this method, carefulness has been found in both the outliers and the non-outliers and a statistically significant difference has been found between the means of the carefulness of the two clusters of students in the non-outlying (more careful) group, i.e. one cluster is more careful than the other. Interestingly, post learning gains did present to be statistically differentiated between the outliers and non-outliers when in the authors' previous work post-test learning gains did not have any relationship to the predictors of carefulness. As a contribution to this field of study, carefulness can exist in varying levels or degrees in students regardless of their level of mastery and creativity. With the outliers identified in this study, a clearer model of student carefulness has resulted: (1) that non-outliers (those who can be considered as careful students) can have significantly varying degrees of carefulness; (2) that post-test learning gains are more significantly pronounced with non-outliers than the outliers; and (3) that carefulness can even exist within the outliers, which explains why the previous work of the authors was able to build the predictive model given the entire dataset even without performing a cluster-based outlier detection (except using the standard deviation as the basis for outlier removal). Educational intervention and pedagogical design can then benefit from this study's results, i.e. carefulness exist in varying levels or degrees and that characteristics exist and differentiate the more careful to the less careful students.

ACKNOWLEDGEMENTS

We would like to thank Physics Playground developers and researchers, Dr. Valerie Shute, Dr. Matthew Ventura, and their colleagues at the Florida State University for collaborating with the authors. We would also like to thank the Ateneo de Manila and Ateneo de Davao University for making this study, as well as the other studies of the authors, possible.

REFERENCES

Baker, R.S. and Yacef, K., 2009. The state of educational data mining in 2009: A review and future visions. JEDM| Journal of Educational Data Mining, 1(1), pp. 3–17.

Banawan, M.P., Andres, J.M.L. and Rodrigo, M.M.T., 2017a. Predicting Student Carefulness in an Educational Game for Physics Using Semi-supervised Learning. In Proc. of the 15th National Conference on Information Technology Education, 19–21 October 2017, Leyte, Philippines.

Banawan, M.P., Rodrigo, M.M.T. and Andres, J.M.L., 2017b. Predicting Student Carefulness within an Educational Game for Physics using Support Vector Machines. In Proc. of the 25th International Conference on Computers in Education (pp. 62–67).

Breunig, M.M., Kriegel, H.P., Ng, R.T. and Sander, J., 2000, May. LOF: identifying density-based local outliers. In ACM sigmod record (Vol. 29, No. 2, pp. 93–104). ACM.

Chandola, V., Banerjee, A. and Kumar, V., 2009. Anomaly detection: A survey. ACM computing surveys (CSUR), 41(3), p.15.

Duckworth, A.L. and Seligman, M.E., 2005. Self-discipline outdoes IQ in predicting academic performance of adolescents. Psychological science, 16(12), pp. 939–944.

Elahi, M., Li, K., Nisar, W., Lv, X. and Wang, H., 2008, October. Efficient clustering-based outlier detection algorithm for dynamic data stream. In Fuzzy Systems and Knowledge Discovery, 2008. FSKD'08. Fifth International Conference on (Vol. 5, pp. 298–304). IEEE.

Gong, Y., Rai, D., Beck, J.E. and Heffernan, N.T., 2009. Does Self-Discipline Impact Students' Knowledge and Learning? International Working Group on Educational Data Mining.

Jain, A.K., 2010. Data clustering: 50 years beyond K-means. Pattern recognition letters, 31(8), pp. 651–666.

Kirby, K.N., Winston, G.C. and Santiesteban, M., 2005. Impatience and grades: Delay-discount rates correlate negatively with college GPA. Learning and Individual Differences, 15(3), pp. 213–222.

Moore, G.R. and Shute, V.J., 2017. Improving learning through stealth assessment of conscientiousness. In Handbook on Digital Learning for K-12 Schools (pp. 355–368). Springer, Cham.

Morris, W., 1969. American heritage dictionary of the English language. American heritage.

Pamula, R., Deka, J.K. and Nandi, S., 2011, February. An outlier detection method based on clustering. In 2011 Second International Conference on Emerging Applications of Information Technology (pp. 253–256). IEEE.

Pelleg, D. and Moore, A.W., 2000, June. X-means: Extending k-means with efficient estimation of the number of clusters. In Icml (Vol. 1, pp. 727–734).

Rodríiguez-Fornells, A. and Maydeu-Olivares, A., 2000. Impulsive/careless problem solving style as predictor of subsequent academic achievement. Personality and Individual Differences, 28(4), pp. 639–645.

Romero, C. and Ventura, S., 2007. Educational data mining: A survey from 1995 to 2005. Expert systems with applications, 33(1), pp. 135–146.

Shute, V.J., Ventura, M. and Kim, Y.J., 2013. Assessment and learning of qualitative physics in newton's playground. The Journal of Educational Research, 106(6), pp. 423–430.

Whimbey, A., 1980. Students Can Learn to Be Better Problem Solvers. Educational Leadership, 37(7), p. 560.

Whimbey, A., Lochhead, J. and Narode, R., 2013. Problem solving & comprehension: A short course in analytical reasoning. Routledge.

Theory and Practice of Computation – Nishizaki et al. (eds)
© 2019 Taylor & Francis Group, London, ISBN 978-0-367-20417-4

Matrix representation and automation of verification of soundness of robustness diagram with time and loop controls

K.M. Agnes & R. Delos Reyes
Department of Computer Science, University of the Philippines, Quezon City, Philippines

J. Malinao
Headstart Business Solutions, Inc., Quezon City, Philippines

R.A. Juayong
Augmented Intelligence Pros, Inc., Quezon City, Philippines

ABSTRACT: Robustness Diagram with Loop and Time Controls (RDLT) is a graph representation of a system. It was designed to build multidimensional workflow models for complex systems modelling. In this paper, a matrix representation of RDLT is proposed. Using this matrix representation, it is shown how activity extraction in RDLTs can be done through computations involving matrix operations and how the soundness of RDLTs can be verified from the results of these computations.

1 INTRODUCTION

A workflow is an automation of a business or scientific process (Weske 2007, Deelman et. al 2009). Workflow models illustrate workflow components to validate and to verify the specifications of workflows (Collet et. al 2001). These models are capable of representing simple and complex dynamic systems in various fields like human resource management (Leopold et. al 2016), manufacturing engineering (Ballarini 2011), and biology (Verdi et. al 2007, Liu & Heiner 2010).

In 2017, a workflow model called Robustness Diagram with Loop and Time Controls (RDLT) (Malinao 2017) was designed to build multidimensional workflow models for complex systems modelling. RDLT is the workflow model that is studied in this work because of several reasons. First, it addresses the gap in literature with regards to modelling and verification of multidimensional workflows. RDLT utilizes all three workflow dimensions (process, resource, and case) (Van der Aalst 1996) in building models of complex systems. Second, RDLT establishes mechanisms to support the persistence and/or volatility requirements for modelling complex systems. One of the difficulties in modelling complex systems is that they generate a large number of states because of their non-linear processes. However, this difficulty is addressed by providing support for the design of persistent and volatile components. RDLT represents these components using reset-bound subsystems (Malinao 2017). Lastly, there are currently no automation tools for RDLT since it was recently introduced. For classical workflow models like Petri nets (PN) (Desel & Esparza 1995), automation tools were created to assist in the design, simulation, and analysis of workflows. Some of the automation tools for PN are the PN Toolbox (Matcovschi et. al 2003), SimHPN (Julvez et. al 2012), GPenSIM (Davidrajuh 2013), LoLA (Schimdt 2000), and INA (Starke & Roche 1992).

In this paper, a matrix representation of RDLT is proposed. In previous literatures, graphical models like PN, Spiking Neural P (SN P) Systems (Zeng et. al 2010), and Evolution-Communication P Systems with Energy (ECP-E) (Juayong & Adorna 2011) were able to be represented by matrices. With their matrix representations, operations on PN, SN P systems, and ECP-E can be computed using simple matrix operations which can be easily programmed for computer simulation. By designing a matrix representation of RDLT, activity extraction in RDLTs can also be done through computations involving matrix operations. Furthermore, this matrix representation can aid in the creation of an automation tool that can simulate such activity extraction and can perform an automated verification of the properties of RDLTs.

2 ROBUSTNESS DIAGRAM WITH LOOP AND TIME CONTROLS

2.1 *Definitions and notations*

Definition 1.1 *Robustness Diagram with Loop and Time Controls (RDLT) A Robustness Diagram with Loop and Time Controls (RDLT) is a graph representation R of a system that is defined as $R = (V, E, \Sigma, C, L, M)$ where*

- *V is a finite set of vertices where every vertex has a type $V_{type} : V \rightarrow \{`b`, `e`, `c`\}$, where `b`, `e`, and `c` means the vertex is either a "boundary object", "entity object", or a "controller", respectively.*

- *E is a finite set of arcs such that $E \subseteq (V \times V) \backslash E'$ where $E' = \{(x, y) | x, y \in V, V_{type}(x) \in \{`b`, `e`\}, V_{type}(y) \in \{`b`, `e`\}\}$.*

- *Σ is a finite non-empty set of symbols.*

- *$C : E \rightarrow \Sigma \cup \{\epsilon\}$ where ϵ is the empty string. Note that for real-world systems, a task $v \in V$, i.e. $V_{type}(v) = `c`$, is executed by a component $u \in V$, $V_{type}(u) \in \{`b`, `e`\}$. This component-task association is represented by the arc $(u, v) \in E$ where $C((u, v)) = \epsilon$. Furthermore, $C((x, y)) \in \Sigma$ represents a constraint to be satisfied to reach y from x. This constraint can represent either an input requirement or a parameter $C((x, y))$ which needs to be satisfied to proceed from using the component/task x to y. $C((x, y)) = \epsilon$ represents a constraint-free process flow to reach y from x or a self-loop when $x = y$.*

- *$L : E \rightarrow \mathbb{Z}^+$ is the maximum number of traversals allowed on the arc.*

- *$M : V \rightarrow \{0, 1\}$ indicates whether $u \in V$ and every $v \in V$ where $(u, v) \in E$ and $C((u, v)) = \epsilon$ induce a subgraph G_u of R known as a reset-bound subsystem (RBS). The RBS G_u is induced with the said vertices when $M(u) = 1$. In this case, u is referred to as the center of the RBS G_u. G_u's vertex set V_{G_u} contains u and every such v, and its arc set E_{G_u} has $(x, y) \in E$ if $x, y \in V_{G_u}$. Finally, $(a, b) \in E$ is called an in-bridge of b if $a \notin V_{G_u}$, $b \in V_{G_u}$. Meanwhile, $(b, a) \in E$ is called an out-bridge of b if $b \in V_{G_u}$ and $a \notin V_{G_u}$. Arcs $(a, b), (c, d) \in E$ are type-alike if $\exists y \in V$ where $(a, b), (c, d) \in Bridges(y)$ with $Bridges(y) = \{(r, s) \in E | (r, s)$ is either an in-bridge or out-bridge of $y\}$ or if $\forall y \in V$, $(a, b), (c, d) \notin Bridges(y)$.*

An RDLT R with 5 vertices, 5 arcs, and 1 RBS is shown in Figure 1. In the figure, the arc attributes of every $(x, y) \in E$ are shown as $L((x, y)) : C((x, y))$ and the RBS G_{x2} of R is enclosed in a box.

2.2 *Vertex-simplification of RDLTs*

With the concept of RBS, RDLT can support the persistence and/or volatility requirements for modelling complex systems. An RBS performs the function of cancellation regions in workflows. It also addresses the problems of encapsulation, memory utility, interactions, and poor control schemes for resets in classical workflow models by imposing topolatical and behavioral requirements to perform resets.

In (Malinao 2017), the RBS of an RDLT R is abstracted to derive a vertex-simplified RDLT G. Activity extraction in G is similar to that of R. Furthermore, verification of the properties of G can be generalized to R. The results of the level-1 and level-2 vertex simplification of the RDLT R in Figure 1 is shown in Figure 3.

Definition 1.2 *Vertex-simplified RDLT A vertex-simplified RDLT $G = (V', E', \Sigma, C', L')$ of $R = (V, E, \Sigma, C, L, M)$ is a multidigraph whose vertices $v \in V$ have $V_{type}(v) = `c`$ where G is derived from R such that the following holds,*

1. $x \in V'$ if any of the following holds,
- *$x \in V$ and $x \notin V_{G_u}$ of an RBS G_u in R, or*
- *there exists an in-bridge $(q, x) \in E$ of $x \in V \cap V_{G_u}$, $q \in V$ of R, or*
- *there exists an out-bridge $(x, q) \in E$ of $x \in V \cap V_{G_u}$, $q \in V$ of R*

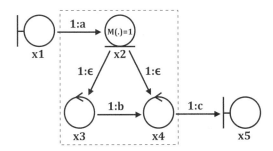

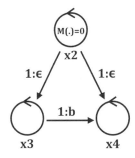

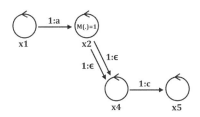

Figure 1. An RDLT R with 2 boundary objects (vertices $x1$ and $x5$), 1 entity object (vertex $x2$), and 2 controllers (vertices $x3$ and $x4$).

Figure 2. The level-1 vertex-simplified RDLT $G1$ of the RDLT R in Figure 1.

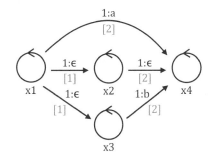

Figure 3. The level-2 vertex-simplified RDLT $G2$ of the RDLT R in Figure 1.

Figure 4. An RDLT R with one of its activity profile obtained by algorithm $\mathcal{A}$.

2. $(x,y) \in E'$ with $C'((x,y)) = C((x,y))$ for $x,y \in V'$ if $(x,y) \in E$

3. $C((x,y)) = \epsilon$ and $L((x,y)) = 1$ if $x,y \in V' \cap V_{G_u}$ and x is an ancestor of y in R and $(x,y) \notin E_{G_u}$.

We refer to this simplification of R as level-1 vertex-simplification of R with respect to every RBS G_u in R. A level-2 vertex-simplification of R with respect to its RBS G_u is the level-1 vertex-simplification of G_u where G_u is treated as an RDLT where the value of the vertex attribute M of u is redefined to 0, i.e. $M(u) = 0$.

2.3 Activity extraction in RDLTs

An activity refers to the execution of a specific ordered set of tasks by the proper resources (Van der Aalst 1996). It was included in the design of RDLT that an RDLT R may contain multiple activities wherein R has multiple inputs and multiple outputs. In this paper, it is considered that RDLTs only have one activity. This means that an RDLT R can only have one input and one output. This is due to the fact that an extended RDLT R' can be derived from a multi-input, multi-output RDLT R such that a new vertex acts as the dummy input and another new vertex acts as the dummy output. It must also be noted that the single input must be a source vertex with no incoming arcs. On the other hand, the single output must be a sink vertex with no outgoing arcs. The proposed algorithm for activity extraction in RDLTs is algorithm $\mathcal{A}$. In order to understand algorithm $\mathcal{A}$, the following definitions are first introduced.

Definition 1.3 *Reachability Configuration* A reachability configuration $S(t)$ in $R = (V, E, \Sigma, C, L, M)$ contains the arcs traversed by $\mathcal{A}$ at time step $t \in \mathbb{N}$.

Definition 1.4 *Activity Profile* A set $S = \{S(1), S(2), \ldots, S(d)\}$ of reachability configurations, $d \in \mathbb{N}$, is an activity profile in $R = (V, E, \Sigma, C, L, M)$ where $\exists (u,v) \in S(1)$ and $(x,y) \in S(d)$ such that $\nexists w, z \in V$ where $(w,u), (y,z) \in E$.

Algorithm $\mathcal{A}$

Input: RDLT R; *Output:* activity profile S; otherwise, $\emptyset$

Steps:

1. Initialize S.
2. For every $(x,y) \in E$, initialize $T((x,y))$ such that $T((x,y)) = (t_1, \ldots, t_n)$ where $n = L((x,y))$ and $t_i \in \mathbb{N}$ is the time a check or traversal is done on (x,y) by $\mathcal{A}$.
3. Start from the source vertex.
4. While the sink vertex is not reached, do the following:
    i. Perform a check by arbitrarily selecting $(x,y) \in E$ where the number of traversals done on (x,y) has not yet reached $L((x,y))$.
    ii. Assign $maxV + 1$ to the leftmost zero of $T((x,y))$. If $\exists (u,x) \in E$, $maxV$ is the largest value from all of $T((u,x))$. Otherwise, $maxV = 0$.
    iii. Evaluate whether (x,y) is an unconstrained arc.
    iv. If (x,y) is an unconstrained arc, traverse (x,y). For every $(v,y) \in E$, either retain or update $T((v,y))$. If $C((v,y)) \in \Sigma$, update the last value in $T((v,y))$ where the last check was done on (v,y) to $MAX + 1$. If $v \in V$ is either a boundary or entity object and $y \in V$ is a controller, update the first value in $T((v,y))$ to $MAX + 1$. MAX is the maximum value from all of $T((v',y)) \; \forall v' \in V$.
    v. If (x,y) is traversed and (x,y) is an out-bridge of $x \in V$, every $T((a,b))$ is reset to the zero vector wherein (a,b) is in the arc set of the RBS where x is part of the vertex set.
    vi. If (x,y) is not an unconstrained arc and no other $(x,y') \in E$ can be selected, backtrack to $a \in V$ where $(a,x) \in E$ and a was previously visited by $\mathcal{A}$ to reach x.
5. If the activity extraction fails, return $\emptyset$. Otherwise, return S.

Definition 1.5 *Unconstrained Arc Let $R = (V, E, \Sigma, C, L, M)$ be an RDLT. An arc $(x,y) \in E$ is unconstrained if $\forall (v,y) \in E$, any of the following holds,*

1. $C((v,y)) \in \{\epsilon, C((x,y))\}$,

2. $|\{t_i \in T((x,y)) | t_i \geq 1\}| \leq |\{t_j \in T((v,y)) | t_j \geq 1\}| \leq L((x,y))$ *if* $C((x,y)), C((v,y)) \in \Sigma$ *and* $C((x,y)) \neq C((v,y))$,

3. $C((v,y)) \in \Sigma$ *and* $C((x,y)) = \epsilon$ *and* $T((v,y)) \neq \vec{0}$.

As stated in Definition 1.5, every $(v,y) \in E$ does not prevent the traversal of (x,y) if any of the three given conditions is satisfied. Condition (1) states that $C((v,y))$ and $C((x,y))$ have the same value or $C((v,y)) = \epsilon$. Condition (2) states that when $C((v,y))$ and $C((x,y))$ are in Σ and they have different values, the number of traversals done on (x,y) has not yet exceeded the number of traversals done on (v,y) and the traversal limit of (v,y). Condition (3) states that (v,y), which imposes a constraint to reach vertex $y \in V$, was already previously explored (either checked or traversed) by $\mathcal{A}$, so it no longer imposes any constraint on the traversal of (x,y).

Shown in Figure 4 is an RDLT R with one of its activity profiles obtained by $\mathcal{A}$. Given this RDLT R, $\mathcal{A}$ starts the activity extraction from the source vertex $x1$ and stops once the sink vertex $x4$ is reached. The red marking beside an arc indicates the time step t that the arc was traversed by $\mathcal{A}$. Together, these red markings represent an activity profile in R which is $S = \{S(1), S(2)\}$ where $S(1) = \{(x1, x2), (x1, x3)\}$ and $S(2) = \{(x1, x4), (x2, x4), (x3, x4)\}$.

To show how this activity profile is obtained, assume that $\mathcal{A}$ arbitrarily selected the arcs in the following sequence: $(x1, x4), (x1, x2), (x2, x4), (x1, x3), (x3, x4)$. When $(x1, x4)$ is selected, $(x1, x4)$ is considered as checked at $t = 1$. Since $x1$ is a source vertex, $maxV = 0$; thus, $T((x1, x4)) = [1]$. However, $(x1, x4)$ cannot yet be traversed at $t = 1$ because $(x1, x4)$ is not an unconstrained arc. This situation also happens when $(x2, x4)$ is checked at $t = 2$. This means that $(x1, x4)$ and $(x2, x4)$ have to wait because the constraint that is imposed by $(x3, x4)$ has not yet been satisfied by the time that $(x1, x4)$ and $(x2, x4)$ were checked. Once $(x3, x4)$ is checked at $t = 2$, all constraints to reach vertex $x4$ have already been satisfied at this instance, so $(x1, x4), (x2, x4)$, and $(x3, x4)$ are traversed at $t = 2$.

The time that $(x1, x4)$ is explored is then updated to $T((x1, x4)) = [2]$. Therefore, the sink vertex $x4$ is only reached at $t = 2$. It must be noted that although the arcs are selected by $\mathcal{A}$ one at a time, arcs that are checked or traversed at the same time step t are simultaneously checked or traversed at t, respectively. Each reachability configuration $S(t)$ in the activity profile S represents the state of R at each time step t. Thus, the state of an RDLT R at any time step t is described by the arcs traversed by $\mathcal{A}$ at t.

3   MATRIX REPRESENTATION OF RDLT

In this section, we proposed that is applicable to RDLTs with or without the presence of RBS. For the former case, we shall first obtain the level-1 and level-2 vertex-simplifications of the RDLT and then use any of them as input to our matrix representation. This vertex-simplification does not affect the activity extraction in the RDLT. Moreover, the verification of properties of an RDLT, e.g. soundness (Malinao 2017), on these level-1 and level-2 vertex-simplifications can be generalized to the original RDLT.

3.1   *State representation*

As mentioned previously, the state of R at any time step t is described by the arcs traversed by $\mathcal{A}$ at t. When an arc is traversed at t, it means that both its traversal limit (attribute L) and its constraint (attribute C) have been satisfied. In this paper, the counter vector and the constraint vector are defined to give information on the state of R with respect to the traversal limit and constraint of the arcs in R, respectively.

Definition 1.6 *Counter Vector Let $R = (V, E, \Sigma, C, L, M)$ be an RDLT and $Q = (e_1, e_2, \ldots, e_q)$ be the finite sequence of arcs in R where $q = |E|$ and $e_i \in E$ is the ith arc of the sequence. The counter vector at time step t is defined as $\alpha(t) = (a_1^{(t)}, a_2^{(t)}, \ldots, a_q^{(t)})$ such that $a_i^{(t)} \in \mathbb{N}$ represents the total number of times arc e_i has been explored from time step 0 to time step t.*

Definition 1.7 *Constraint Vector Let $R = (V, E, \Sigma, C, L, M)$ be an RDLT and $Q = (e_1, e_2, \ldots, e_q)$ be the finite sequence of arcs in R where $q = |E|$ and $e_i \in E$ is the ith arc of the sequence. The constraint vector at time step t is defined as $\beta(t) = (b_1^{(t)}, b_2^{(t)}, \ldots, b_q^{(t)})$ such that*

$$b_i^{(t)} = \begin{cases} C(e_i)_y, & \text{if (arc } e_i \text{ is currently checked but cannot yet} \\ & \text{be traversed at time step } t) \text{ or (arc } e_i = (x, y) \\ & \text{with } C(e_i) = \epsilon \text{ is not checked but there exists} \\ & \text{arc } e_j = (v, y) \text{ that is currently checked)} \\ & \text{where } C(e_i) \text{ is the attribute } C \text{ of arc } e_i; \\ -C(e_i)_y, & \text{if arc } e_i = (x, y) \text{ with } C(e_i) \in \Sigma \text{ is not checked} \\ & \text{but there exists arc } e_j = (v, y) \text{ that is currently} \\ & \text{checked where } C(e_i) \text{ is the attribute } C \text{ of arc } e_i; \\ 0_y, & \text{otherwise.} \end{cases}$$

It can be observed that each of the possible values of $b_i^{(t)} \in \beta(t)$ has a subscript $y \in V$. This subscript is a vertex indicator which associates each constraint of $(x, y) \in E$ to the destination vertex y. This association is important because constraints that are imposed by (x, y) and every $(v, y) \in E$ are only local to y.

In order to provide a snapshot of the state of R at any time step t, the state vector is defined. The state vector is simply an aggregation of the counter vector and the constraint vector because both the traversal limit and constraint of the arcs in R are essential in describing the state of R at t.

Definition 1.8 *State Vector Let $\alpha(t)$ be the counter vector at time step t and $\beta(t)$ be the constraint vector at time step t. The state vector at time step t is defined as $\rho(t) = [\alpha(t), \beta(t)]$.*

Given an RDLT R, the state vector at $t = 0$ can already be obtained by following the definitions stated above. The state vector $\rho(0)$ is called the initial state vector. Using the RDLT R in Figure 4 and assuming that the finite sequence of arcs in R is $((x1,x2),(x1,x3),(x1,x4),(x2,x4),(x3,x4))$, the initial state vector is $\rho(0) = [\alpha(0), \beta(0)]$ where $\alpha(0) = (0,0,0,0,0)$ and $\beta(0) = (0_{x2}, 0_{x3}, 0_{x4}, 0_{x4}, 0_{x4})$. These values of $\alpha(0)$ and $\beta(0)$ make sense since no arcs are explored yet at $t = 0$.

From the initial state vector $\rho(0)$ where only the source vertex of R is reached, it is desired to obtain a state vector $\rho(d)$ where the sink vertex of R is reached at time step d. In this paper, this is achieved by using matrices to perform activity extraction in RDLTs.

3.2 Components for activity extraction

In algorithm $\mathcal{A}$, arcs are explored at every time step. In order to represent the arcs that are chosen to be explored at each time step, the explored arcs vector is defined. It must be noted that among the arcs that can be explored at t, there must always be at least one of them that is chosen to be explored at t.

Definition 1.9 *Explored Arcs Vector Let $R = (V, E, \Sigma, C, L, M)$ be an RDLT and $Q = (e_1, e_2, \ldots, e_q)$ be the finite sequence of arcs in R where $q = |E|$ and $e_i \in E$ is the ith arc of the sequence. The explored arcs vector at time step t is defined as $\gamma(t) = (g_1{}^{(t)}, g_2{}^{(t)}, \ldots, g_q{}^{(t)})$ such that*

$$
g_i{}^{(t)} = \begin{cases} 1, & \text{if arc } e_i = (x,y) \text{ is chosen to be explored at time} \\ & \text{step } t \text{ where vertex } x \text{ was already reached before} \\ & \text{time step } t; \\ 0, & \text{otherwise.} \end{cases}
$$

When $(x,y) \in E$ is explored at t, the constraint of every incoming arc $(v,y) \in E$ of vertex $y \in V$ determines whether (x,y) will only be checked at t or will be traversed at t. In this paper, the incoming arcs vector is defined to represent these incoming arcs. Also, the C-attribute vector is defined to represent the constraint of every arc in R. It must be recalled that ϵ represents a constraint-free process flow. Thus, (v,y) does not prevent the traversal of (x,y) when $C((v,y)) = \epsilon$.

Definition 1.10 *Incoming Arcs Vector Let $R = (V, E, \Sigma, C, L, M)$ be an RDLT, $Q = (e_1, e_2, \ldots, e_q)$ be the finite sequence of arcs in R where $q = |E|$ and $e_i \in E$ is the ith arc of the sequence, and $\gamma(t) = (g_1{}^{(t)}, g_2{}^{(t)}, \ldots, g_q{}^{(t)})$ be the explored arcs vector at time step t. The incoming arcs vector at time step t is defined as $\phi(t) = (p_1{}^{(t)}, p_2{}^{(t)}, \ldots, p_q{}^{(t)})$ such that*

$$
p_i{}^{(t)} = \begin{cases} 1, & \text{if } (g_i{}^{(t)} = 1) \text{ or } (g_i{}^{(t)} = 0 \text{ and } C(e_i) = \epsilon_y \text{ and} \\ & \exists g_j{}^{(t)} = 1) \text{ where } e_i = (x,y), e_j = (v,y), \text{ and } C(e_i) \\ & \text{is the attribute } C \text{ of arc } e_i; \\ -1, & \text{if } g_i{}^{(t)} = 0 \text{ and } C(e_i) \in \Sigma \text{ and } \exists g_j{}^{(t)} = 1 \text{ where} \\ & e_i = (x,y), e_j = (v,y), \text{ and } C(e_i) \text{ is the attribute } C \\ & \text{of arc } e_i; \\ 0, & \text{otherwise.} \end{cases}
$$

Definition 1.11 *C-Attribute Vector Let $R = (V, E, \Sigma, C, L, M)$ be an RDLT and $Q = (e_1, e_2, \ldots, e_q)$ be the finite sequence of arcs in R where $q = |E|$ and $e_i \in E$ is the ith arc of the sequence. The C-attribute vector of R is defined as $\vec{C} = (c_1, c_2, \ldots, c_q)$ such that $c_i = C(e_i)_y$ where $C(e_i)$ is the attribute C of $e_i = (x,y)$.*

4 ACTIVITY EXTRACTION THROUGH COMPUTATIONS INVOLVING MATRIX OPERATIONS

4.1 Monitoring the arcs' traversal limits

In algorithm $\mathcal{A}$, an arc $(x,y) \in E$ can only be explored if (x,y) has not yet reached its traversal limit. This is why $T((x,y))$ is updated whenever (x,y) is explored by $\mathcal{A}$ to keep track of the number of times that (x,y) has already been explored. It is shown in Lemma 1.1 how the state of R with respect to the arcs' traversal limit can be monitored from the counter vector and the explored arcs vector.

Lemma 1.1 *Let R be an RDLT, $Q = (e_1, e_2, \ldots, e_q)$ be the finite sequence of arcs in R where $q = |E|$, $\alpha(t-1)$ be the counter vector at time step $t-1$, and $\gamma(t)$ be the explored arcs vector at time step t. Then the counter vector at time step t can be obtained by $\alpha(t) = \alpha(t-1) + \gamma(t)$.*

4.2 Monitoring the arcs' constraints

Aside from the traversal limit, the constraint of the arcs in R must also be monitored to be able to describe the state of R at each time step. In order to understand how these constraints are being monitored, the following definitions are first introduced. As a recall, the notation Σ is a finite non-empty set of symbols and the notation ϵ is the empty string. In addition, the notation $-\Sigma$ is also a finite non-empty set of symbols containing the same elements in Σ but with a negative sign. The literal sign function accepts an element in the set $\Sigma \cup -\Sigma \cup \{0, \epsilon\}$ and extracts its sign. It is similar to the sign function for real numbers but accepts a different set of elements. The literal element-wise multiplication deals with two vectors that have elements from different sets. One vector has elements in the set $\{1, 0, -1\}$ while the other vector has elements in the set $\Sigma \cup \{\epsilon\}$. The multiplication of the elements in these vectors is similar to that of algebraic multiplication. The unrefreshed constraint vector at time step t shows which among the constraint of the arcs in R are currently satisfied at t.

Definition 1.12 *Literal Sign Function*
Let A be an element in the set $\Sigma \cup -\Sigma \cup \{0, \epsilon\}$. The literal sign function of A is defined as

$$sign(A) = \left\{ \begin{array}{ll} 1, & if\ A \in \Sigma \cup \{\epsilon\}; \\ 0, & if\ A \in \{0\}; \\ -1, & if\ A \in -\Sigma. \end{array} \right.$$

Definition 1.13 *Literal OR*
Let A, B, and C be elements in the set $\Sigma \cup -\Sigma \cup \{0, \epsilon\}$. The literal OR of A and B is defined as $A \vee B = C$ such that $(|A| = |B|)$ or $(A \in \Sigma \cup -\Sigma \cup \{\epsilon\}$ and $B = 0)$ or $(A = 0$ and $B \in \Sigma \cup -\Sigma \cup \{\epsilon\})$ where

$$C = \left\{ \begin{array}{ll} A, & if\ (sign(A) = 1)\ or\ (sign(A) = -1\ and\ sign(B) \neq 1)\ or \\ & (sign(A) = sign(B) = 0); \\ B, & if\ (sign(B) = 1\ and\ sign(A) \neq 1)\ or\ (sign(B) = -1 \\ & and\ sign(A) = 0). \end{array} \right.$$

Definition 1.14 *Literal Element-Wise Multiplication*
Let A, B, and C be $1 \times m$ vectors where $A_i \in \{1, 0, -1\}$, $B_i \in \Sigma \cup \{\epsilon\}$, and $C_i \in \Sigma \cup -\Sigma \cup \{0, \epsilon\}$ for all $1 \leq i \leq m$. The literal element-wise multiplication of A and B is defined as $A \odot B = C$ such that

$$C_i = \left\{ \begin{array}{ll} B_i, & if\ A_i = 1; \\ 0, & if\ A_i = 0; \\ -B_i, & if\ A_i = -1. \end{array} \right.$$

Definition 1.15 *Unrefreshed Constraint Vector*
Let $\beta(t-1)$ be the constraint vector at time step $t-1$, $\phi(t)$ be the incoming arcs vector at time step t, and $\vec{C}$ be the C-attribute vector of R. The unrefreshed constraint vector at time step t is defined as $\omega(t) = \beta(t-1) \vee (\phi(t) \odot \vec{C})$.

Definition 1.16 *Refresh Function*
Let $\omega(t) = (w_1^{(t)}, w_2^{(t)}, \ldots, w_q^{(t)})$ be the unrefreshed constraint vector at time step t. The refresh function of $\omega(t)$ is defined as $refresh(\omega(t)) = Z$ where $Z = (z_1, z_2, \ldots, z_q)$ such that

$$z_i = \left\{ \begin{array}{ll} 0_y, & if\ e_i = (x, y)\ is\ traversed\ at\ time\ step\ t; \\ w_i, & if\ e_i\ cannot\ yet\ be\ traversed\ at\ time\ step\ t. \end{array} \right.$$

There are two possible scenarios to reach a vertex $y \in V$ at time step t. First, all the constraints to reach vertex y are currently satisfied at t. This means that all the incoming arcs of vertex y have been checked on or before time step t. These satisfied constraints are represented in the unrefreshed constraint vector at t as those elements in the set $\Sigma \cup \{\epsilon\}$ with a subscript y. Second, not all of the incoming arcs of vertex y are currently checked at t, but those arcs that have been checked are unconstrained arcs. Thus, they can still be traversed at t, so vertex y is still reached at t. If vertex y is to be visited again later on, either one of these scenarios must occur once more. Therefore, the refresh function is introduced so that when vertex y is reached, all the constraints to reach vertex y are refreshed. This indicates that those constraints need to be satisfied again in order to visit y. It is shown in Lemma 1.2 how the state of R with respect to the arcs' constraint can be monitored using the refresh function.

Lemma 1.2 *Let R be an RDLT, $Q = (e_1, e_2, \ldots, e_q)$ be the finite sequence of arcs in R where $q = |E|$, and $\omega(t)$ be the unrefreshed constraint vector at time step t. Then the constraint vector at time step t can be obtained by $\beta(t) = refresh(\omega(t))$.*

4.3   *Computing for the next state vector*

Theorem 1 *Let R be an RDLT, $Q = (e_1, e_2, \ldots, e_q)$ be the finite sequence of arcs in R where $q = |E|$, $\alpha(t-1)$ be the counter vector at time step $t - 1$, $\gamma(t)$ be the explored arcs vector at time step t, $\beta(t-1)$ be the constraint vector at time step $t - 1$, $\phi(t)$ be the incoming arcs vector at time step t, and $\vec{C}$ be the C-attribute vector. Then the state vector at time step t can be obtained by*

$$[\alpha(t), \beta(t)] = [\alpha(t-1) + \gamma(t), refresh(\beta(t-1) \vee (\phi(t) \odot \vec{C}))]$$

It is explained in Theorem 1 how the next state vector can be computed from the current state vector. Going back to the RDLT R in Figure 4, the initial state vector is $\rho(0) = [\alpha(0), \beta(0)]$ where $\alpha(0) = (0,0,0,0,0)$ and $\beta(0) = (0_{x2}, 0_{x3}, 0_{x4}, 0_{x4}, 0_{x4})$. This is under the assumption that the finite sequence of arcs in R is $((x1,x2), (x1,x3), (x1,x4), (x2,x4), (x3,x4))$. Given R and this sequence of arcs, the C-attribute vector of R can also be obtained which is $\vec{C} = (\epsilon_{x2}, \epsilon_{x3}, a_{x4}, \epsilon_{x4}, b_{x4})$.

By Theorem 1, the state vector at $t = 1$ can be computed from the state vector at $t = 0$. The arcs that can be explored at $t = 1$ are $(x1,x2), (x1,x3),$ and $(x1,x4)$ since only the source vertex $x1$ is reached at $t = 0$. Thus, the explored arcs vector can have 2^3 possible combinations. Assume that $(x1,x2), (x1,x3),$ and $(x1,x4)$ are all chosen to be explored at $t = 1$. It follows that the explored arcs vector at $t = 1$ is $\gamma(1) = (1,1,1,0,0)$ and the incoming arcs vector at $t = 1$ is $\phi(1) = (1,1,1,1,-1)$. The counter vector at $t = 1$ can then be obtained by $\alpha(1) = \alpha(0) + \gamma(1)$, which is equal to $(1,1,1,0,0) = (0,0,0,0,0) + (1,1,1,0,0)$. It can be seen in $\alpha(1)$ that $(x1,x2), (x1,x3),$ and $(x1,x4)$ have already been explored once while $(x2,x4)$ and $(x3,x4)$ have not yet been explored. Likewise, the unrefreshed constraint vector at $t = 1$ can be obtained by $\omega(1) = \beta(0) \vee (\phi(1) \odot \vec{C})$ which is equal to $(\epsilon_{x2}, \epsilon_{x3}, a_{x4}, \epsilon_{x4}, -b_{x4}) = (0_{x2}, 0_{x3}, 0_{x4}, 0_{x4}, 0_{x4}) \vee$
$((1,1,1,1,-1) \odot (\epsilon_{x2}, \epsilon_{x3}, a_{x4}, \epsilon_{x4}, b_{x4}))$. From $\omega(1)$, the constraint vector at $t = 1$ can be obtained by $\beta(1) = refresh(\omega(1))$ which is equal to $(0_{x2}, 0_{x3}, a_{x4}, \epsilon_{x4}, -b_{x4}) =$
$refresh((\epsilon_{x2}, \epsilon_{x3}, a_{x4}, \epsilon_{x4}, -b_{x4}))$.

It can be seen from $\omega(1)$ that the constraints to reach vertices $x2$ and $x3$ have already been satisfied (since they only have 1 incoming arc and those arcs were explored). Thus, vertices $x2$ and $x3$ are reached at $t = 1$. The values of the corresponding elements of $(x1,x2)$ and $(x1,x3)$ in $\beta(1)$ are then refreshed to 0_{x2} and 0_{x3}, respectively. Moreover, it can be seen from $\beta(1)$ that the constraint imposed by $(x3,x4)$, which is $-b_{x4}$, has a negative sign. This means that $(x3,x4)$ is preventing the traversal of the other incoming arcs of vertex $x4$. In this example, the constraint imposed by $(x3,x4)$ is preventing the traversal of $(x1,x4)$. Thus, $(x1,x4)$ is only checked at $t = 1$. Arc $(x1,x4)$ has to wait until the constraint imposed by $(x3,x4)$ is satisfied before $(x1,x4)$ can be traversed.

From the results of these computations, the state vector at $t = 1$ is $\rho(1) = [\alpha(1), \beta(1)]$ where $\alpha(1) = (1,1,1,0,0)$ and $\beta(1) = (\epsilon_{x2}, \epsilon_{x3}, a_{x4}, \epsilon_{x4}, -b_{x4})$.

Continuing the computation to solve for the state vector at $t = 2$, assume that the explored arcs vector at $t = 2$ is $\gamma(2) = (0,0,0,1,1)$. Consequently, the incoming arcs vector at $t = 2$ is $\phi(2) = (0,0,-1,1,1)$. It must be noted that $(x2,x4)$ and $(x3,x4)$ can already be explored at $t = 2$ since vertices $x2$ and $x3$ were reached at $t = 1$. Thus, the counter vector at $t = 2$ can be obtained by $\alpha(2) = \alpha(1) + \gamma(2)$ which is equal to $(1,1,1,1,1) = (1,1,1,0,0) + (0,0,0,1,1)$.

16

It can be seen in $\alpha(2)$ that all arcs have already been explored once. This means that they have all reached their traversal limit. If any of these arcs is chosen to be explored again, it will lead to a state of R that is invalid because one of the arcs will have exceeded its traversal limit.

Likewise, the unrefreshed constraint vector at $t = 2$ can be obtained by $\omega(2) = \beta(1) \vee (\phi(2) \odot \vec{C})$ which is equal to $(0_{x2}, 0_{x3}, a_{x4}, \epsilon_{x4}, b_{x4}) = (0_{x2}, 0_{x3}, a_{x4}, \epsilon_{x4}, -b_{x4}) \vee$ $((0, 0, -1, 1, 1) \odot (\epsilon_{x2}, \epsilon_{x3}, a_{x4}, \epsilon_{x4}, b_{x4}))$.

From $\omega(2)$, the constraint vector at $t = 2$ can be obtained by $\beta(2) = refresh(\omega(2))$ which is equal to $(0_{x2}, 0_{x3}, 0_{x4}, 0_{x4}, 0_{x4}) = refresh((0_{x2}, 0_{x3}, a_{x4}, \epsilon_{x4}, b_{x4}))$.

It can be seen from $\omega(2)$ that all constraints to reach vertex $x4$ are satisfied. Thus, the values of their corresponding elements in $\beta(2)$ are refreshed to 0_{x4}. It must also be noted that at this instance, the sink vertex $x4$ has already been reached, so the computation stops here.

The state vector $\rho(d)$ where the sink vertex is reached at time step d is called a final state vector. In this example, the state vector at $t = 2$ which is $\rho(2) = [\alpha(2), \beta(2)]$ where $\alpha(2) = (1, 1, 1, 1, 1)$ and $\beta(2) = (0_{x2}, 0_{x3}, 0_{x4}, 0_{x4}, 0_{x4})$ is a final state vector.

5 EVALUATING THE FINAL STATE VECTOR

Once a final state vector is obtained, it must first be evaluated to determine if it is "valid". A final state vector is considered valid when the final state vector is obtained such that all traversal requirements have been satisfied. If a final state vector is determined to be valid, it can then be evaluated if it is also "sound". A valid final state vector is considered sound when all conditions of the soundness of RDLTs have been met. The formal definitions of these properties are provided in the succeeding subsections.

5.1 *Valid final state vector*

The computations discussed in Section 4 may lead to a final state vector that is invalid. An invalid final state vector is obtained when the number of times an arc has been explored has exceeded its traversal limit and/or when the sink vertex cannot be reached because of some constraints. Otherwise, a valid final state vector is obtained. In any of these cases, the computation stops and a final state vector is obtained. This is why the obtained final state vector must be evaluated to determine if it is valid. The space and time complexity to compute for all possible final state vectors is $O(|E|)$ and $O(2^{|E|})$, respectively. In Definition 1.17, condition (1) states that all elements in the counter vector of the final state vector have not exceeded the traversal limit of their corresponding arc. On the other hand, condition (2) states that all elements in the constraint vector of the final state vector must be equal to 0 with their corresponding subscript. This means that all the arcs that were chosen to be explored to reach the sink vertex are unconstrained arcs. By Definition 1.17, the final state vector that was computed in the example in Section 4.3 is a valid final state vector.

Definition 1.17 *Valid Final State Vector*
Let $\alpha(d)$ be the counter vector at time step d and $\beta(d)$ be the constraint vector at time step d. A final state vector $\rho(d) = [\alpha(d), \beta(d)]$ is a valid final state vector if the following conditions hold,

1. $a_i^{(d)} \leq L(e_i) \; \forall a_i^{(d)} \in \alpha(d)$ *where $L(e_i)$ is the attribute L of arc e_i, and*

2. $b_i^{(d)} = 0_y \; \forall b_i^{(d)} \in \beta(d)$.

Theorem 2 *There exists an activity profile S in R generated by algorithm $\mathcal{A}$ if and only if there exists a valid final state vector.*

Once a final state vector is determined to be valid, an activity profile S in R can be constructed from the series of unrefreshed constraint vectors and the series of constraint vectors that were obtained from the computations. The corresponding arcs of the positive constraints in $\omega(t)$ that were refreshed to 0 (with their corresponding subscript) in $\beta(t)$ are the arcs traversed at t. Thus, the set containing those arcs is the reachability configuration $S(t)$. In the example in Section 4.3, the unrefreshed constraint vectors are $\omega(1) = (\epsilon_{x2}, \epsilon_{x3}, a_{x4}, \epsilon_{x4}, -b_{x4})$ and $\omega(2) = (0_{x2}, 0_{x3}, a_{x4}, \epsilon_{x4}, b_{x4})$

whereas the constraint vectors are $\beta(1) = (0_{x2}, 0_{x3}, a_{x4}, \epsilon_{x4}, -b_{x4})$ and $\beta(2) = (0_{x2}, 0_{x3}, 0_{x4}, 0_{x4}, 0_{x4})$. Thus, the obtained reachability configurations are $S(1) = \{(x1, x2), (x1, x3)\}$ and $S(2) = \{(x1, x4), (x2, x4), (x3, x4)\}$. These reachability configurations comprise the activity profile S in R which is $S = \{S(1), S(2)\}$. It can be observed that this activity profile S is the same activity profile S obtained by $\mathcal{A}$ from the graph representation of R. On the other hand, given the activity profile $S = \{S(1), S(2)\}$ where $S(1) = \{(x1, x2), (x1, x3)\}$ and $S(2) = \{(x1, x4), (x2, x4), (x3, x4)\}$ which is generated by $\mathcal{A}$, a valid final state vector can be obtained. This is achieved after a sequence of arcs in R is fixed. If the same set of arcs in each reachability configuration $S(t)$ is chosen to be explored at each explored arcs vector $\gamma(t)$, then $\gamma(1) = (1, 1, 0, 0, 0)$ and $\gamma(2) = (0, 0, 1, 1, 1)$. Using these explored arcs vector, a final state vector can be obtained which is $\rho(2) = [\alpha(2), \beta(2)]$ where $\alpha(2) = (1, 1, 1, 1, 1)$ and $\beta(2) = (0_{x2}, 0_{x3}, 0_{x4}, 0_{x4}, 0_{x4})$. By Definition 1.17, this final state vector is a valid final state vector.

Definition 1.18 *Total Explored Arcs Vector*
Let $\gamma(t)$ be the explored arcs vector at t. The total explored arcs vector is defined as $\gamma(*) = \gamma(1) + \gamma(2) + \ldots + \gamma(d)$ where d is the time step that the sink vertex is reached.

Theorem 3 *There exists an activity profile S in R generated by algorithm $\mathcal{A}$ if and only if there exists a total explored arcs vector $\gamma(*)$ such that $[\alpha(1), \beta(1)] = [\alpha(0) + \gamma(*), refresh(\beta(t-1) \vee (\phi(t) \odot \vec{C}))]$ where $\rho(0) = [\alpha(0), \beta(0)]$ is the initial state vector and $\rho(1) = [\alpha(1), \beta(1)]$ is a valid final state vector.*

Looking back at the RDLT R in Figure 4, the initial state vector is $\rho(0) = [\alpha(0), \beta(0)]$ where $\alpha(0) = (0, 0, 0, 0, 0)$ and $\beta(0) = (0_{x2}, 0_{x3}, 0_{x4}, 0_{x4}, 0_{x4})$. In Section 4.3, the explored arcs vectors that were selected are $\gamma(1) = (1, 1, 1, 0, 0)$ and $\gamma(2) = (0, 0, 0, 1, 1)$. Using this example, the total explored arcs vector is $\gamma(*) = (1, 1, 1, 1, 1)$. By Theorem 3, a final state vector is obtained by $[\alpha(1), \beta(1)] = [\alpha(0) + \gamma(*), refresh(\beta(0) \vee (\phi(1) \odot \vec{C}))]$ which is equal to
$[(1, 1, 1, 1, 1), (0_{x2}, 0_{x3}, 0_{x4}, 0_{x4}, 0_{x4})] =$
$[(0, 0, 0, 0, 0) + (1, 1, 1, 1, 1), refresh((0_{x2}, 0_{x3}, 0_{x4}, 0_{x4}, 0_{x4}) \vee$
$((1, 1, 1, 1, 1) \odot (\epsilon_{x2}, \epsilon_{x3}, a_{x4}, \epsilon_{x4}, b_{x4}))].$

By Definition 1.17, $\rho(1) = [\alpha(1), \beta(1)]$ is a valid final state vector. From this valid final state vector, an activity profile S can be constructed which is $S = \{S(1), S(2)\}$ where $S(1) = \{(x1, x2), (x1, x3)\}$ and $S(2) = \{(x1, x4), (x2, x4), (x3, x4)\}$. Again, this activity profile is the same activity profile S obtained by $\mathcal{A}$ from the graph representation of R.

On the other hand, given an activity profile S generated by $\mathcal{A}$, a total explored arcs vector $\gamma(*)$ can be computed from S. This can be achieved after fixing the order of the arcs in R. For every reachability configuration $S(t)$ in S, 1 is added to the corresponding element of $(x, y) \in E$ in the total explored arcs vector $\gamma(*)$ if (x, y) is in $S(t)$. Using the same example above, it can be seen that given $S = \{S(1), S(2)\}$ where $S(1) = \{(x1, x2), (x1, x3)\}$ and $S(2) = \{(x1, x4), (x2, x4), (x3, x4)\}$, the computed total explored arcs vector is $\gamma(*) = (1, 1, 1, 1, 1)$. Using this $\gamma(*)$, it was shown previously that a valid final state vector can be obtained from the initial state vector.

Definition 1.19 *Transition*
Let $\rho(t)$ be the state of RDLT R at time step $t \in \mathbb{N}$. A transition from state $\rho(t-1)$ to state $\rho(t)$, denoted by $\rho(t-1) \xrightarrow{\gamma_t} \rho(t)$, is a change in the state of R from $\rho(t-1)$ to $\rho(t)$ brought by the explored arcs vector at t, $\gamma(t)$.

Let $\rho(0)$ be the initial state of RDLT R and $\rho(t), t \in \mathbb{N}$, be a valid final state of RDLT R. The total traversed arcs vector from $\rho(0)$ to $\rho(t)$, denoted by $\rho(0) \xrightarrow{\gamma_*} \rho(t)$, is a change in the state of R from the initial state to the final state where $\gamma_* = \gamma(1) + \gamma(2) + \ldots + \gamma(t)$.

5.2 *Sound final state vector*

Given a valid final state vector, it can also be verified if an RDLT is sound (Malinao 2017) by determining if the valid final state vector is sound. A sound final state vector is obtained when all conditions of the soundness of RDLTs have been met. Among the many properties of workflows, the soundness property is the one verified in this work because many other properties are implied by it. Furthermore, by verifying the soundness of workflows, potential errors in the workflow's design can already be identified (Van der Aalst 1996).

Definition 1.20 *Soundness of RDLTs (Malinao 2017)*
An RDLT R is sound if for a source vertex w and a sink vertex f, there exists an activity profile $S = \{S(1), S(2), \ldots S(k)\}$ where $(w, v) \in S(1), (q, f) \in S(k), v, q \in V, S(k + 1) = \emptyset$, and the following conditions hold:

1. *there is at least one vertex $v \in V$, where $(u, v) \in S(j)$, that connects to another vertex $q \in V$, where $(v, q) \in S(j + 1)$,*

2. *no other arc that does not end at the sink vertex f is included in the last reachability configuration $S(k)$ of S,*

3. *an arc (x, y) is always traversed at time $t < k$ and $y \in V$ is connected to at least one vertex that has been previously reached, and*

4. *all arcs in R have been used at least once.*

Definition 1.21 *Sound Final State Vector*
Let $\alpha(d)$ be the counter vector at time step d, $\beta(d)$ be the constraint vector at time step d, and $\omega(d)$ be the unrefreshed constraint vector at time step d. A valid final state vector $\rho(d) = [\alpha(d), \beta(d)]$ is a sound final state vector if the following conditions hold,

1. $a_i^{(d)} > 0 \; \forall a_i^{(d)} \in \alpha(d)$, *and*

2. *if $w_i^{(d)} \neq 0_y$ and $b_i^{(d)} = 0_y$, then vertex y is the sink vertex*
   $\forall w_i^{(d)} \in \omega(d)$ *and* $\forall b_i^{(d)} \in \beta(d)$ *where* $e_i = (x, y)$.

In Definition 1.21, condition (1) states that all elements in the counter vector of the final state vector is greater than 0. This means that all arcs in R must have been explored at least once as stated in condition (iv) of Definition 1.20. On the other hand, condition (2) states that all arcs traversed at the final time step d are incoming arcs of the sink vertex. This satisfies condition (ii) of Definition 1.20. It must be noted that conditions (i) and (iii) of Definition 1.20 are always satisfied because of the property of the explored arcs vector. As stated in Definition 1.9, an arc $(x, y) \in E$ can only be chosen to be explored at t if the initial vertex $x \in V$ of (x, y) was already reached before time step t. Moreover, at least one of the arcs that can be explored at t must be chosen to be explored at t.

Theorem 4 *An RDLT R is sound if and only if there exists a sound final state vector.*

Using the RDLT R in Figure 4, it was shown in Section 4.3 that a final state vector is obtained from the proposed computations. This final state vector is $\rho(2) = [\alpha(2), \beta(2)]$ where $\alpha(2) = (1, 1, 1, 1, 1)$ and $\beta(2) = (0_{x2}, 0_{x3}, 0_{x4}, 0_{x4}, 0_{x4})$. In Section 5.1, it was determined that this final state vector is a valid final state vector. It was also discussed that an activity profile S can be constructed from the series of unrefreshed constraint vectors and the series of constraint vectors that were obtained from the computations. At $t = 2$ where the sink vertex is reached, the unrefreshed constraint vector is $\omega(2) = (0_{x2}, 0_{x3}, a_{x4}, \epsilon_{x4}, b_{x4})$ and the constraint vector is $\beta(2) = (0_{x2}, 0_{x3}, 0_{x4}, 0_{x4}, 0_{x4})$. It can be seen that every element in $\alpha(2)$ is greater than 0. Moreover, all the constraints of the arcs in $\omega(2)$ that were refreshed to 0 (with their corresponding subscript) in $\beta(2)$ are incoming arcs of the sink vertex $x4$. By Definition 1.21, this valid final state vector is a sound final state vector and by Theorem 4, the RDLT R in Figure 4 is sound.

It was mentioned in Section 3 that this matrix representation can also represent RDLTs with RBS and can be used to verify their soundness. Given an RDLT R with RBS, a level-1 and level-2 vertex-simplification will be performed on R. The vertex-simplified RDLTs obtained from the level-1 and level-2 vertex-simplification of R are RDLTs without RBS. Thus, the matrix representation of RDLT still holds. Moreover, if a sound final state vector can be obtained from the level-1 and level-2 vertex simplified RDLTs of R, it means that both the level-1 and level-2 vertex simplified RDLTs are sound. It follows that the entire RDLT R is sound.

6   CONCLUSIONS

In this paper, a matrix representation of RDLT is proposed. Using this matrix representation, activity extraction in RDLTs can be done through computations involving simple matrix operations. Morever, the soundness of RDLTs can be verified from the results of these computations.

This proposed matrix representation of RDLT can aid in the automation of the simulation of activity extraction in RDLTs and of the verification of soundness of RDLTs. It may also be studied further to see how it can be used to verify other properties of RDLTs.

REFERENCES

Ballarini P., Djafri H., Duflot M., Haddad S., & Pekergin H. 2011. Petri nets compositional modeling and verification of flexible manu-facturing systems.

Belhajjame K., Vargas-Solar G., & Collet C. 2001. A flexible workflow model for process-oriented applications. volume 1: pages 72–80.

Davidrajuh R. 2013. General purpose petri net simulator (gpensim).

Deelman E., Gannon D., Shields M., & Taylor I. 2009. Workflows and e-science: An overview of workflow system features and capabilities. volume 25: pages 528–540.

Desel J. & Esparza J. 1995. *Free Choice Petri Nets*. Cambridge University Press.

Jensen K,. Kristenses L. M, & Mailund T. 2012. The sweep-line state space exploration method. volume 4: pages 169–179.

Juayong R. A. & Adorna H. 2011. A matrix representation for computations on ecp systems with energy.

Julvez J., Mahulea C, & Vazquez C. 2012. Simhpn: A matlab toolbox for simulation, analysis and design with hybrid petri nets. volume 6: pages 806–817.

Julvez J., Mahulea C, & Vazquez C. 2014. Matlab tools for the analysis of petri net models.

Kaplan H. 2007. *Handbook on Data Structures and Application: Persistent Data Structures*. CRC Press.

Kleijn H. C. M. & Spieksma F. M. 2013. Coverability and extended petri nets.

Korf R. E. and Schultze P. 2005. Large-scale parallel breadth-first search. volume 5: pages 1380–1385.

Leopold H., Mendling J., & Gunther O. 2016. What we can learn from quality issues of bpmn models from industry. volume 33: pages 26–33.

Lima I., Perkusich A., & Figueiredo J. 1996. An interactive petri net tool for modeling, analysis and simulation of complex systems.

Liu F. & Heiner M. 2010. Conceptual-level workflow modeling of scientific experiments using nmr as a case study.

Malinao J. A. 2017. *On Building Multidimensional Workflow Models for Complex Systems Modelling*. PhD thesis.

Matcovschi M., Mahulea C., & Pastravanu O. 2003. Petri net toolbox for matlab.

Murata T. 1989. Petri nets: Properties, analysis and applications. volume 77: pages 541–580.

Schmidt K. 2000. Lola: A low level analyser. pages 465–474.

Starke P. H. & Roche S. 1992. Ina: Integrated net analyzer (reference manual).

Tarjan R. 1972. Depth-first search and linear graph algorithms. volume 1: pages 146–160.

Van der Aalst W. M. P. 1996. Structural characterizations of sound workflow nets. volume 9623.

Van der Aalst W. M. P. 1998. The application of petri-nets to workflow management. volume 8: pages 21–66.

Verdi K. K., Ellis H., & Gryk M. 2007. R. Conceptual-level workflow modeling of scientific experiments using nmr as a case study. volume 8:31.

Weske M. 2007. *Business Process Management: Concepts, Languages, Architectures*. Springer Berlin Heidelberg New York.

Zeng X., Adorna H., Martinez del Amor M. A, Pan L., & Perez-Jimenez M. J. 2010. Matrix representation of spiking neural p systems. volume 6501.

Theory and Practice of Computation – Nishizaki et al. (eds)
© 2019 Taylor & Francis Group, London, ISBN 978-0-367-20417-4

Interoperable system with authentication and authorization for IoT

J.E.P. Avenido, F.J.R. Caldejon, J.M.D. Ortaliz & G.G. Cu
De La Salle University, Manila, Philippines

ABSTRACT: The Internet of Things has become the latest point of interest in the IT industry. Due to this, many companies and individuals are beginning to make new innovations and conduct more research regarding IoT. As it always is when new IT innovations emerge, information security is a must, hence there has been researches on what the ideal security measures should be when it comes to IoT. However, one problem in IoT is with each new infrastructure and different security protocols are implemented. There is also no authentication and authorization protocol that can handle different types of infrastructures in one internetwork. The aim of this study is to make a system that can authorize and authenticate devices joining an IoT network, regardless of their infrastructure. With the proposed system, different infrastructure devices were able to communicate with one another. A device running on 802.15.4 was able to send a 256-byte packet to a device running on 802.11 with a latency of 300.111 milliseconds, while a device running on 802.11 was able to send a 256-byte packet to a device running on 802.15.4 with a latency of 1035.087 milliseconds.

1 INTRODUCTION

Today, most of society is connected on the Internet via desktops, laptops, or mobile devices. Aside from these traditional devices, there are now new technologies that have been developed, and are being developed that enable other objects to connect to the Internet to provide different kinds of services. These new technologies are part of the concept called the Internet of Things (IoT). In IoT, small computers are used to record information about its environment and exchange that information to similar devices. These can also be used to respond based on the data it receives. These small devices are useful for times wherein a traditional computer would not be suitable.

Since IoT is a relatively new point of interest in the IT industry, it is still lacking when it comes to standardization[1]. There have been several yet varying contributions to different aspects of IoT. This includes how security and privacy is implemented in IoT. Because of this, there is a lack of interoperability in regard to IoT infrastructures. Different infrastructures require different protocols for communication and for authentication and authorization. The lack of standardization in the implementation of IoT causes incompatibility issues, making it difficult for devices using a different infrastructure to join the system.

This heterogeneity of IoT devices leads to a problem when it comes to security. Despite being different from traditional networks, IoT is still susceptible to common cyber-attacks such as denial of service. Due to IoT's heterogeneity when it comes to security, there is a need for an interoperable solution to authenticate and authorize IoT devices. Without an interoperable solution designed to be able to authenticate and authorize heterogeneous IoT devices, there would be issues in terms of implementation, convenience, and deployment of IoT technologies.

This study aims to develop a system that authenticates sensor nodes with current existing infrastructures; authorizes communication and logging services for sensor nodes; implement a gateway that allows communication between sensor nodes with different infrastructures; and to implement simple services that the sensor nodes use for storing data or receiving commands.

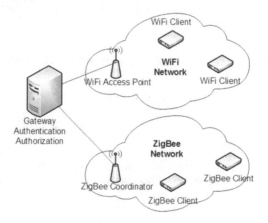

Figure 1.   System topology.

2   SYSTEM OVERVIEW

As shown in Fig. 1, the system will be comprised of a server and a number of clients. These clients can be of differing infrastructures with each other, but will be able to communicate with one another by passing their packets to the server, who will then relay the packet to the intended recipient client. For the overlay network, regardless of the infrastructure, every packet must first pass through the server.

The infrastructures focused on in the study were 802.11 (WiFi), and 802.15.4 (ZigBee). A gateway was configured to receive all packets, regardless of the infrastructure. This gateway will be the one to relay the packet to a client of either the same infrastructure, or a different infrastructure.

2.1   *Server*

The server will act as the gateway, as well as provide the authentication and authorization services. The gateway is the point of intersection between all devices where all traffic passes through. The authentication server, authorization server, and middleware are integrated in the gateway as separate modules. Because the server fulfills a number of services in the network, it is not considered a constrained device.

A Digi XBee PRO (S2) transceiver, which controls the 802.15.4 section of the system, was connected to the server. The transceiver was configured to run as a coordinator in transparent(AT) mode and to broadcast every transmission to the Personal Area Network (PAN). The server was also connected to a WiFi access point and was installed with a message broker software called RabbitMQ, which controls the 802.11 section of the system, and the server was set as the message broker. Three topics were initialized: one topic was used by the server to listen for incoming 802.11 packets, another topic was used by the server to transmit packets to the 802.11 devices, the last topic was used by the server to reply to specific 802.11 client services. The server was configured to publish packets in fanout mode, hence all client nodes subscribed to the topics will receive the same server packets.

2.2   *ZigBee client*

The ZigBee client was a Raspberry Pi 3 Model B with a Digi XBee PRO (S2) transceiver connected via serial connection. The transceiver was configured to run as a router in AT mode and all transmissions is directly sent to the coordinator.

Table 1. Handshake packet format.

	Header	Phase	Payload
Example	00	00	0013A20040E7353E

Table 2. Service packet format.

	Header	Type	Src	Dst	Payload	HMAC
Example	01	00	12	14	<Push>	<HMAC>

2.3 *WiFi client*

The Wifi Client was a Raspberry Pi 3 Model B connected to the same access point as the server. The client was configured to know that the server was the broker.

2.4 *Packet format*

In order for the server to properly identify the process it must execute for the packets it receives, a specific packet format was designed.

There are two main types of packets in the system: handshake packets, and service packets. Headers were used to differentiate the two types of packets. For handshake packets, a header of b'\x00' was used, while a header of b'\x01' was used for service packets.

As shown in Table 1, handshake packets are comprised of a header, the phase number, and the payload. The phase number corresponds to the current phase in which the client is currently on in the authentication handshake process. The payload contains the actual message that the client is sending to the server for the current handshake phase. Table 1 shows a sample handshake packet for Phase 1 which contains the client's MAC Address as the payload.

As shown in Table 2, service packets are comprised of a header, the service type, the source node, the destination node, the payload, and the keyed-hash message authentication code (HMAC). The service type identifies what kind of service is being requested upon by the source node to the destination node. The source and destination node fields are the node IDs of the two nodes. The payload contains the message that the source node is sending to the destination node. The HMAC is a computed value added at the end of every service packet used for authentication.

3 IMPLEMENTATION

3.1 *Handshake*

Before a node can be considered part of the IoT network, it must first go through an authentication handshake with the server. The handshake is a series of packet exchanges between a client and the server wherein encrypted information is sent to one another in order to develop a secure connection between the two. The handshake is composed of four phases. The handshake design and sequence is loosely based on the Datagram Transport Layer Security (DTLS) handshake. To prevent denial of service (DoS) attacks, DTLS implements a stateless cookie exchange wherein when the client sends a ClientHello message to the server, the server responds with a HelloVerifyRequest message containing a generated stateless cookie. The client must retransmit the ClientHello message with the received cookie added[4]. As shown in Fig. 2, the handshake sequence is as follows:

Phase 1: The client initiates the handshake by sending an authentication request to the server. The authentication request payload includes the client's physical address. Once the server receives the

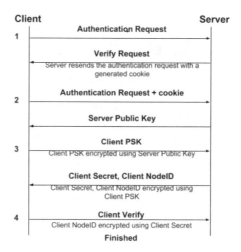

Figure 2.   Handshake sequence diagram.

authentication request, it first checks if the packet is a valid authentication request. After validation, the server would resend the authentication request packet, with a generated cookie attached.

The inclusion of the cookie is to prevent DoS attacks. For the server to consider the authentication request to be legitimate, it must receive back the authentication request with the correct cookie from the client. The lack or error in the client cookie will signify that the authentication request is not legitimate and could be a sign of a DoS attack, i.e. an attacker node keeps sending an authentication request over and over.

Phase 2: Once the client receives the authentication request with the cookie, the client will simply resend it back to the server. After receiving the request with the valid client cookie, the server will then send its public key to the client.

This part of the handshake requires the use of RSA encryption. The server will send its public key to the client, who will then use it for encryption. When receiving a reply, the server will use its private key for decryption.

Phase 3: The client will use the server public key it received to be able to send its pre-shared key to the server securely. The server will use its private key to decrypt the client's pre-shared key. Then, the server will verify the validity of the pre-shared key by comparing it with its copy of the key. After this verification, the server will encrypt the client's secret and node ID using the pre-shared key.

This part of the handshakes requires AES encryption. The server will send the proper node credentials to the client, encrypted using the pre-shared key. The client will decrypt it by also using the pre-shared key.

Phase 4: Once the client receives the reply from the server, it will decrypt the message using its pre-shared key to acquire its node ID. This node ID will act as the client's unique identifier in the overlay network. The node ID is needed when the client node is to send service packets to the server. The secret is also pertinent whenever the client will send a service packet as it is used for authentication checks via the use of HMAC.

For verification that the client did indeed receive its assigned node ID and secret without any fragmentation, the client will send its node ID encrypted with its secret. When the server receives this reply from the client, it will decrypt it using the secret to confirm that the node ID that the client received was correct.

The server keeps track of the current phase of all the expected authenticating nodes. Initially, all the unauthenticated nodes will start at Phase 1. Clients whose phase is set to 1 is considered unauthenticated, furthermore these unauthenticated clients do not have a secret, nor a node ID, making them unable to send service packets to the server.

This authentication handshake was designed to be unreliable. If at any point the server or the client does not receive a reply within a certain amount of time, the handshake will expire. In the server side, the server has a timer for each phase. If at that certain phase the timer runs out, the handshake will expire. In the client side, the client waits a certain time to receive a reply from the server. If the server does not reply in time, the client program will terminate, and the handshake will be incomplete. If the handshake expires, the server will reset the client's phase to Phase 1.

3.2 *Services*

Once a client has finished the handshake and has been successfully authenticated, it can be considered as a node in the overlay network. As part of the network, a node can send service packets to another node in the network.

The two main types of services implemented in the system is 'Push' and 'Pull'. The push service is used whenever a node is to send data, or a command to another node. In this study, a source node sends a service packet to another node with a light-emitting diode connected to it. Upon receiving the service packet, the destination node parses the packet in order to get the payload. A specific message is needed in order for the destination node to execute the code to make the LED light up. Receiving a packet containing anything but the light triggering message will result in the light being turned off. The pull service is used whenever a node needs to acquire data from another node. This was implemented in the study by having a node send a pull request to another node with a DHT11 Temperature and Humidity Sensor connected to it in order to get the temperature or humidity. Once the destination node receives the service packet, it parses it to get the payload. If the message is, <temp>, the destination node will execute the code to get the temperature. If the message is, <hum>, the destination node will execute the code to get the humidity. After getting the desired data, the destination node will form a reply packet to send back to the source node. If the destination node receives a pull request packet with anything but the message 'temp' or 'hum', it will not process the request.

When sending service packets, the node will make use of node IDs as identifiers. It will set its own node ID as the source node, and the recipient node's ID as the destination node. Due to the design of the system in which there is a gateway server, every packet is sent to the server, and the server will be the one to forward the packet to its proper destination.

To ensure that a valid node did send the packet to the server, and that the packet went through the server first before reaching the destination node, an HMAC check is done in both the server and the destination node. Before sending a packet to the server, the source node will compute for an HMAC by concatenating the packet message and its secret, and hashing it using the MD5 hashing algorithm. Once the server receives the packet, it will authenticate that the source node is who it says it to be. The server will parse the packet in order to separate the packet message and the HMAC. It will compute for its own HMAC by concatenating the packet message and its copy of the source node secret, then hashing it with MD5. It will compare the received HMAC with its own computed HMAC. If the hashes are the same, then the node has been authenticated. If the hashes are different, then the node is not authenticated, and the packet is dropped.

After authentication, the server will check if the service is authorized. The server has an access control list which contains a whitelist of allowed actions. It checks if there is an entry for that service being done by that source to that destination. The presence of an entry means that the service is authorized. No such entry in the access control list means that the service is not allowed.

Because the design of the system if unreliable, there are no acknowledgements. The server does not send a message to the source node regarding if the destination node received the service packet. Hence, the source node will not know whether the destination node received the packet and was able to process the service, nor if the destination node did not receive the service packet because the service is unauthorized.

3.3 *Server state diagram*

As the gateway in the system, the server is in a recurring 'Waiting' state. It can be seen in Fig. 3 that after each process, the server will return to its 'Waiting' state until it receives a packet. After

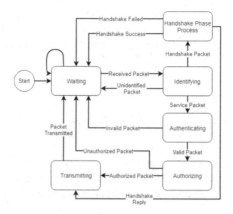

Figure 3.　Server state diagram.

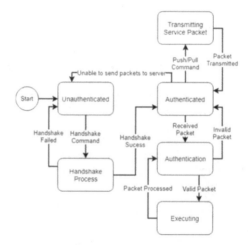

Figure 4.　Client state diagram.

receiving a packet, it will first identify what kind of packet it received. When receiving a handshake packet, it will check the phase to determine which handshake phase process it will execute. After each execution, the server will transmit a packet back to the client. Then, it will return to its 'Waiting' state until it receives another packet. Any error or handshake failure will have the server return to its 'Waiting' state. When receiving a service packet, the server will undergo authentication of the packet to ensure that the source node is a legitimate authenticated node. If the packet fails authentication, the server will stop the process, drop the packet, and go back to 'Waiting'. If it passes authentication, the server will then do authorization of the packet before sending it to the destination. The authorization is done so that no unauthorized activity will be done in the network. If the packet passes the authorization process, it will transmit the authorized packet to the destination node before going back to its 'Waiting' state. Failing the authorization process will have the server drop the packet and return to its 'Waiting' state until it receives another packet.

3.4　Client state diagram

As shown in Fig. 4, the client initially starts at an "Unauthenticated" state. To get to an 'Authenticated' state, the client must first successfully finish the authentication handshake with the server. A handshake command from the user would initiate the handshake process to start. Any error or

Table 3. Authentication handshake test cases.

Test Case	Expected Result	Result
Incorrect authentication packet format	Failed authentication	Failed authentication
Invalid MAC Address	Failed authentication	Failed authentication
Invalid PSK	Failed authentication	Failed authentication
Unable to reply with cookie	Failed authentication	Failed authentication
Sending service packet without authentication	Dropped Service Packet	Dropped Service Packet
Valid authentication packet	Successful authentication	Successful authentication

failure during any phase of the handshake would result in the client remaining unauthenticated. Successfully finishing the handshake, the client would then be considered to be authenticated. In its 'Authenticated' state, the client is to be idle until it either receives a user command or receives a packet from the server. When the authenticated client receives a packet from the server, most probably a service packet from another node, it will first authenticate the packet to verify that the packet went through the server. After successful authentication, the client will execute the service. After execution, the client will become idle again. Packets that fail authentication will also lead the client to return to its idle "Authenticated" state. If the client receives a service command, i.e. "Push" or "Pull", it will transmit a service packet with the correct parameters to the server. If the client becomes idle for too long, i.e. the server not receiving any activity from the client, the client will return to its 'Unauthenticated' state in the server-side. Because of this, the packets that the client would send to the server would be dropped. In this case, the client is unaware that the server has deemed it inactive. User intervention is needed in order to observe that the client is unable to send packets to the server and that an authentication handshake must commence once again.

4 TESTS AND RESULTS

4.1 *Handshake*

The authentication handshake was designed in such a way that whenever there is any error in the packet message or the packet format, the server will deem the handshake as a failure. The authentication handshake was tested in order to verify that any error in any part of the handshake would result in a failed authentication. The test cases and the results are shown in Table 3.

Test case A was done to test if an invalid packet format would be processed by the server. The server parses every packet it receives and properly identifies the process to follow. Because the packet sent had an invalid format, the server did not process the packet.

Test case B was done to verify that only expected authenticating nodes are able to successfully finish the authentication handshake. The server has a list of client MAC addresses that it refers to identify if the client can be part of the overlay network. As expected, a client with an invalid MAC address was not able to be authenticated.

Test case C was done to check that only valid pre-shared keys are accepted. The server has a list of client pre-shared keys. During Phase 3 of the handshake, the client sends its copy of the pre-shared key to the server. An invalid pre-shared key would result in the handshake to fail.

Test case D was done to test the effectiveness of the part of the handshake that prevents denial of service attacks. During Phase 2, the server is expecting the client to resend its authentication handshake with the server-generated cookie added to it. As expected, the lack of cookie resulted in a failed authentication.

Test case E was done to verify that only authenticated nodes are able to send service packets in the overlay network. The test was done by having an unauthenticated node send a service packet. Because the node did not go through the authentication handshake, it does not have its assigned node ID and secret. The server dropped the service packet due to the lack of the necessary attributes.

Test case F was a valid authentication test. The client was properly configured with the correct parameters needed to successfully finish the handshake. As expected, a valid authentication packet resulted in a successful authentication handshake.

Aside from testing the effectiveness of the authentication handshake, the latency and success rate were recorded. The authentication handshake was done 25 times between a ZigBee client and the server, and between a WiFi client and the server. The handshake test was done with different second intervals in between each handshake in order to observe the effect it would have on the latency. The results of the authentication handshake tests with five-second intervals up to ten-second intervals are shown in Table 4. With only a five-second interval in between handshakes, the ZigBee handshake test had a 64% success rate, with 16 out of 25 handshakes finishing successfully. This shows that even with a five-second interval, a bottleneck could occur within the ZigBee communication in the network. The fastest handshake finished at 835.217 milliseconds, while the longest handshake finished at 2518.790 milliseconds. As the interval between handshakes increases, the ZigBee handshake test garnered improvements in its performance. However, the success rate seemed to still be sporadic, having varying numbers of success and fails for different intervals. At ten-second intervals, the ZigBee handshake test still experienced failures. The ZigBee handshake failed attempts showed that the handshake mostly failed during Phase 3 of the handshake. The failed attempts were due to a server-side problem wherein the server was unable to validate the

Table 4.   Authentication handshake latency (in milliseconds).

Interval	Metric	ZigBee	WiFi
5 seconds	Mean	1312.609 ms	513.413 ms
	Min Value	835.217 ms	376.602 ms
	Max Value	2518.790 ms	1053.582 ms
	Success	16	25
	Fail	9	0
6 seconds	Mean	1132.497 ms	714.490 ms
	Min Value	835.458 ms	341.733 ms
	Max Value	1824.265 ms	1169.363 ms
	Success	25	25
	Fail	0	0
7 seconds	Mean	976.932 ms	708.774 ms
	Min Value	823.522 ms	443.793 ms
	Max Value	1333.174 ms	1537.875 ms
	Success	21	25
	Fail	4	0
8 seconds	Mean	867.374 ms	476.968 ms
	Min Value	815.053 ms	365.853 ms
	Max Value	1291.669 ms	631.749 ms
	Success	24	25
	Fail	1	0
9 seconds	Mean	1019.136 ms	817.423 ms
	Min Value	819.370 ms	473.459 ms
	Max Value	1937.973 ms	1288.784 ms
	Success	20	25
	Fail	5	0
10 seconds	Mean	936.554 ms	890.982 ms
	Min Value	820.804 ms	475.001 ms
	Max Value	1763.229 ms	1735.095 ms
	Success	23	25
	Fail	2	0

phase of the client, although the client sent a correctly phased packet. A locking problem was observed wherein the server was prone to have a dirty read in between updating the handshake phase in the Phase table and fetching the current phase in the Phase table. On the other hand, the WiFi handshake test had a 100% success rate across the board. For every second interval done, i.e. from five seconds to ten seconds with a one second increment, the WiFi handshake did not experience any failures. However, it is still possible for a WiFi handshake to fail as it can be seen in the results that there are times wherein the handshake could take longer than the average time. The deviation could stem from a probable collision of packets during the fast two-way communication during the authentication handshake. Probable connection timeouts with the message queue broker could also cause a WiFi handshake to fail. The WiFi handshake was also recorded to be generally faster than the ZigBee handshake. At the five-second interval test, the fastest handshake finished at 376.602 milliseconds, while the longest handshake finished at 1053.582 milliseconds.

4.2 Services

In sending service packets, the server checks its access control list to determine if the action is authorized. The access control list contains a whitelist of allowed services from a specific source node to a specific destination node. To verify the effectiveness of the authorization module of the server, tests were conducted. The test cases included sending an authorized packet and an unauthorized packet. An unauthorized service packet was sent out wherein the source node was not allowed to send that type of service to the destination node. As expected, the server was able to identify that the packet was unauthorized and did not forward the packet to the intended recipient. The testing showed that authorized packets were forwarded by the server to the destination node.

The latency of sending service packets were also recorded. The tests were done by making a node send a push service packet to another node with an increasing size in payload. It is to be noted that before the packet reaches the destination node, it must first go through authentication and authorization by the server. The tests conducted were: from a WiFi node to a WiFi node (WF-WF), from a ZigBee node to a ZigBee node (ZB-ZB), from a WiFi node to a ZigBee node (WF-ZB), and from a ZigBee node to a WiFi node (ZB-WF). Each test case was performed 5 times. The results of the tests are shown in Table 5.

It can be observed that overall, transmission of packet from WiFi node to WiFi node has the fastest transmission time. Its average time of 292.697 milliseconds was the fastest out of all the tests in transmitting a packet size of 256 bytes. The ZigBee to ZigBee communication test showed that it takes more time for a packet to reach the destination node in the case that both source and destination node are ZigBee nodes. ZigBee to ZigBee communication yielded the slowest transmission rates for every packet size increase, having an average of 1348.450 milliseconds when sending 256-byte packets. The difference in the speed of the WiFi to WiFi communication and the ZigBee communication can be attributed to 802.11 generally having higher performance compared to 802.15.4, which is more suited for resource-constraint networks because of its low power consumption[5]. The WiFi to ZigBee transmission also yielded a fast transmission rate yet showed longer times as the size of the packet increased. In sending 4 bytes to 32 bytes, the WiFi to ZigBee transmission showed to be the second fastest. However, as the number of bytes increased, it got slower. When sending a packet size of 256 bytes, its transmission rate rivaled that of ZigBee to ZigBee communication, having an average of 1035.087 milliseconds. The slow transmission time could be attributed to possible bottlenecking due to the transmission going from a fast bandwidth infrastructure to a slower one. On the other hand, the ZigBee to WiFi communication had a steadier increase in the transmission time as the size of the packets increased with its average in sending 256-byte packets being 300.111 milliseconds. While it was slower compared to the WiFi to ZigBee communication at the start, it had better performance when sending bigger sized packets. In contrast, the ZigBee to WiFi transmission is not experiencing a delay because the receiver infrastructure is able to keep up with the bandwidth of the sender.

29

Table 5. Communication Latency (in milliseconds).

Bytes	WF-WF	ZB-ZB	WF-ZB	ZB-WF
4	6.081	189.786	33.117	98.491
	3.467	187.687	25.256	100.936
	7.832	182.148	28.421	93.296
	3.043	182.705	40.978	96.999
	4.479	178.100	33.583	108.346
Avg.	4.980	184.085	32.271	99.613
8	9.215	194.541	81.139	107.014
	11.134	191.923	96.245	106.378
	8.370	201.850	91.150	111.684
	15.256	216.003	84.858	106.792
	4.686	193.558	83.622	105.886
Avg.	9.732	199.575	87.403	107.551
16	5.845	227.735	96.760	126.127
	16.199	224.134	92.256	127.690
	8.089	222.702	96.659	120.366
	8.101	228.108	94.212	125.865
	16.243	225.977	91.237	130.034
Avg.	10.896	225.731	94.225	126.016
32	14.086	302.437	109.262	157.523
	46.479	300.923	125.332	160.794
	14.393	296.549	119.880	158.287
	25.233	308.419	125.560	164.662
	15.882	304.671	115.562	157.140
Avg.	23.215	302.600	119.119	159.681
64	19.936	525.440	294.705	219.904
	70.186	523.511	245.329	219.911
	16.465	517.893	242.971	219.471
	10.499	515.260	284.988	228.558
	30.786	512.935	303.991	223.618
Avg.	29.575	519.008	274.397	222.292
128	118.642	655.303	351.976	284.178
	94.785	649.178	294.012	289.643
	48.386	646.789	320.275	293.562
	293.470	659.027	303.841	294.433
	50.111	657.951	358.138	281.350
Avg.	131.143	653.650	325.648	288.633
256	536.986	1381.573	1007.795	302.895
	280.152	1346.334	1080.790	294.934
	156.573	1354.064	1001.078	308.180
	269.499	1333.473	1036.014	301.366
	220.276	1326.805	1049.760	293.181
Avg.	292.697	1348.450	1035.087	300.111

5 CONCLUSION

The developed system was able to authenticate client nodes of two different infrastructures. It was also able to authorize communication and services between the client nodes. A middleware and gateway system was implemented that facilitated the communication between client nodes with different infrastructures. ZigBee clients took more time to finish the authentication handshake compared to WiFi clients. The WiFi client showed to have a 100% success rate, with probable failures due to connection timeouts with the message queue broker, or due to packet collision during the fast two-way transmission of packets. On the other hand, the ZigBee handshake had inconsistent results. It was observed that having more than a five-second interval in between authentication handshakes would yield a higher chance of success; the failed attempts were due to a problem in the server wherein it was unable to correctly validate the phase of the client, resulting in the server terminating the handshake.

In terms of communication between the nodes, WiFi to WiFi communication was the fastest with an average of 292.697 milliseconds when sending 256-byte packets. Next, ZigBee to WiFi communication with an average of 300.111 milliseconds. In sending fewer number of bytes, WiFi to ZigBee communication was the second fastest but got slower as the number of bytes increased. When sending 256-byte packets, it averaged 1035.087 milliseconds. The difference between the ZigBee to WiFi communication and the WiFi to ZigBee communication lies in the transition between the two different infrastructures. With ZigBee to WiFi communication, it's a slower infrastructure going to a faster infrastructure. On the other hand, the WiFi to ZigBee communication was slower due to the receiver infrastructure possibly not being able to keep up with the faster bandwidth of the sender. Lastly, the ZigBee to ZigBee communication was the slowest overall with an average of 1348.450 milliseconds when sending 256-byte packets.

REFERENCES

R. Sutaria and R. Govindachari, Making sense of interoperability: Protocols and Standardization initiatives in IoT. 2013 [Online]. Available: http://www.cymbet.com/pdfs/Low_power_IoT_ComNet_2013_Mindtree.pdf

L. Liang et al, "A Denial of Service Attack Method for an IoT System," 2016 8th International Conference on Information Technology in Medicine and Education (ITME), Fuzhou, China, 2016, pp. 360–364.

J. Ko et al, Beyond Interoperability – Pushing the Performance of Sensor Network IP Stacks. 2011 [Online]. Available: http://dunkels.com/adam/ko11beyond.pdf

E. Rescorla and N. Modadugu. (2012). Datagram Transport Layer Security Version 1.2, RFC 6347 [Online]. Available: https://tools.ietf.org/html/rfc6347

K. S. Ting, G. K. Ee, C. K. Ng, N. K. Noordin and B. M. Ali, "The performance evaluation of IEEE 802.11 against IEEE 802.15.4 with low transmission power," *The 17th Asia Pacific Conference on Communications*, Sabah, 2011, pp. 850–855.

Theory and Practice of Computation – Nishizaki et al. (eds)
© 2019 Taylor & Francis Group, London, ISBN 978-0-367-20417-4

A characterization on necessary conditions of realizability for reactive system specifications

Takashi Tomita
Japan Advanced Institute of Science and Technology, Ishikawa, Japan

Shigeki Hagihara
Tohoku University of Community Service and Science, Yamagata, Japan

Masaya Shimakawa
Tokyo Institute of Technology, Tokyo, Japan

Naoki Yonezaki
Tokyo Denki University, Tokyo, Japan

ABSTRACT: This paper focuses on verification for specifications of reactive systems. A reactive system is an open system that interacts with an uncontrollable external environment continuously, and it is often required to be highly safe and reliable. However, the realizability checking for a given specification is very costly, so that we need effective methods to detect and analyze defects of unrealizable specifications for refining them efficiently.

We introduce a systematic characterization on necessary conditions of the realizability. This characterization is based on quantifications for inputs and outputs in early/late behaviors, and reveals four essential aspects of realizability: exhaustivity, strategizability, preservability and stability. Additionally, the characterization derives new necessary conditions which enable us to classify defects of unrealizable specifications systematically and hierarchically.

1 INTRODUCTION

1.1 *Background*

Most practical systems are open systems that interact with uncontrollable external environments continuously. Such open systems are often modeled as *reactive systems*, and required to be highly safe and reliable. *Automatic synthesis* from formal specification have been studied widely (Büchi & Landweber 1969, Pnueli & Rosner 1989, Rosner 1992, Kupferman & Vardi 2005, Schewe & Finkbeiner 2007, Filiot et al. 2009, Ehlers 2012, Bohy et al. 2012) as an ideal process to develop such safe and reliable reactive systems. This is because it has no manual (i.e. error-prone) phase except for describing the specification. If the specification has no defect, we can obtain a perfect program. That is, the automatic synthesis is also *realizability checking* of the specification.

A specification with defects will have to be fixed. Unfortunately, realizability checking of reactive system specification is extremely costly (Pnueli & Rosner 1989, Abadi et al. 1989, Rosner 1992) in general. So it is not feasible to make a specification realizable by refining and realizability-checking repeatedly. We need a method to detect and analyze defects of a given unrealizable specification efficiently and effectively. Mori & Yonezaki (1993) and Yoshiura (2004) introduced three necessary conditions of realizability and their decision procedures. Based on whether the necessary conditions hold or not, we can classify defects of unrealizable specifications.

1.2 *Contributions*

The contributions of the paper are: (1) systematic characterization on necessary conditions of realizability, (2) four essential aspects of realizability: *exhaustivity*, *strategizability*, *preservability* and *stability*, (3) new necessary conditions derived from the characterization, which can classify defects of unrealizable specifications in detail, and (4) the hierarchy results. The characterization is based on how system/environment behaviors are quantified in early and late stage. Additionally, it is applicable to known necessary conditions, clarifies the four essential aspects of realizability, and derives new necessary conditions. By using the information of whether the necessary conditions hold or not, we can classify defects of specifications in detail on the viewpoint of the essential aspects. The detailed classification will be helpful for considering how to refine the specifications. We also show the hierarchy theorem of necessary conditions.

1.3 *Related work*

Reactive system synthesis from formal specification is equivalent to realizability checking for the specification, and it have studied widely (Büchi & Landweber 1969, Pnueli & Rosner 1989, Rosner 1992, Kupferman & Vardi 2005, Schewe & Finkbeiner 2007, Filiot et al. 2009, Ehlers 2012, Bohy et al. 2012). The computational complexity of realizability checking is costly in most cases, e.g. LTL realizability checking is 2EXPTIME-complete (Pnueli & Rosner 1989, Rosner 1992).

So, when a given specification is unrealizable, it is strongly required to extract useful information for efficiently refining the specification. One approach is to check necessary conditions of realizability (Mori & Yonezaki 1993, Yoshiura 2003, Shimakawa et al. 2013). Whether necessary conditions hold or not corresponds with whether certain characteristics are missing or not in the specification. Therefore, we can classify defects of unrealizable specifications based on necessary conditions checking. This paper introduces a characterization on the necessary conditions, and also new necessary conditions. The characterization enable us to classify the defects systematically in detail.

Necessary conditions are useful for defect component extraction. Hagihara et al. (2014) focused on a certain necessary condition, and proposed a method to extract minimal components that implies violation of the necessary condition. Imperfect synthesis from specifications meeting necessary conditions is another application technique. Yoshiura & Yonezaki (2000) proposed a method to compose an imperfect (but preferable) reactive system based on another certain necessary condition. The techniques are outside of the scope of the paper.

2 PRELIMINARIES

2.1 *Reactive systems*

An open system interacting with an environment (e.g. user, external models, etc.) is often modeled as a *reactive system*. A typical instance of such systems is a controller, which gives control signals to a target module and receives their feedback continuously. In formally, a reactive system has characteristics as follows.

  i. A reactive system can (resp., cannot) control its outputs to (resp., inputs from) an environment.
 ii. The outputs at each step must be determined based on a past behavior (i.e. a sequence of inputs and outputs until then).

Let $\mathcal{I}$ and $\mathcal{O}$ be disjoint sets of atomic propositions that mean the occurrences of input and output events controlled by the environment and system, respectively. Formally, a reactive system is defined as follows.

Definition 1. (Reactive system) *A reactive system is a reaction function* $r : (2^{\mathcal{I}})^+ \to 2^{\mathcal{O}}$.

The set of all possible reactive systems is denoted by $\mathcal{R}$. For an infinite sequence $\alpha = a_0 a_1 a_2 \cdots \in (2^{\mathcal{I}})^\omega$ of inputs from the environment, an infinite sequence $r(a_0) r(a_0 a_1) r(a_0 a_1 a_2) \cdots \in (2^{\mathcal{O}})^\omega$ of outputs of a reactive system r for α is denoted by $r^\omega(\alpha)$.

Definition 2. (Behavior) *A behavior of a reactive system r for an infinite input sequence α is a stepwise union of α and an infinite output sequence $r^\omega(\alpha)$ produced by r.*

For an infinite input sequence $\alpha = a_0 a_1 a_2 \cdots \in (2^{\mathcal{I}})^\omega$ and infinite output sequence $\beta = b_0 b_1 b_2 \cdots \in (2^{\mathcal{O}})^\omega$, a stepwise union $(a_0 \cup b_0)(a_1 \cup b_1)(a_2 \cup b_2) \cdots \in (2^{\mathcal{I} \cup \mathcal{O}})^\omega$ of them is denoted by $\langle \alpha, \beta \rangle$. We can divide an infinite input (resp., output) sequence α (resp., β) into (i) a finite input (resp., output) prefix $\bar{\alpha}$ (resp., $\bar{\beta}$) and (ii) a infinite input (resp., output) suffix $\hat{\alpha}$ (resp., $\hat{\beta}$) such that $\alpha = \bar{\alpha} \cdot \hat{\alpha}$ (resp., $\beta = \bar{\beta} \cdot \hat{\beta}$). For a finite input sequence $\bar{\alpha} = a_0 a_1 \cdots a_n \in (2^{\mathcal{I}})^*$, a finite output sequence $r(a_0) r(a_0 a_1) \cdots r(a_0 a_1 \cdots a_n) \in (2^{\mathcal{O}})^*$ of a reactive system r for $\bar{\alpha}$ is denoted by $r^*(\bar{\alpha})$.

2.2 Specifications

A *specification* is a description of what a system should and should not do. Typically, a formal specification is given by a formula in Linear Temporal Logic (LTL) (Pnueli 1977) or ω-automaton. They divide possible behaviors into satisfied or accepted ones and the others. Usually, the satisfied or accepted ones are considered as desirable behaviors of a reactive system. In this paper, we use the following definition.

Definition 3. (Specification) *A specification is a set $\mathcal{S} \subseteq (2^{\mathcal{I} \cup \mathcal{O}})^\omega$ of desirable behaviors of a reactive system.*

A reactive system has to be able to respond outputs suitable for a given specification step by step for any input sequence. Conversely, a reactive system specification must be not only *satisfiable* (i.e. consistent), but also *realizable*.

Definition 4. (Satisfiability) *A specification $\mathcal{S}$ is* satisfiable if

$$\exists \alpha \in (2^{\mathcal{I}})^\omega, \beta \in (2^{\mathcal{O}})^\omega : \langle \alpha, \beta \rangle \in \mathcal{S}, \tag{1}$$

i.e. $\mathcal{S}$ is not empty.

Definition 5. (Realizability) *A specification $\mathcal{S}$ is* realizable if

$$\exists r \in \mathcal{R} : \forall \alpha \in (2^{\mathcal{I}})^\omega : \langle \alpha, r^\omega(\alpha) \rangle \in \mathcal{S}. \tag{2}$$

If a given ω-regular specification is realizable, we can synthesize a reactive system realizing it algorithmically (Büchi & Landweber 1969, Pnueli & Rosner 1989, Rosner 1992). Otherwise, we need to defect and analyze defects of the specification, and then refine it.

Note that Equation (2) is equivalent to:

$$\forall a_0 \in 2^{\mathcal{I}} : \exists b_0 \in 2^{\mathcal{O}} : \forall a_1 \in 2^{\mathcal{I}} : \exists b_1 \in 2^{\mathcal{O}} : \cdots : \langle a_0 a_1 \cdots, b_0 b_1 \cdots \rangle \in \mathcal{S}. \tag{3}$$

3 CHARACTERIZATION ON NECESSARY CONDITIONS OF REALIZABILITY

In this section, we firstly introduce known necessary conditions of realizability. Then we propose a characterization, which can systematically deal with them and reveals some essential aspects of realizability.

3.1 Known necessary conditions

Mori & Yonezaki (1993) and Yoshiura (2004) provided some necessary conditions and its decision procedures for a given ω-regular specification. By using the decision procedures, we can classify types of the defects.

Definition 6. (Strong satisfiability (Mori & Yonezaki 1993, Yoshiura 2004)) *A specification $\mathcal{S}$ is* strongly satisfiable if

$$\forall \alpha \in (2^{\mathcal{I}})^\omega : \exists \beta \in (2^{\mathcal{O}})^\omega : \langle \alpha, \beta \rangle \in \mathcal{S}. \tag{4}$$

If a given specification $\mathcal{S}$ is unrealizable but strongly satisfiable, a previsional system, which can prerecognize a whole input sequence, can produce a suitable output. However, such system is of course not realistic because the environment can select inputs adaptively. If S is not strongly satisfiable, there exists a *bad input sequence* α such that $\langle \alpha, \beta \rangle \notin S$ for any $\beta \in (2^{\mathcal{O}})^\omega$. That is, the environment can force violation of the specification without considering what a reactive system responds at all.

Definition 7. (Preservably stepwise satisfiability (Mori & Yonezaki 1993, Yoshiura 2004)) *A specification S is* preservably stepwisely satisfiable if

$$\exists r \in \mathcal{R} : \forall \bar{\alpha} \in (2^{\mathcal{I}})^* : \exists \hat{\alpha} \in (2^{\mathcal{I}})^\omega, \hat{\beta} \in (2^{\mathcal{O}})^\omega : \langle \bar{\alpha}\hat{\alpha}, r^*(\bar{\alpha})\hat{\beta} \rangle \in S. \tag{5}$$

A witness system r in Equation (5) *preserves* the satisfiability of S. In other words, r realizes the safety component of S. If a specification is not preservably stepwisely satisfiable, the environment can force its violation within certain steps with only a certain adaptive input prefix for any system.

Definition 8. (Preservably stepwisely strong satisfiability (Mori & Yonezaki 1993, Yoshiura 2004)) *A specification S is* preservably stepwisely strongly satisfiable if

$$\exists r \in \mathcal{R} : \forall \bar{\alpha} \in (2^{\mathcal{I}})^*, \hat{\alpha} \in (2^{\mathcal{I}})^\omega : \exists \hat{\beta} \in (2^{\mathcal{O}})^\omega : \langle \bar{\alpha}\hat{\alpha}, r^*(\bar{\alpha})\hat{\beta} \rangle \in S. \tag{6}$$

A witness system r in Equation (6) preserves the strong satisfiability of S. Even if S is preservably stepwisely strongly satisfiable, it may be unrealizable. If a specification is not preservably stepwisely strongly satisfiable, the environment can force its violation with a certain adaptive input suffix for any system.

Note that the above two necessary conditions were originally named simply as *stepwise satisfiability* and *stepwisely strong satisfiability*, respectively (Mori & Yonezaki 1993, Yoshiura 2004).

3.2 *Characterization by quantification matrix*

The known necessary conditions of realizability, introduced by Mori & Yonezaki (1993) and Yoshiura (2003), are given by quantifications on (i) input prefix, (ii) output prefix, (iii) input suffix and (iv) output suffix. Table 1 shows matrices of how to quantify them in satisfiability, realizability and the necessary conditions. The subscript numbers means the order of occurrences of quantifications. The item "r_1" in "Output" row means that an output prefix/suffix is bounded by a reactive system quantified existentially and primarily.

We use this quantification matrix to characterize necessary conditions of realizability. The quantifications on input prefix and suffix mean the *exhaustivity* on inputs, while those on output prefix and suffix mean the *strategizability* on outputs. Note the asymmetry on inputs and outputs. Inputs are uncontrollable for a system so that we need finally to consider any cases. Outputs are controllable for a reactive system, however, the system must determine it step by step. Therefore, a r-quantification on output prefix (resp., suffix) must precedes a $\forall$-/$\exists$-quantification on input prefix (resp., suffix). Otherwise, the r-quantification is just equivalent to a $\exists$-quantification on output prefix (resp., suffix).

Table 1. Quantification matrices for satisfiability, realizability and necessary conditions introduced by Mori & Yonezaki (1993) and Yoshiura (2004).

(i) Sat.

	Prefix	Suffix
Input	$\exists_1$	$\exists_1$
Output	$\exists_1$	$\exists_1$

(ii) Real.

	Prefix	Suffix
Input	$\forall_2$	$\forall_2$
Output	r_1	r_1

(iii) Str. Sat.

	Prefix	Suffix
Input	$\forall_1$	$\forall_1$
Output	$\exists_2$	$\exists_2$

(iv) Pres. Step. Sat.

	Prefix	Suffix
Input	$\forall_2$	$\exists_3$
Output	r_1	$\exists_3$

(v) Pres. Step. Str. Sat.

	Prefix	Suffix
Input	$\forall_2$	$\forall_2$
Output	r_1	$\exists_3$

In the other perspective, the quantifications on input and output prefixes mean how *preservatively* a system can behave on an early stage, while those on input and output suffixes mean how *stably* a system can behave on a late stage. Note the asymmetry on prefix and suffix. The length of suffix must have infinite, however, that of prefix may have any finite value, including 0. Additionally, in a realistic situation, prefix precedes suffix so that the order of occurrences of quantifications follows it.

4 NEW NECESSARY CONDITIONS

The characterization in the previous section derives new necessary conditions of realizability. In this section, we introduce some meaningful ones of them. Based on whether they hold or not, we can classify types of defects in a given unrealizable specification in more detail.

4.1 *New behavior-based necessary conditions*

Strong satisfiability does not guarantee the existence of a realistic reactive system with some property. In this sense, strong satisfiability is a behavior-based necessary conditions of realizability. Based on the characterization in the previous section, we can obtain new behavior-based necessary conditions of realizability (Table 2).

Definition 9. (Prefixally semi-strong satisfiability) *A specification S is* prefixally semi-strong satisfiable if

$$\forall \bar{\alpha} \in (2^{\mathcal{I}})^* : \exists \hat{\alpha} \in (2^{\mathcal{I}})^\omega, \beta \in (2^{\mathcal{O}})^\omega : \langle \bar{\alpha}\hat{\alpha}, \beta \rangle \in S. \tag{7}$$

If a given specification S is not prefixally semi-strongly satisfiable, there exists a *bad input prefix* $\bar{\alpha}$ that forces violation of S within certain steps without considering what a reactive system responds at all.

Definition 10. (Suffixally semi-strong satisfiability) *A specification S is* suffixally semi-strongly satisfiable if

$$\forall \hat{\alpha} \in (2^{\mathcal{I}})^\omega : \exists \bar{\alpha} \in (2^{\mathcal{I}})^*, \beta \in (2^{\mathcal{O}})^\omega : \langle \bar{\alpha}\hat{\alpha}, \beta \rangle \in S. \tag{8}$$

If a given specification S is not suffixally semi-strongly satisfiable, there exists a *bad input suffix* $\hat{\alpha}$ that forces violation of S from any time without considering what a reactive system responds at all. Note that the quantification for an input suffix $\hat{\alpha}$ precedes the others contrary to a realistic situation in this property. By changing the order of occurrences of the quantifications into a realistic one, we can obtain a variant of the suffixally semi-strong satisfiability.

Definition 11. (Suffixally semi-properly strong satisfiability) *A specification S is* suffixally semi-properly strongly satisfiable if

$$\exists \bar{\alpha} \in (2^{\mathcal{I}})^*, \bar{\beta} \in (2^{\mathcal{O}})^{|\bar{\alpha}|} : \forall \hat{\alpha} \in (2^{\mathcal{I}})^\omega : \exists \hat{\beta} \in (2^{\mathcal{O}})^\omega : \langle \bar{\alpha}\hat{\alpha}, \bar{\beta}\hat{\beta} \rangle \in S. \tag{9}$$

Table 2.   Quantification matrices for new behavior-based necessary conditions.

(i) Pref. Semi-Str. Sat.

	Prefix	Suffix
Input	$\forall_1$	$\exists_2$
Output	$\exists_2$	$\exists_2$

(ii) Suff. Semi-Str. Sat.

	Prefix	Suffix
Input	$\exists_2$	$\forall_1$
Output	$\exists_2$	$\exists_2$

(iii) Suff. Semi-Prop. Str. Sat.

	Prefix	Suffix
Input	$\exists_1$	$\forall_2$
Output	$\exists_1$	$\exists_3$

(iv) Prop. Str. Sat.

	Prefix	Suffix
Input	$\forall_1$	$\forall_3$
Output	$\exists_2$	$\exists_4$

Table 3.   Quantification matrices for new preservability-based necessary conditions.

(i) Prop. Pres. Step. Sat.

	Prefix	Suffix
Input	$\forall_2$	$\exists_3$
Output	r_1	r_1

Table 4.   Quantification matrices for stability-based necessary conditions.

(i) Stab. Step. Sat.

	Prefix	Suffix
Input	$\exists_1$	$\forall_2$
Output	$\exists_1$	r_1

(ii) Stab. Step. Str. Sat.

	Prefix	Suffix
Input	$\forall_1^{\geq n}$	$\forall_3$
Output	$\exists_2$	r_2

If a given specification $\mathcal{S}$ is not suffixally semi-properly strongly satisfiable, for any input prefix $\bar{\alpha}$, the environment can make an *adaptive bad input suffix* $\hat{\alpha}$ that forces violation of $\mathcal{S}$ with considering what a reactive system responds for it. Similarly, by changing the order of occurrences of the quantifications, we can obtain a variant of the strong satisfiability.

Definition 12. (Properly strong satisfiability) *A specification $\mathcal{S}$ is* properly strongly satisfiable if

$$\forall \bar{\alpha} \in (2^{\mathcal{I}})^* : \exists \bar{\beta} \in (2^{\mathcal{O}})^{|\bar{\alpha}|} : \forall \hat{\alpha} \in (2^{\mathcal{I}})^{\omega} : \exists \hat{\beta} \in (2^{\mathcal{O}})^{\omega} : \langle \bar{\alpha}\hat{\alpha}, \bar{\beta}\hat{\beta} \rangle \in \mathcal{S}. \tag{10}$$

This is the two-phase strong satisfiability. If a given specification $\mathcal{S}$ is not properly strongly satisfiable, there exists a *probing input prefix* $\bar{\alpha}$ such that the environment can make an adaptive bad input suffix that forces violation of the specification with considering what a reactive system responds for the input prefix. Note that any input prefix is a probing one if $\mathcal{S}$ is not suffixally semi-properly strongly satisfiable.

4.2   New preservability-based necessary conditions

The witness system of preservably stepwise (strong) satisfiability can preserve just the (strong) satisfiability of the specification, and it cannot produced a suitable output suffix $\hat{\beta}$ even for any convenient input suffix $\hat{\alpha}$. Based on the characterization in the previous section, we can obtain new preservability-based necessary conditions of realizability (Table 3).

Definition 13. (Properly preservably stepwise satisfiability) *A specification $\mathcal{S}$ is* properly preservably stepwisely satisfiable if

$$\exists r \in \mathcal{R} : \forall \bar{\alpha} \in (2^{\mathcal{I}})^* : \exists \hat{\alpha} \in (2^{\mathcal{I}})^{\omega} : \langle \bar{\alpha}\hat{\alpha}, r^*(\bar{\alpha}\hat{\alpha}) \rangle \in \mathcal{S}. \tag{11}$$

The witness system r of properly preservably stepwise satisfiability can preserve the satisfiability of $\mathcal{S}$ for any input prefix, as well as those of preservably stepwise satisfiability. Additionally, it can produce an output suffix suitable for a certain convenient input suffix. Note that a strategy to produce such output suffixes is unified with that to preserve the satisfiability.

4.3   Stability-based necessary conditions

Mori & Yonezaki (1993) and Yoshiura (2004) focused on only preservability, did not on stability. Based on the characterization in the previous section, we can obtain stability-based necessary conditions of realizability (Table 4).

Definition 14. (Stably stepwise satisfiability) *A specification $\mathcal{S}$ is* stably stepwisely satisfiable if

$$\exists r \in \mathcal{R}, \bar{\alpha} \in (2^{\mathcal{I}})^*, \bar{\beta} \in (2^{\mathcal{O}})^{|\bar{\alpha}|} : \forall \hat{\alpha} \in (2^{\mathcal{I}})^{\omega} : \langle \bar{\alpha}\hat{\alpha}, \bar{\beta}r^{\omega}(\hat{\alpha}) \rangle \in \mathcal{S}. \tag{12}$$

For convenient prefixes of input $\bar{\alpha}$ and output $\bar{\beta}$, the witness system r of stably stepwise satisfiability can behave suitably for any output suffix $\hat{\alpha}$ after then. That is, stably stepwise satisfiability means the existence of stable sets of states (represented by r) and the reachability to them (guaranteed by $\bar{\alpha}$ and $\bar{\beta}$). Note that, in different from the relation between Equations (5) and (11), Equation (12) is equivalent to the following formula:

$$\exists r' \in \mathcal{R}, \bar{\alpha} \in (2^{\mathcal{I}})^* : \forall \hat{\alpha} \in (2^{\mathcal{I}})^\omega : \langle \bar{\alpha}\hat{\alpha}, r'^\omega(\bar{\alpha}\hat{\alpha}) \rangle \in \mathcal{S}. \tag{13}$$

This is because, from witnesses r, $\bar{\alpha}$ and $\bar{\beta}$ of Equation (12), we can construct a witness r' of Equation (13) such that $r'^*(\bar{\alpha}) = \bar{\beta}$ and $r'^\omega(\bar{\alpha}\hat{\alpha}) = r'^*(\bar{\alpha})r^\omega(\hat{\alpha})$. This difference is derived from the asymmetry of prefix and suffix.

Definition 15. (Stably stepwisely strong satisfiability) *A specification $\mathcal{S}$ is stably stepwisely n-strongly satisfiable if*

$$\forall m \in \mathbb{R}^{\geq n}, \bar{\alpha} \in (2^{\mathcal{I}})^m : \exists \bar{\beta} \in (2^{\mathcal{O}})^m, \exists r \in \mathcal{R} : \forall \hat{\alpha} \in (2^{\mathcal{I}})^\omega : \langle \bar{\alpha}\hat{\alpha}, \bar{\beta}r^\omega(\hat{\alpha}) \rangle \in \mathcal{S}. \tag{14}$$

The stably stepwisely n-strongly satisfiable becomes closer to realizability when n becomes smaller, and finally becomes the same if n is 0. If $\mathcal{S}$ is stably stepwisely n-strongly satisfiable, there exists an output prefix $\bar{\beta}$ suitable for any input prefix $\bar{\alpha}$ with the length greater than or equal to n and a witness system r that can behave suitably for any output suffix $\hat{\alpha}$ after then. That is, stably stepwise strongly satisfiability means the existence of stable sets of states (represented by r) and the strong reachability to them (guaranteed by the existence of $\bar{\beta}$ suitable for any $\bar{\alpha}$) after certain steps. Note that a witness system of stably stepwise satisfiability is fully strategized, however, that of stably stepwise strong satisfiability is not. This is derived from a trade-off between exhaustivity on inputs and strategizability on outputs.

5   HIERARCHY THEOREM AND DEFECT CLASSIFICATION

In this section, we introduce a hierarchy theorem of the necessary conditions, and give an idea to classify defects of a given unrealizable specification.

Let ***Real***, ***StabStrSat***, ***StabSat***, ***PresStrSat***, ***PropPresSat***, ***PresSat***, ***PropStrSat***, ***StrSat***, ***PrefSemiStrSat***, ***SuffSemiPropStrSat***, ***SuffSemiStrSat***, and ***Sat*** be sets of specifications meeting realizability, stably stepwisely strong satisfiability, stably stepwise satisfiability, preservably stepwisely strong satisfiability, properly preservably stepwise satisfiability, preservably stepwise satisfiability, properly strong satisfiability, strong satisfiability, prefixally semi-strong satisfiability suffixally semi-properly strong satisfiability, suffixally semi-strong satisfiability, and satisfiability, respectively. We have:

Theorem 1. (Hierarchy theorem)

$$StabSat \subset StabStrSat \subseteq Real, \tag{15}$$

$$SuffSemiStrSat \subset SuffSemiPropStrSat \subset StrSat \subset PropStrSat \subset PresStrSat \subset Real, \tag{16}$$

$$Sat \subset PrefSemiStrSat \subset PresSat \subset PropPresSat \subset Real, \tag{17}$$

$$PresSat \subset PresStrSat, \tag{18}$$

$$PropStrSat \subset StabStrSat, \tag{19}$$

$$PrefSemiStrSat \subset StrSat, \tag{20}$$

$$SuffSemiPropStrSat \subset StabSat, \tag{21}$$

$$Sat \subset SuffSemiStrSat. \tag{22}$$

Proof for Theorem 1 *The given inclusiveness of the sets are trivial from Definitions 4–15. The properness of the relations except for **StabStrSat** $\subseteq$ **Real** can be confirmed with the existence of witness specifications. There is no enough space to give them so that they are omitted from the paper.* □

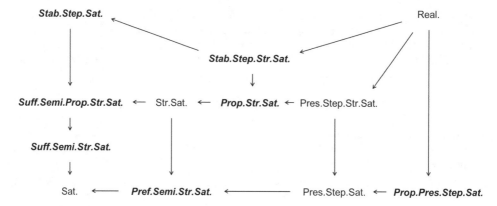

Figure 1. Summary of hierarchy of necessary conditions of realizability.

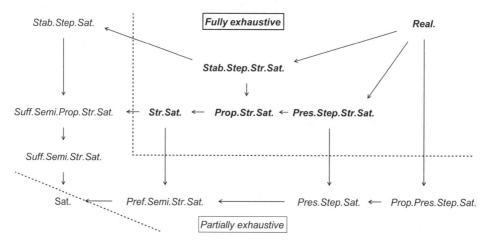

Figure 2. Classification of necessary conditions on exhaustivity on inputs.

The hierarchy illustrated in Theorem 1 is summarized as Figure 1. Bold italic-typed necessary conditions are introduced newly in this paper. An inclusion between conditions that can not derived from the partial order on the inclusion relation does not hold.

The necessary conditions in the hierarchy are given based on quantification matrices and the quantifications reflect four aspects of realizability: exhaustivity, strategizability, preservability and stability. Therefore, by recognizing whether the necessary conditions hold or not, we can explain which aspects of realizability are missing in a given specification. Note again that there is a trade-off between exhaustivity on inputs and strategizability on outputs. A specification can be relaxed (i.e. refined) (1) by strengthening constraints for environment or (2) by weakening those for reactive system. Even if an unrealizable specification is inexhaustive (resp., unstrategizable), it may be possible to make it realizable by refining constraints for reactive system (resp., environment). So, it is probably difficult to find how should we refine an unrealizable specification based on the viewpoints of exhaustivity and strategizability (Figs 2 and 3).

While, it is relatively easier to find that based on the viewpoints of preservability and stability (Figs 4 and 5). We can recognize that an unrealizable specification has detects in the early (resp., late) stage of behaviors when it is (i) stable (resp., preservable) or (ii) impreservable (resp., unstable). The detects in the early stage can be assumed to be related with initial conditions of system and environment. On the other hand, those in the late stage can be assumed to be related to continuous

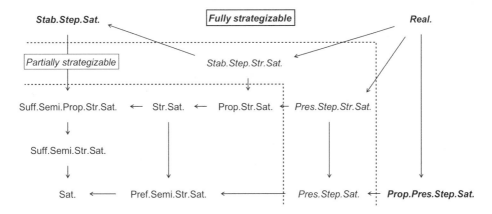

Figure 3. Classification of necessary conditions on stragegizability on outputs.

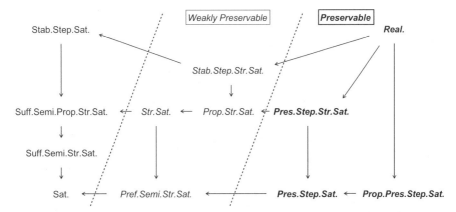

Figure 4. Classification of necessary conditions on preservability of satisfiability.

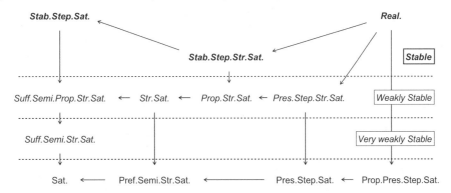

Figure 5. Classification of necessary conditions on stability of satisfiability.

operations. In LTL specification, constraints of continuous operations are given by **G**-formulae[1]. We can try to refine the specification based on these natural assumption.

---

[1] '□' symbol is often used for representing the **G**-operator.

6 CONCLUSIONS AND FUTURE WORK

In this paper, we firstly proposed a systematic characterization on necessary conditions of realizability, based on quantification matrices. A quantification matrix shows how system/environment behaviors are quantified in early and late stage. From the viewpoint of quantification matrices, we found four essential aspects of realizability: exhaustivity, strategizability, preservability and stability. Additionally, we introduced new necessary conditions derived from the characterization and showed the hierarchy theorem among them. By using the information of whether the necessary conditions hold or not, we can recognize which aspects of realizability are missing in a given unrealizable specification.

A future direction is to develop a systematic and integrated method and tool: (1) to check the necessary conditions, (2) to extract core components implying violations of the necessary conditions, and (3) to compose an imperfect (but preferable) reactive system based on necessary conditions checking.

ACKNOWLEDGMENT

This work was supported by JSPS KAKENHI Grant Number JP17K17763.

REFERENCES

Abadi, M. at al. 1989. Realizable and unrealizable specifications of reactive systems. *Automata, Languages and Programming, Lecture Notes in Computer Science* 372: 1–17.

Bohy, A. et al. 2012. Acacia+, a tool for LTL synthesis. *Computer Aided Verification, Lecture Notes in Computer Science* 7358: 652–657.

Büchi, J.R. & Landweber, L.H. 1969. Solving sequential conditions by finite-state strategies. *Transactions of the American Mathematical Society* 138: 295–311.

Ehlers, R. 2012. Symbolic bounded synthesis. *Formal Methods in System Design* 40(2): 232–262.

Filiot, E. et al. 2009. An antichain algorithm for LTL realizability. *Computer Aided Verification, Lecture Notes in Computer Science* 5643: 263–277.

Hagihara, S. et al. 2014. Minimal strongly unsatisfiable subsets of reactive system specifications. *29th ACM/IEEE International Conference on Automated Software Engineering (ASE '14)*: 629–634.

Kupferman, O. & Vardi, M. 2005. Safraless decision procedures. *46th Annual IEEE Symposium on Foundations of Computer Science (FOCS 2005)*: 531–540.

Mori, R. & Yonezaki, N. 1993. Several realizability concepts in reactive objects. *Information Modelling and Knowledge Bases IV, Frontiers in Artificial Intelligence and Applications* 16: 407–424.

Pnueli, A. 1977. The temporal logic of programs. *18th Annual Symposium on Foundations of Computer Science*: 46–57.

Pnueli, A. & Rosner, R. 1989. On the synthesis of a reactive module. *16th ACM SIGPLAN-SIGACT Symposium on Principles of Programming Languages (POPL '89)*: 179–190.

Rosner, R. 1992. Modular synthesis of reactive systems. PhD thesis, Weizmann Institute of Science.

Schewe, S. & Finkbeiner, B. 2007. Bounded synthesis, *Automated Technology for Verification and Analysis, Lecture Notes in Computer Science* 4762: 474–488.

Shimakawa, M. et al. 2013. SAT-based bounded strong satisfiability checking of reactive system specifications. *Information and Communication Technology, Lecture Notes in Computer Science* 7804: 60–70.

Yoshiura, N. & Yonezaki, N. 2000. Program synthesis for stepwise satisfiable specification of reactive system. *International Symposium on Principles of Software Evolution*: 58–67.

Yoshiura, N. 2004. Decision procedures for several properties of reactive system specifications. *Software Security - Theories and Systems, Lecture Notes in Computer Science* 3233: 154–173.

Theory and Practice of Computation – Nishizaki et al. (eds)
© 2019 Taylor & Francis Group, London, ISBN 978-0-367-20417-4

An empirical analysis of a combination of the Bradley-Fayyad-Reina clustering algorithm and Kohonen Maps for Big Data applications

D.D. Delos Santos & A. Azcarraga

Software Technology, De La Salle University, Taft Avenue, Metro Manila, Philippines

ABSTRACT: Clustering algorithms tackle the problem of grouping similar data points in a dataset. Self-Organizing Maps, or Kohonen Maps is an example of a clustering algorithm that is commonly used for grouping and data visualization, but it falls into the pitfall of not being able to completely or effectively cluster a dataset that is extremely big or extremely complex due to its relatively slow training time. The researchers propose using Bradley-Fayyad-Reina clustering as a preprocessing step to first summarize the dataset so SOM can be used and trained, and provide an empirical analysis and testing framework to evaluate the given algorithm.

Keywords: Algorithm Design and Analysis, Clustering, Experimental Algorithmics, Big Data, BFR Clustering, SOM

1 INTRODUCTION

Clustering algorithms generally aim to tackle the problem of grouping together similar data points in a data space. This family of clustering algorithms are generally used for fields including data analytics, data mining, data compression or summarization, and other applications, to either summarize, form groups out of data, or visualize the data to streamline analysis. An example of a clustering algorithm with a focus on visualization is the Kohonen Map/Self-Organizing Map (SOM) (Kohonen, 1998), where a topological data structure is fitted to a dataset and can be mapped onto a 2D space.

Problems in clustering arise when datasets start scaling out of the capabilities of current commonly-used clustering algorithms, such as when the applications start scaling up into Big Data. For example, a naïve implementation of the Density-Based Spatial Clustering of Applications with Noise (DBSCAN) (Ester, Kriegel, Sander, & Xu, 1996) clustering algorithm very quickly becomes unusable for larger datasets with its big-O of $O(n^2)$ with respect to dataset size. SOM also starts running into problems when storing the entire dataset into RAM becomes infeasible. This causes the algorithm to either slow down, due to requiring querying a storage for data, and paging a space in the RAM for that data, or simply become incompatible with Big Data. Other algorithms are created solely for the purpose of handling Big Data and can be used as a data preprocessing step to make the dataset more amenable to more commonly-used algorithms. The Bradley-Fayyad-Reina clustering algorithm (Bradley, Fayyad, & Reina, 1998) is one of these algorithms extended for usage in Big Data applications and may be used to quickly create cluster prototypes for SOM to visualize.

The proponents of this paper propose an experimental framework for an empirical analysis of algorithms and show that a SOM can be extended to be used for Big Data applications by preprocessing first using BFR and then visualizing the resultant cluster prototypes by taking them as data points to train a SOM. This provides a center-based cluster visualization of a dataset in Big Data.

2 ALGORITHM OVERVIEW

2.1 *Bradley-Fayyad-Reina clustering*

The Bradley-Fayyad-Reina (BFR) clustering algorithm is a variant of k-means clustering that is built to handle large volumes of data, by only needing one pass to cluster an entire dataset, compared to k-means, which needs more than one iteration for its clusters to converge and return a solution. The BFR algorithm does not try to hold every point in memory, but instead stores statistical information of all the clusters it generates in memory, holding the assumption that every cluster is distributed as a Gaussian distribution around its centroid.

The algorithm starts by using a normal in-memory algorithm, k-means, for example, and starts with an initial clustering of a sample of the dataset. The algorithm then makes use of a Discard Set (DS) and a Compression Set (CS) as sets of clusters of points, and a Retain Set (RS) as a set of data points to keep track of the clusters. The algorithm will then start querying data from the database, and proceed to summarize them as one of the members of one of the three sets. The algorithm terminates when all the data is processed or the termination criteria has been reached.

2.1.1 Algorithm pseudocode
(i) Instantiate a DS, CS, and an RS
(ii) Query a batch of points from the DB and perform an in-memory clustering algorithm (usually k-means)
(iii) While there are still points in the DB or termination criteria is not reached,
  (a) Query a batch of points from the DB and place the batch in the RAM buffer
  (b) For each point in the RAM buffer, check whether there is a set within DS or a CS that has a high probability of containing the point
  (c) If so, add the point to the set
  (d) Otherwise, add the point to the RS
  (e) After a specified number of batch queries, try to cluster RS using an in-memory clustering algorithm and check whether it fits the requirements of being a CS/merging with another CS/DS
(iv) Instantiate a DS, CS, and an RS

2.1.2 Initial analysis
The main factors that affect the BFR algorithm's time complexity include the dataset size n, the cluster count k, and the dimensionality of the dataset d. Since the BFR algorithm is not an iterative algorithm unlike k-means clustering or SOM, the algorithm operates independently of an iterator variable. At worst case, the algorithm should perform at O(nkd). The memory requirements of the algorithm add the main factor page size p, because the algorithm's main strength is that it does not need to hold all of the data in memory. The final memory complexity of the BFR algorithm is O(pd + kd).

2.2 Kohonen maps/self-organizing maps

The Kohonen Map or the Self-Organizing Map (SOM) is an algorithm that uses an Artificial Neural Network (ANN) to map a data space by using data points from the dataset as training data for the ANN. The SOM is commonly used for its topological consistency, which is preserved due to the learning function of the ANN taking a whole neighborhood of nodes into account for each update. This allows the SOM to be 'unwrapped' and allows visualization of a dataset in a 2D or 3D space dependent on the size of map used even if the dataset was originally too high-dimensional.

2.2.1 Algorithm
(i) Instantiate an m × m map of points
(ii) While the grid position has not converged yet or a target iteration count has not been reached,
  (a) Randomly sample a point from the dataset
  (b) Find the closest neuron in the map
  (c) Update by pulling the closest neuron and its neighbors closer to the data point

2.2.2 Initial analysis
The main factors that affect the SOM's time complexity include the iteration count i, the dataset size n, the dimensionality of each point d, and the number of nodes there are on the map, or m^2. The most defining operation for the time complexity of SOM is that for each iteration, one has to calculate

the distance between the sample point and each neuron in the grid, resulting to a time complexity of $O(idm^2)$. Due to the algorithm needing a large number of iterations to satisfactorily capture the dataset, the algorithm generally performs at least n iterations, and this causes the algorithm to be considered as slower than other linear clustering algorithms. Memory-wise, the algorithm's factors are the same as above, and because SOM is an in-memory algorithm, it must save all points and all the neurons in memory, returning a memory complexity of $O(nd + md)$.

3   EXPERIMENTAL FRAMEWORK

3.1   *Data synthesis*

A data synthesis program generating randomly-created datasets scaling on size and dimensionality based on parameters such as mean position, standard deviation, dataset size, and dimensionality, was implemented to create controlled experiments. The data synthesis program can be used to create different distributions of data and can be tweaked to create handmade datasets for testing and evaluation purposes.

The synthetic datasets generated for use in the study include a randomly generated dataset of size 1,000,000 for memory and time complexity testing with regards to dataset size, a randomly generated dataset with 10,000 elements and 2048 dimensions for the testing of memory and time complexity with regards to dimensionality, and four 2D datasets of size 100,000 for more specific solution quality testing.

3.2   *Experiment design*

The experiments are designed to show and highlight specific strengths and weaknesses of each method. The main goal of each experiment is to create a focused factor-by-factor analysis of each algorithm to show the change in their own respective time complexities and memory complexities as a dataset scales up into Big Data. The experiments are designed as described in McGeoch's *A Guide to Experimental Algorithmics* (2012), and generally use doubling-up experiments to gauge how the algorithms scale up into Big Data.

3.2.1   *Algorithm implementations*
The two algorithms to be used in the study are the Bradley-Fayyad-Reina Clustering algorithm, and the Kohonen Map / Self-Organizing Map algorithm. The algorithms were implemented on an Intel core i5 laptop using Java 1.7, and were modified dependent on the experiment done to count the number of important operations taken by the clustering algorithm. The experiments will be run on BFR only, SOM only, and then BFR + SOM.

3.2.2   *Time complexity experiment*
The time complexity experiments were conducted by first modifying the algorithms by adding an instruction counter to the code of each algorithm. Every non-instantiation non-function call operation was counted as an instruction, and power operations are counted separately. The algorithm then undergoes two different experiments: dataset size and dimensionality.

For the dataset size tests, each algorithm is run on a random sample of the 2-dimensional size-1m dataset with an initial sample size of 120, then the sample size is scaled up by 2 for subsequent runs, up until a maximum sample size of 983,040. The instruction counts are then logged, and saved into a file for storage. After five runs of this process, the average instruction count for each point in dataset size is taken and an approximate time complexity based on dataset size is calculated via polynomial regression.

For the dimensionality experiment, each algorithm is run on a random sample of features from the 2048-dimensional dataset, starting from a sample size of 2, then scaling up by a factor of 2 to the maximum size of 2048 dimensions. The instruction counts are then logged, and saved into a file for storage. After five runs of this process, the average instruction count for each point in dimensionality is taken and an approximate time complexity based on dimensionality is calculated via polynomial regression.

3.2.3 *Memory complexity experiment*

Like for the time complexity experiments, the memory complexity experiments were conducted by first modifying the algorithms by adding an memory counter to the code of each algorithm. Every instantiation operation done in code increments the counter based on how much data in bytes is allocated memory. The algorithm then undergoes two different experiments: dataset size and dimensionality.

For the dataset size test, each algorithm is run on a random sample of the 2-dimensional size-1m dataset with an initial sample size of 120, then the sample size is scaled up by 2 for subsequent run, up until a maximum sample size of 983,040. The memory usage is then logged, and saved into a file for storage. After five runs of this process, the average memory usage for each point in dataset size is taken and an approximate memory complexity based on dataset size is calculated via polynomial regression.

For the dimensionality experiment, each algorithm is run on a random sample of features from the 2048-dimensional dataset, starting from a sample size of 2, then scaling up by a factor of 2 up to the maximum size of 2048 dimensions. The memory usage is then logged, and saved into a file for storage. After five runs of this process, the average memory usage for each point in dimensionality is taken and an approximate memory complexity based on dimensionality is calculated via polynomial regression.

3.2.4 *Solution quality experiment*

Solution quality experiments were conducted by running the algorithms on the four hand-crafted 2D datasets of size 100,000 and comparing the resultant solution qualities from different solution quality indices. The chosen solution quality indices used include the Dunn Validity Index (DI), the Davies-Bouldin Index (DBI), and the Silhouette Index (SI). The indices were chosen and from both their usage in relation to the algorithms above, and their individual qualities; the DI is a measure taking the worst/largest cluster into account, scoring higher if the worst cluster is tight and well-spaced from the other clusters (Dunn, 1973), the DBI being an index that evaluates the separation and tightness/density of the clusters (Davies & Bouldin, 1979), and SI being an index looking at the silhouettes of each cluster and evaluating based on the average silhouette fit based on a scoring function (Rousseew, 1987).

4 EXPERIMENT RESULTS AND ANALYSIS

4.1 *Time complexity experiment*

The time complexity experiments were done on the BFR, SOM, and BFR+SOM implementations with an included instruction count, and polynomial regression was done on the final instruction counts for each data size scaling up to about 1 million data points and then was tabulated for data size tests, and dimensionalities scaling up to 2048. The results were recorded in Tables 1 and 2. There was no significant difference found between the time complexities of BFR and the combination of algorithms with regards to both factors of dataset size and dimensionality.

Table 1.   Time complexity – dataset size experiment.

Algorithm	Big-O (time)	Largest Term
BFR	$O(n)$	4.18×10^2 n
SOM	$O(n)$	9.50×10^1 n
BFR + SOM	$O(n)$	4.20×10^2 n

Table 2. Time complexity – dimensionality experiment.

Algorithm	Big-O (time)	Largest Term
BFR	O(d)	1.82×10^6 d
SOM	O(d)	2.33×10^6 d
BFR + SOM	O(d)	1.81×10^6 d

4.2 Memory complexity experiment

Like for the time complexity experiments, the memory complexity experiments were executed on the BFR, SOM, and BFR+SOM implementations with an included memory timer, and polynomial regression was done on the final memory byte counts for each data size scaling up to about 1 million data points and then was tabulated. Also similar to the time complexity experiments, there was no significant difference found between the time complexities of BFR and the combination of algorithms with regards to both factors of dataset size and dimensionality.

Table 3. Memory complexity – dataset size experiment.

Algorithm	Big-O (time)	Largest Term
BFR	O(n)	2.01×10^1 n
SOM	O(n)	4.30×10^1 n
BFR + SOM	O(n)	2.03×10^1 n

Table 4. Memory complexity – dimensionality experiment.

Algorithm	Big-O (time)	Largest Term
BFR	O(d)	2.02×10^1 d
SOM	O(d)	4.28×10^1 d
BFR + SOM	O(d)	2.03×10^1 d

4.3 Solution quality experiment

4.3.1 Uniform datasets test

The uniform datasets test is done on a dataset with 10,000 elements split into 4 normal distributions arranged in a square in flat 2D space. BFR trades off some information loss for speed when clustering, and does worse than SOM when working with datasets, but the combination of BFR + SOM manages to get closer solution qualities to SOM than BFR.

Table 5. Uniform datasets test.

Algorithm	DI (highest)	DBI (closest to 0)	SI (closest to 1)
BFR	2.51×10^{-5}	7.13×10^0	3.16×10^3
SOM	7.07×10^{-3}	5.47×10^{-1}	4.66×10^{-1}
BFR + SOM	1.78×10^{-3}	5.81×10^{-1}	4.50×10^{-1}

4.3.2 Differing variances test

The differing variances test is done on a dataset with 10,000 elements split into 4 different variance cases, one for a very low variance leading to a dense cluster, one for a very loose variance leading to a sparse cluster, one with a tight variance in one dimension but a loose variance in another, and one with the reverse.

Table 6.   Differing datasets test.

Algorithm	DI (highest)	DBI (closest to 0)	SI (closest to 1)
BFR	2.03×10^{-5}	1.17×10^{0}	1.35×10^{-1}
SOM	1.13×10^{-1}	2.07×10^{-1}	7.42×10^{-1}
BFR + SOM	8.11×10^{-2}	5.53×10^{-1}	6.28×10^{-1}

4.3.3 *Intersecting datasets test*

The intersecting datasets test is done on a dataset with 10,000 elements in 2D space where the distribution of points made to be clusters intersect each other. The algorithms seem to have found a bit of difficulty in clustering the intersecting datasets, as the scores are comparatively lower (or higher, in the case for DBI) across the board.

Table 7.   Intersecting datasets test.

Algorithm	DI (highest)	DBI (closest to 0)	SI (closest to 1)
BFR	8.52×10^{-5}	2.87×10^{0}	1.37×10^{-2}
SOM	1.15×10^{-3}	2.07×10^{-1}	7.42×10^{-1}
BFR + SOM	8.11×10^{-2}	5.53×10^{-1}	6.28×10^{-1}

5   RECOMMENDATIONS AND FUTURE WORK

The research focused on the strengths and weaknesses of using the Bradley-Fayyad-Reina clustering algorithm as a preprocessing step to simplify a large dataset so that one can use the Self-Organizing Maps algorithm for datasets under Big Data applications, but only studying the algorithms under an empirical lens using synthetic data. This study can be extended by studying the effects of real data of large datasets on the BFR-SOM combination, specifically for domains that require a center-based clustering algorithm.

Another possible extension of the research is to use other clustering algorithms designed for Big Data applications, (e.g. CLARANS or BIRCH), as different clustering algorithms have different objectives and clustering models and may be able to model other datasets in different domains in a more suitable manner.

REFERENCES

Bradley, P. S., Fayyad, U., & Reina, C. (1998). *Scaling clustering algorithms to large databases*. In Proceedings of the fourth international conference on knowledge discovery and data mining (pp. 9–15). AAAI Press.

Davies, D.; Bouldin, D. (1979). *A Cluster Separation Measure*. IEEE Transactions on Pattern Analysis and Machine Intelligence.

Dunn, J. C. (1973). *A Fuzzy Relative of the ISODATA Process and Its Use in Detecting Compact Well-Separated Clusters*. Journal of Cybernetics (pp. 32–57).

Ester, M.; Kriegel, H.P.; Sander, J.; Xu, X. (1996). *A density-based algorithm for discovering clusters in large spatial databases with noise*. Proceedings of the Second International Conference on Knowledge Discovery and Data Mining (pp. 226–23). AAAI Press.

Kohonen, T. (1988). *Neurocomputing: Foundations of research*. In J. A. Anderson & E. Rosenfeld (Eds.), (pp. 509–521). Cambridge, MA, USA: MIT Press.

McGeoch, C. C. (2012). *A guide to experimental algorithmics* (1st ed.). New York, NY, USA: Cambridge University Press.

Theory and Practice of Computation – Nishizaki et al. (eds)
© 2019 Taylor & Francis Group, London, ISBN 978-0-367-20417-4

A Bayesian network approach for estimating product substitution using only POS data

J.M.B. Cortez & A.A.R. Yamzon
Cobena Business Analytics and Strategy, Taguig City, National Capital Region, Philippines

ABSTRACT: In retail, whenever an item is unavailable, customers may decide to purchase other items instead. We define the substitution rate between product A and B as the probability that, if product A is unavailable, a customer who originally wanted product A would purchase product B instead. Normally, estimating substitution rates requires both inventory and Point-of-Sale (POS) data. However, many retailers may not have inventory data with the expected granularity and reliability. Our approach for estimating substitution rates uses only POS data, produces confidence estimates and can be implemented at scale using methods such as Stochastic Variational Inference (Hoffman, Blei, Wang & Paisley, 2013). We test our approach using simulated POS data and find that our estimates have sufficient accuracy without using inventory data. We further demonstrate that the resulting substitution rates can be used to simulate changes in inventory and assortment policies and gauge impact on revenue and profit.

1 INTRODUCTION AND RELATED STUDIES

In order to maximize limited shelf space and resources, it is important for retailers to understand customer product substitution behavior. Whenever an item a customer intends to purchase is not available, this customer may purchase another product instead or not purchase anything at all. By estimating the substitution rates between products, retailers can improve policies on product assortment and estimate effects when they opt to drop or reduce inventory of specific products.

In order to estimate product substitution rates, it is often necessary to access both Point-of-Sale (POS) data and inventory status data (Anupindi, Dada, & Gupta, 1998; Kök & Fisher, 2007; Musalem, Olivares, Bradlow, Terwiesch, & Corsten, 2010; Vulcano, Van Ryzin, & Ratliff, 2012). However, many retailers do not track inventory at a sufficient granularity to complement POS data. Dehoratius and Raman (2008) studied a number of branches of a particular retailer and found that 65% of inventory records were inaccurate. When inventory data is unavailable or unreliable, retailers must rely solely on POS data to estimate product substitution rates.

Having inventory data is ideal for estimating substitution rates because there is ground truth of the out-of-stock periods of each product. Substitution only occurs if there is a product that is out-of-stock. However, we do not need to know the actual inventory levels (the number of units available per product per time interval) to estimate substitution rates. We only need to know the inventory status: whether a product is in stock or out-of-stock within a time interval. Without inventory data, we aimed to estimate the inventory status instead of the inventory level.

We propose a two-phase method to estimate product substitution rates of a single store: In the first phase, we estimate inventory status during each time interval in the POS. To this end, we borrow the method of Karabati, Tan and Öztürk (2009) which is based on the number of consecutive time intervals of zero-sales.

In the second phase, we formulate a Bayesian Network model which estimates product substitution rates and demand rates. Current solutions to estimating product substitution rates use

Quadratically Constrained Quadratic Programming (QCQP) (Karabati, Tan & Öztürk, 2009), and Bayesian networks (Letham, B. Letham, L. M., & Rudin, 2016).

A Bayesian network is a directed acyclic graph (DAG) where each node represents a random variable and the edges represent the probabilistic dependencies among the random variables (Ben-Gal, 2008). The demand and substitution rates are represented as nodes in the Bayesian network. They are random variables initially set with prior distributions. Bayesian inference on the Bayesian network provides a way to update the prior distributions using data (Heckerman, 1998). After Bayesian inference, we could use an estimator (e.g. taking the mean or median) on the posterior distributions to come up with point estimates of the demand and substitution rates.

The Bayesian network formulation provides several advantages over QCQP:

1. Provides a convenient language for expressing how latent variables (i.e. the demand and substitution rates) affect the observed variables (i.e. unit sales) through the conditional dependences (i.e. the edges) between the random variables (i.e. the nodes) in the Bayesian network (Ahmed, Aly, Gonzalez, Narayanamurthy, Smola, 2012), (Blei, Kucukelbir, McAuliffe, 2017).
2. Perform inference at scale by methods such as Stochastic Variational Inference. (Hoffman, Blei, Wang & Paisley, 2013)
3. A Bayesian network model allows us to draw further insights regarding the latent variables by sampling from their respective posterior distributions. In particular, we could measure the uncertainty and variance of the latent variable from the sampled histogram. (Eshky, 2008)
4. Prior domain knowledge regarding the latent variables can be injected to Bayesian network solutions through the specification of their prior distributions. (Davidson-Pilon, 2015)

Compared to the Bayesian network formulation by Letham et al., our two-phase method does not require inventory data and can rely on just POS data. By combining the estimation of inventory status (first phase) with product substitution rate and demand rate estimation (second phase), retailers can improve on their product assortment even if only POS data is available.

2 METHODOLOGY

2.1 *Estimating inventory status*

We borrow the method of Karabati, Tan and Öztürk (2009) for estimating inventory status of every product i from the POS data. The goal is to find the inventory status $I_i \in \{0, 1\}^T$ where T is the total number of time intervals in the POS data of the store. This method starts with first estimating the demand rate λ_i and then finding the critical length n_i.

We first assume that product demand follows a Poisson distribution, a common choice for modeling customer arrivals (Mingola, 2013). With the Poisson distribution, we assume that: the demand for product i occurs at a constant rate (i.e. λ_i units sold on average per time interval), and the demand of product i occur independently across time intervals. The interpretation of the length of a single time interval is up to the modeler. It could be 30 seconds, 1 minute, 5 minutes, etc. The λ_i parameter could be rescaled to fit the preferred time scale.

We can think of the POS data of product i as vector $V_i \in \mathbb{N}^T$ where V_i's entries are the unit sales per time interval and T is the total number of time intervals in the POS data of the store. For example, $V_i = [4, 3, 7, 10]$ means 4 units of product i were sold within the first 30 minutes, 3 units were sold in the next 30 minutes, etc, assuming a time interval length is set at 30 minutes. The entire POS data of a store is the matrix $V = [V_1, V_2, \ldots, V_n]$ where n is the total number of products.

Notice that zero sales observations during any time interval may be due to zero demand or unavailability (out-of-stock) of the product. This implies that it is impossible to tell if there was indeed zero demand if the unit sales within a time interval was zero. This means that the distribution of demand is zero-truncated (Cohen, 2016). Thus we estimate the demand rate λ_i using the Zero Truncated Poisson (Grogger & Carson, 1991).

We compute for the maximum likelihood estimates of the demand rates by maximizing the log-likelihood function of the Zero Truncated Poisson distribution as given in Equation 1. Since there is no closed form solution for maximizing this function, we use numerical methods to optimize. In particular, we used the scipy library in Python for numerical optimization.

$$\ln(L(\lambda_i)) = (\sum x_{it}) \ln(\lambda_i) - n \ln(e^{\lambda_i} - 1) - \ln(\prod x_{it}!) \tag{1}$$

Wherein λ_i is the rate parameter of the distribution, in this case the demand rate, x_{it} is the unit sales on time interval t, and L is the likelihood function.

For each product, we compute the critical length n_i. The critical length is defined as the minimum number of consecutive zero-sales time intervals which has a probability of occurring less than a specified threshold ε, assuming that the product demand is Poisson distributed. Given the estimated demand rate $\hat{\lambda}_i$, the critical length, is given Equation 2. (Karabati, Tan and Öztürk, 2009)

$$\frac{-\ln(\varepsilon)}{\hat{\lambda}_i} - 1 < n_i < \frac{-\ln(\varepsilon)}{\hat{\lambda}_i} \tag{2}$$

Using the critical length n_i, find all the consecutive time intervals (of length n_i or more) of zero sales for product i. Fill-in all these time intervals with 0 (representing out-of-stock) in the inventory status I_i. As an example, if $n_i = 4$ and $V_i = [0, 1, 3, 0, 0, 0, 0, 0, 6, 2]$, then $I_i = [1, 1, 1, 0, 0, 0, 0, 0, 1, 1]$

2.2 Inference of demand and substitution rates

With the inventory status already estimated in section 2.1. We can proceed to infer the substitution rates. We formulate the system as a Bayesian Network. We use the following indices for notation: i and j for product indices, and t for the time interval.

Our model considers the following latent variables:

$$\lambda_i = the\ demand\ rate\ for\ product\ i$$
$$\alpha_{ij} = probability\ of\ substituting\ product\ j\ if\ product\ i\ is\ unavailable$$

Note that the demand rate mentioned here in section 2.2 is different from the demand rate in section 2.1. The former distinguishes sales coming from the product demand and sales coming from substitution, while the latter does not.

Our model requires the following parameters:

$$S_{it} = the\ observed\ unit\ sales\ of\ product\ i\ during\ time\ interval\ t$$
$$I_{it} = 1\ if\ product\ i\ is\ in\ stock\ during\ time\ interval\ t;\ 0\ otherwise$$

The expected sales of an available product during each time interval is expressed as the expected arrivals of customers who demand the product itself plus expected substitutions from other products which are out-of-stock. Therefore, the sales of each product during each time intervals can be represented as shown in Equation 3.

$$S_{it} = I_{it}(Poisson(\lambda_i) + \sum_{j \neq i}^{J}(1 - I_{jt})\alpha_{ji}Poisson(\lambda_j)) \tag{3}$$

We apply a logit transformation to latent variable α_{ij} to allow prior distributions with all-real number domains. Since the α_{ij} take on values between 0 and 1, an appropriate prior distribution would have been the Beta distribution, since it has domain between 0 and 1. But the Beta distribution has been found to be difficult to work with in practice. We denote the transformed variable as β_{ij}.

$$\beta_{ij} = ln(\frac{\alpha_{ij}}{1 - \alpha_{ij}}) = logit(\alpha_{ij}) \tag{4}$$

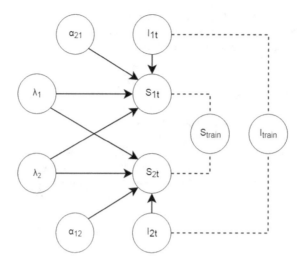

Figure 1.   Sample graph with 2 products.

The resulting formulation is Equation 5.

$$S_{it} = I_{it}(Poisson(\lambda_i) + \sum_{j \neq i}^{J}(1 - I_{jt})Sigmoid(\beta_{ji})Poisson(\lambda_j)) \tag{5}$$

We, however, found that the following formulation in Equation. 6, where the latent variables are all within one Poisson function, is more tractable in implementation. In Edward, the Python library used to implement the Bayesian network, there is no guarantee to successfully perform inference on deterministic functions of random variables (in this case, sum of Poisson random variables). This is because it does not automatically infer Edward random variable classes given operations.

$$S_{it} = Poisson(I_{it}(\lambda_i + \sum_{j \neq i}^{J}(1 - I_{jt})Sigmoid(\beta_{ji})\lambda_j)) \tag{6}$$

Depending on the solution method, a Bernoulli distribution may be applied to the variable β_{ji} for a more accurate representation. However, we find that for Variational Inference solutions, it is sufficient to maintain β_{ji} as a coefficient.

Figure 1 shows a sample graph representation with 2 products.

In the graph, S_{train} represents the actual sales observations, while I_{train} represents the actual Inventory status observations. In the model, these are depicted by S and I matrices respectively. Here, notice that observed variable S_{1t} depends on the latent variables $\lambda_1, \lambda_2, \alpha_{21}$, and the observed variable S_{2t} depends on the latent variables $\lambda_1, \lambda_2, \alpha_{12}$. Both the observed variables (S_{1t}, S_{2t}), and the latent variables ($\lambda_1, \lambda_2, \alpha_{12}, \alpha_{21}$) are nodes (i.e. random variables) in the Bayesian network. The variables I_{1t} and I_{2t} are deterministic variables (not random variables) that only affect S_{1t}, S_{2t} directly as constant coefficients.

We also represent Equation 6 using matrix operations, for conveniently expressing it in probabilistic programming libraries such as Edward. (Ongoing development of the Edward library has since been migrated to Google's Tensorflow Probability.) We denote T as the total number of time intervals and N as the total number of products. The matrix formulation is shown in Equation 7.

$$S = Poisson(I \circ (A + (B \circ C))) \tag{7}$$

where

$$A = Ones(1, T) \circ \boldsymbol{\lambda}$$
$$B = Ones(T, N) - \boldsymbol{I}$$
$$C = (Ones(1, T) \circ \boldsymbol{\lambda}) \cdot Sigmoid(\boldsymbol{\beta})$$

Above, **S** is a T by N matrix representing the sales of each product during each time interval, **I** is a T by N matrix representing the availability of each product during each time interval, $\boldsymbol{\lambda}$ is a 1 by N matrix of random variables representing the demand rate for each product, and $\boldsymbol{\beta}$ is an N by N matrix of random variables representing the logit transformed substitution rates between products. *Ones(a, b)* represents a two-dimensional tensor (i.e. a matrix) of ones with dimensions *a* and *b*. The ∘ operator represents element-wise multiplication and the · operator represents matrix multiplication.

We use variational inference using KL divergence on our Bayesian Network using Gamma priors for the λ_i, since λ_i is strictly positive and the Gamma distribution has positive domain. For the β_{ij}, since it can take on all real numbers, Normal priors were used.

3 A CASE-STUDY USING SIMULATED DATA

3.1 *Simulation*

To test our methodology, we simulate a retailer selling 5 products. Figure 2 illustrates our simulation model.

Customers for each product arrive following a Poisson process with rate λ_i. If the product demanded by a customer is not available, he substitutes following rates α_{ij}. Each product is assigned a Reorder point. Whenever the inventory level of a product goes below this inventory level, the store requests a restock. The amount requested is the amount which would fill the capacity for the product. The restock arrives after a lead time, which follows an Exponential distribution with mean ρ_i. The parameters for our simulation are detailed in Table 1 and Table 2. We simulate 200,000 time intervals to produce sample POS data and Inventory status.

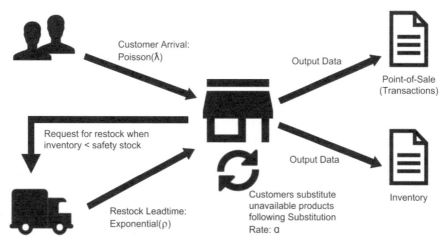

Figure 2.   Illustration of simulation model.

Table 1. Details of products used in simulation.

Product	Demand Rate λ_i	Mean Restock Lead Time ρ_i	Capacity Consumption	Reorder Point	Revenue per Unit	Unit Cost	Fixed Ordering Cost
a	0.1	250	1/750	10	6	2	150
b	0.05	250	1/1000	5	6	3	160
c	0.2	200	1/500	5	15	7	265
d	0.0833	450	1/500	10	8	3	165
e	0.04	550	1/250	10	10	5	180

Table 2. Substitution rates between products used in simulation.

Substitution Rate α_{ij}		jth product				
		a	b	c	d	e
ith	A	–	0.25	0	0	0
product	B	0.8	–	0	0	0
	C	0	0	–	0	0
	D	0.1	0	0	–	0.5
	E	0	0	0	0.9	–

Table 3. Accuracy of estimated inventory for each product.

Product	Correctly classified Stock-Out	Correctly classified Available	Wrongly classified as Stock-Out	Wrongly classified as Available	Overall Accuracy
a	41,253	156,284	1,050	1,414	0.9845
b	32,039	161,935	3,879	2,148	0.9697
c	82,791	113,249	1,605	2,356	0.9802
d	32,321	165,990	715	975	0.9916
e	22,960	175,137	421	1,483	0.9905

3.2 Estimating inventory status

Using the inventory estimation method proposed by Karabati, S., Tan, B., & Öztürk, Ö C. (2009) with parameter $\epsilon = 1 \times 10^{-4}$ we are able to estimate the inventory status for each product as shown in Table 3.

3.3 Inference of demand and substitution rates

We use the estimated inventory as input for variational inference together with the actual sales observations. We use Gamma prior distributions for the latent variables λ_i, with a concentration parameter of 2.0 and rate parameter of 0.2. We use Normal prior distributions for latent variables β_{ij} with location parameter 0.0 and scale parameter 1.0.

We use Lognormal posterior distributions for latent variables λ_i and Normal posterior distributions for latent variables β_{ij}. We apply Variational Inference with 50000 iterations then estimate variables by taking the mean of 500 samples from resulting posterior distributions. We apply a Sigmoid transformation to variable β_{ij} to derive the estimated substitution rates α_{ij}. Our estimates are detailed in Table 4 and Table 5.

Table 4. Estimates for latent variable λ_i using estimated inventory.

Product	Estimated Demand Rate $\widehat{\lambda}_i$	Simulated Demand Rate λ_i
a	0.0988	0.1
b	0.0471	0.05
c	0.1935	0.2
d	0.0804	0.0833
e	0.0389	0.04

Table 5. Estimates for variable α using estimated inventory.

		\multicolumn{10}{c}{jth Product}									
		a		b		c		d		e	
		$\widehat{\alpha}$	α	$\widehat{\alpha}$	α	$\widehat{\alpha}$	α	$\widehat{\alpha}$	α	$\widehat{\alpha}$	α
ith Product	a	–	–	0.244	0.25	0.053	0	0.037	0	0.024	0
	b	0.758	0.8	–	–	0.113	0	0.087	0	0.040	0
	c	0.010	0	0.013	0	–	–	0.020	0	0.009	0
	d	0.138	0.1	0.043	0	0.077	0	–	–	0.489	0.5
	e	0.081	0	0.081	0	0.174	0	0.764	0.9	–	–

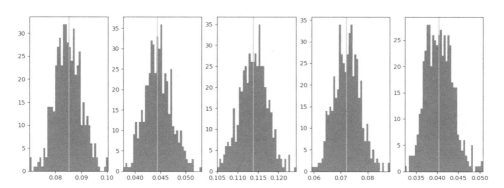

Figure 3. Posterior predictive check reference distributions.

We find that the estimates $\widehat{\alpha}$ are remarkably accurate when compared to the actual simulated substitution rates. We evaluate the accuracy of our solution by computing the Root Mean Squared Error (RMSE) of the inferred sales values against the actual sales values. Using the estimated inventory status, we obtain a RMSE of 0.267.

Furthermore, we conduct a Posterior Predictive Check on the mean sales value simulated by the model. The Posterior Predictive Check is a method for checking whether the posterior distribution is capable of accurately simulating the observed data. (Gelman, Meng, and Stern, 1996) We draw 500 samples from the posterior distribution of sales. Note that each sample is a matrix with dimensions I by T wherein I is the number of products and T is the number of time intervals.

For each sample, we take the mean sales value for each product to obtain a reference distribution. We compare this to the mean sales of each product from the training data and visually inspect the resulting distribution. Figure 3 illustrates the reference distribution for each product.

We find that the mean values from the training data fall into high probability regions for each product, suggesting that the model is able to accurately simulate sales values.

We also demonstrate that the uncertainty surrounding each inferred latent variable can be estimated by sampling from their respective posterior distributions. Figure 4 illustrates the reference distributions for variable α obtained by taking 500 samples.

Observe that histograms along the diagonal, which represent products' substitution probability to themselves, have wide posterior distributions. This is because the inference solution is unable to find samples for these variables and is therefore highly uncertain about their values. Estimates with higher certainty produce narrower distributions. Furthermore, measures of dispersion, such as interquartile range, standard deviation and confidence intervals, can be used to quantify uncertainty in each estimate.

3.4 Simulating impact of policy changes

We demonstrate how a retailer can gauge the impact of assortment modifications. We use the estimated demand and substitution rates to produce simulations of several cases. In each case, we measure the revenue gained during the time horizon, costs and resulting profit. In our base case, the retailer carries all 5 products. We simulate 200,000 time intervals. The results of our base case are shown in Table 6.

In the base case, the overall profit is 238,001 monetary units. In case 1, the retailer drops Product b from his assortment and does not reallocate the capacity previously occupied by Product b. The results of case 1 are shown in Table 7.

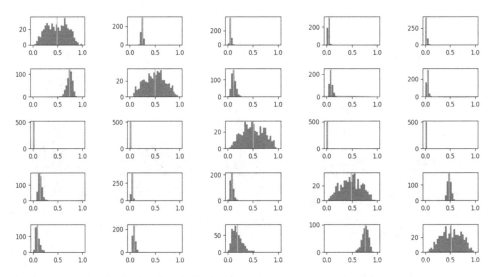

Figure 4.   Posterior distributions for substitution rates.

Table 6.   Results of base case simulation.

	Product a	Product b	Product c	Product d	Product e	Total
Revenue	111,840	59,400	430,425	105,184	66,620	773,469
Units Sold	18,640	9,900	28,695	13,148	6,662	77,045
Out-of-stock Periods	21,940	10,313	54,111	52,751	62,410	201,525
Unit Costs	37,240	29,250	200,165	39,150	33,200	339,005
Storage Costs	7,867	8,709	6,461	6,322	5,585	34,943
Ordering Costs	19,950	8,000	79,765	23,925	29,880	161,520
Profit	46,783	13,441	144,034	35,787	−2,045	238,001

Table 7. Results of case 1 simulation.

	Product a	Product b	Product c	Product d	Product e	Total
Revenue	140,850	–	429,690	113,768	69,300	753,608
Units Sold	23,475	–	28,646	14,221	6,930	73,272
Out-of-stock Periods	28,492	–	58,315	48,265	62,287	197,359
Unit Costs	46,760	–	200,165	44,160	34,580	323,915
Storage Costs	7,514	–	6,231	6,542	5,713	26,000
Ordering Costs	25,050	–	79,765	25,905	31,140	161,860
Profit	61,526	–	143,529	37,161	−2,133	241,833

Table 8. Results of case 2 simulation.

	Product a	Product b	Product c	Product d	Product e	Total
Revenue	154,044	–	429,000	110,392	65,700	759,136
Units Sold	25,674	–	28,600	13,799	6,570	74,643
Out-of-stock Periods	13,935	–	57,621	53,425	68,483	193,464
Unit Costs	51,040	–	199,500	41,310	32,600	324,450
Storage Costs	16,840	–	6,271	6,184	5,369	34,665
Ordering Costs	13,200	–	79,500	25,245	29,340	147,285
Profit	72,964	–	143,729	37,653	−1,609	252,736

Table 9. Results of case 3 simulation.

	Product a	Product b	Product c	Product d	Product e	Total
Revenue	146,016	–	475,965	115,640	70,040	807,661
Units Sold	24,336	–	31,731	14,455	7,004	77,526
Out-of-stock Periods	23,528	–	43,786	42,003	56,956	166,273
Unit Costs	48,498	–	221,760	43,125	34,840	348,223
Storage Costs	9,771	–	8,766	8,646	7,440	34,623
Ordering Costs	20,550	–	69,960	20,625	24,120	135,255
Profit	67,197	–	175,479	43,244	3,640	289,560

In case 1, the overall profit is 241,833 monetary units. Observe that Product b accounted for 59,400 revenue in the base case; yet, the retailer only loses 19,861 in revenue. This is because Product a enjoys increased sales by substituting for Product b. In case 2, the retailer drops Product b and reallocates the capacity previously occupied by Product b to Product a. The results of case 2 are shown in Table 8.

In case 2, the overall profit is 252,736. The retailer obtains higher profit than case 1 due to reduced out-of-stock periods and ordering costs for Product 1. In case 3, the retailer drops Product b and reallocates the capacity previously occupied by Product b equally among the remaining products. The results of case 3 are shown in Table 9.

In case 3, the overall profit is 289,560. The retailer obtains even higher profit than cases 1 and 2 due to increase sales of remaining products. This would suggest that dropping Product B and reallocating its capacity equally would be a profitable policy change for the retailer. Note that this insight is only applicable for the given set of input parameters.

4 RESULTS AND RECOMMENDATIONS

We provide a two-step formulation to estimate product substitution rates using solely POS data. In the first step, we estimate the inventory status during each time interval by examining the length of consecutive zero-sales time intervals. In the second step, we perform Bayesian inference on a Bayesian network and estimate substitution rates between each product pair by taking the mean of each posterior distribution.

Using simulated data, we find that our approach provides accurate estimates both without using inventory data. We also demonstrate that uncertainty surrounding inferred substitution rates can be estimated by examining the dispersion of the posterior distribution.

We simulate changes in assortment policy and demonstrate estimation of impact on revenue and profit for each case. The simulation demonstration showed that dropping product b and reallocating the capacity equally among the remaining products leads to higher profit than keeping all products.

Our approach uses POS data from one retailer store to make estimates. We assume that there are sufficient sample time intervals for each product pair (i,j) such that product i is out-of-stock and product j is available. In some cases, a retailer may find have few stock-out periods in a single store but sufficient samples when data from several stores are combined. Further study can be pursued for estimating substitution rates by pooling POS data of multiple stores.

We also assumed that the demand of products is Poisson distributed. Another area of further study is to model demand taking into account seasonality using non-homogeneous Poisson processes. This will lead to modifications in both estimating the out-of-stock periods and the demand and substitution rates. The out-of-stock periods would be estimated using a zero-truncated version of the non-homogeneous Poisson process.

REFERENCES

Ahmed, A., Aly, M., Gonzalez, J., Narayanamurthy, S., & Smola, A. J. 2012. Scalable inference in latent variable models. In *Proceedings of the fifth ACM international conference on Web search and data mining* (pp. 123–132). ACM.

Andrieu, C., De Freitas, N., Doucet, A., & Jordan, M. I. 2003. An introduction to MCMC for machine learning. *Machine learning*, *50*(1–2), 5–43.

Anupindi, R., Dada, M., & Gupta, S. 1998. Estimation of consumer demand with stock-out based substitution: An application to vending machine products. *Marketing Science*, *17*(4), 406–423.

Ben-Gal, I. 2008. Bayesian networks. *Encyclopedia of statistics in quality and reliability*, *1*.

Blei, D. M., Kucukelbir, A., & McAuliffe, J. D. 2017. Variational inference: A review for statisticians. *Journal of the American Statistical Association*, *112*(518), 859–877.

Cohen, A. C. 2016. *Truncated and censored samples: theory and applications*. CRC press.

Cohen Jr, A. C. 1954. Estimation of the Poisson parameter from truncated samples and from censored samples. *Journal of the American Statistical Association*, *49*(265), 158–168.

Davidson-Pilon, C. 2015. *Bayesian methods for hackers: probabilistic programming and Bayesian inference*. Addison-Wesley Professional.

Dehoratius, N., & Raman, A. 2008. Inventory Record Inaccuracy: An Empirical Analysis. Management Science,54(4), 627–641. doi:10.1287/mnsc.1070.0789

Dillon, J. V., Langmore, I., Tran, D., Brevdo, E., Vasudevan, S., Moore, D., ... & Saurous, R. A. 2017. TensorFlow Distributions. *arXiv preprint arXiv:1711.10604*.

Eshky, A. 2008. Bayesian methods of parameter estimation. *University of Edimburgh School of Informatics*.

Gelman, A., Meng, X. L., & Stern, H. 1996. Posterior predictive assessment of model fitness via realized discrepancies. *Statistica sinica*, 733–760.

Grogger, J. T. and Carson, R. T. 1991, Models for truncated counts. J. Appl. Econ., 6: 225–238. doi:10.1002/jae.3950060302

Heckerman, D. 1998. A tutorial on learning with Bayesian networks. In *Learning in graphical models* (pp. 301–354). Springer, Dordrecht.

Hoffman, M. D., Blei, D. M., Wang, C., & Paisley, J. 2013. Stochastic Variational Inference. Journal of Machine Learning Research,14, 1303–1347.

Karabati, S., Tan, B., & Öztürk, Ö C. 2009. A method for estimating stock-out-based substitution rates by using point-of-sale data. IIE Transactions,41(5), 408–420. doi:10.1080/07408170802512578

Kök, A. G., & Fisher, M. L. 2007. Demand estimation and assortment optimization under substitution: Methodology and application. *Operations Research*, *55*(6), 1001–1021.

Letham, B., Letham, L. M., & Rudin, C. 2016. Bayesian Inference of Arrival Rate and Substitution Behavior from Sales Transaction Data with Stockouts. Proceedings of the 22nd ACM SIGKDD International Conference on Knowledge Discovery and Data Mining - KDD 16. doi:10.1145/2939672.2939810

Mingola, P. 2013. A Study of Poisson and Related Processes with Applications.

Musalem, A., Olivares, M., Bradlow, E. T., Terwiesch, C., & Corsten, D. 2010. Structural estimation of the effect of out-of-stocks. *Management Science*, *56*(7), 1180–1197.

Ranganath, R., Gerrish, S., & Blei, D. 2014. Black box variational inference. In *Artificial Intelligence and Statistics* (pp. 814–822).

Reyes-Castro, L. I., & Abad, A. G. 2016. A Dynamic Bayesian Network Model for Inventory Level Estimation in Retail Marketing. *arXiv preprint arXiv:1604.01075*

Vulcano, G., Van Ryzin, G., & Ratliff, R. 2012. Estimating primary demand for substitutable products from sales transaction data. *Operations Research*, *60*(2), 313–334.

Theory and Practice of Computation – Nishizaki et al. (eds)
© 2019 Taylor & Francis Group, London, ISBN 978-0-367-20417-4

Reliability rating of news-related posts on Facebook using sentiment analysis

M.A. Solis, Q.J. San Juan & L.L. Figueroa
Department of Computer Science, University of the Philippines Diliman, Diliman Quezon City, Metro Manila, Philippines

ABSTRACT: Social media websites and applications contain data spanning sponsored contents, and shared information. Accessible information-sharing in these platforms makes the propagation of misinformation or fake news faster. In this study, the authors created a Bayes reliability classifier of news articles using topic generation and sentiment analysis. News articles were scraped from Facebook and selected news sites' RSS feeds, and were pre-processed to populate topics and rate sentiments. Furthermore, articles were fed in a classifier that outputs value for each article based on its topics and sentiment. The generated values for each article were tested against a threshold the researchers flagged as standard reliability value. From the results, it can be concluded that news articles from popular local news companies are reliable as they yielded positive statistical mean and positive-neutral statistical mode for sentiment rating. Moreover, news articles from a certain Facebook account known for its strong political statements were classified unreliable.

1 INTRODUCTION

Facebook, a social media platform that started in 2004, has evolved, from its original goal of providing a medium for people to connect with each other over the Internet, into numerous features such as a communication platform for existing media companies and new-sprung media entities. However, this expansion of the reach of Facebook and other social media sites, in general, has been the venue of people who serve their self-interests either for business or partisanship. This leads to the spread of misleading news. Furthermore, social media users are not responsible enough to research on the topic of articles and posts that appear on their respective timelines. In effect, they easily share these news articles without further research and verification.

As the Philippines is tagged as one of the social media capitals of the world, Filipinos spent fairly most of their time on Facebook. They rely on it most of the time being updated on the current affairs or happenings surrounding them. They got updated by reading some articles that appear on their timelines.

In this paper, the researchers added or rather integrated previously used technologies into an application that also aims to aid Facebook users to be aware of the different news that appears in their feeds. The researchers then used different known technologies, platforms, and processes to finally arrive in a working application. The researcher also created an algorithm they consider to be a good fit for checking the reliability of a news article.

2 REVIEW OF LITERATURE

There have been a number of applications developed before that dwell on detecting false or made-up news, but there has been a limited number of published journals dwelling on this topic – fake news detection. One study that tackled this topic is the study pioneered by Victoria Rubin. In her study together with other two researchers, they presented a "hybrid" approach wherein it analyzes both the semantics and syntax of articles (Conroy et al., 2015). The study concluded that this approach which combines the linguistic cues and network analysis produces a significant output in deception detection.

Apart from journals, there have been movements from Facebook to battle the issue of fake news. Just recently, Facebook has released an article that details the possible roots and the solutions to the problem of fake news and misinformation. It states on the article that Facebook will run series of research and development that will dwell on these three key areas as specified in the article: disrupting economic incentives, building new products, and helping people make more informed decisions (Mosserri, 2017). Also, the article also contained the different ongoing and done programs on Facebook that also try to solve the issue. These programs are the Facebook Journalism Project and the News Integrity Initiative among others.

Apart from the actions of the developers of Facebook, there are also some private organizations that want to have their fair share of solving the problem of misinformation. One is the 'this is fake' by Slate which is a Chrome extension or plugin that detects fake news (Oremus, 2016). It works via using collective information discrimination by the Slate developers and Facebook users.

In the succeeding sections, two approaches to false news detection will be further discussed.

2.1 *Linguistic approaches*

To avoid being caught, deceptors use their language effectively to hide. Language "leakage" in certain verbal aspects that are difficult to recognize such as frequencies and patterns of pronoun, conjunction, and negative emotion word usage are arduous to observe even in the attempt of most liars to control what they are saying (Feng & Hirst, 2013). Linguistic approach's primary goal is to detect instances of such leakage or, so-called "predictive deception cues" found in the content of a message.

According to (Conroy et al, 2015), the "bag of word" is the simplest method of representing texts. In this approach, cues of deception can be revealed when the individual grams or "n-grams" (multiword) frequencies are aggregated and analyzed. The biggest shortcoming of this approach also roots from its simplicity. Moreover, the method focuses on the isolated n-gram of which the useful context information is removed. However, a great number of deception detection researchers found still this method effective when used together with other complementary analyses.

2.1.1 *Deep syntax*

Analysis of word use is often not enough in predicting deception. Deeper language structures (syntax) have been analyzed to predict instances of deception. Deep syntax analysis is implemented through Probability Context-Free Grammars (PCFG). Sentences are transformed to a set of rewrite rules (a parse tree) to describe syntax structure or example noun and verb phrases, which are in turn rewritten by their syntactic constituent parts. The final set of rewrites produces a parse tree with a certain probability assigned. This method is used to distinguish rule categories for deception detection with 85-91% accuracy (depending on the rule category used).

2.1.2 *Semantic analysis*

An alternative approach to deception cues is researched upon as signals of truthfulness by characterizing the degree of compatibility between a personal experience (e.g., a hotel reviews) as compared to a content "provided" extracted from an analogous data collection. This approach is an extension of the n-gram plus syntax model by incorporating profile compatibility modules, exhibiting the addition of this approach significantly enhances the classification performance (Feng & Hirst, 2013). The inclusion of contradictions or omissions of facts present in profiles on similar topics is an angle being observed when the deceptive writer has no actual experience of the event or object. When it comes to product reviews, a truthful review is more likely to make similar comments about that parts of the products as other truthful reviews. Pulled content from keywords constitutes of attribute: descriptor pair. By comparing the descriptions of the writer's personal experience and profiles, veracity assessment is a function of compatibility scores: 1. Compatibility with the existence of some distinct aspect. 2. Compatibility with some of the general aspect description such as service or location. An approximation of 91% accuracy of prediction of falsehood is shown with this method.

This method is demonstrated as useful in the above context but has so far been restricted to the application domain. Two potential limitations have been identified in this method: the ability to identify alignment between attributes and descriptors have been heavily depending on enough amount of extracted content for profiles and the adversity of rightfully associating descriptors with extracted attributes.

2.1.3 *Rhetorical structure and discourse analysis*
CMC communication and news content have also shown deception cues at the discourse level. Rhetorical Structure Theory (RST) analytic framework achieves a description of discourse that describes instances of rhetoric relations between elements of linguistic. Deceptive and truthful messages have exhibited systematic differences in terms of their coherence and structure has been combined with a Vector Space Model (VSM) that evaluates search message's position in multi-dimensional RST space accordingly to its distance to truth and deceptive centers (Rubin & Lukoianova, 2014). The prominent use of certain rhetorical relations can indicate deception at this linguistic analysis level.

2.1.4 *Classifiers*
The automated numerical analysis uses sets of word and category frequencies. Training of "classifiers" in Support Vector Machines (SVM) (Zhang et al., 2012) and Naive Bayesian models (Oraby et al., 2015) are of common use. Predicting of instances of future deception is effective when a mathematical model is sufficiently trained from pre-coded models as the basis of numeric clustering and distances. A new experimentation on the net effect of the different clustering methods and distance functions between data points is molded by the different clustering methods and distance functions accuracy of SVM(Strehl et al., 2000). Naive Bayes algorithms create a classification based on aggregated evidence of the correlation between a given variable (e.g. syntax) and the other variables present in the model (Mihalcea et al., 2009).

Sentiment classification(Pang & Lee, 2008) is based on the presumed behavior that deceivers use unintended emotional communication, judgment or evaluation of an effective state (Markowitz & Hancock, 2011). Distinguishing feeling from fact-based arguments by incorporating learned patterns of argumentation style classes is also possible using syntactic patterns. Performance is better than a random guess by 16% in the area of studies of business communication. The language of deceptive executives shows fewer non-extreme positive emotions (Larcker & Zakolyukina, 2012). Human judgment and SVM classifiers exhibited 86% performance accuracy on negative deceptive opinion spam (Ott et al., 2013). Overproduction of negative emotion terms are produced by fake negative reviewers compared relative to the truthful reviews. These are ruled out as result of "leakage cues" but the tendency of the deceivers to exaggerate deception they are trying to convey.

Hybrid approaches such as these linguistic approaches all rely on language usage, and its corresponding analysis shows a promising result. Nevertheless, finding emerging patterns from topic-specific studies such as product reviews and business may have limited generalisable result towards real-time veracity news detection.

2.2 *Network approaches*

As real-time content on current events is being immensely prevalent through micro-blogging applications such as Twitter, deception analysis tools are more needed than before. Using network properties and behavior are ways to extend content-based approaches that focus on deceptive language and leakage cues to predict deception.

2.2.1 *Linked data*
Scalable computation fact-checking methods may make use of knowledge networks may represent a significant leap. False "factual statement" can manifest a form of deception because they can be

extracted and examined together with findable statements about the known world. To evaluate the truth of new statements, this approach utilizes the existing body of collective human knowledge. Querying existing knowledge networks are used by this method use. Publicly available structured data such as DBpedia ontology, or the Google Relation Extraction Corpus (GREC).

A predicate relationship can be used to connect the inherently structured data network. Effective reduction of fact-checking to a simple network analysis is feasible as the computation of the simple shortest path. Extracted fact statements produce queries that are assigned semantic proximity as a function of the transitive relationship of the predicate and subject via other nodes. The nearer the nodes, the higher the probability that a specific subject-predicate-object statement is true.

Exploitation of several so-called 'network effect' variables can be utilized to derive truth probability (Ciampaglia et al., 2015) so the outlook for using structured data repositories for fact-checking remains a possibility. From a few existing published works in this area, sample-facts-based results from four diverse subject areas range from 61% to 95%. Measurement of success was based on whether the machine was able to identify higher true values to true statements than false ones (Ciampaglia et al., 2015). However, a problem rests on the truth that statements must be present in a pre-existing knowledge repository.

2.2.2 Social network behavior

One of the most notions of trust in social media is the authentication of identity. The increasing amount of news in the form of the current events through micro-blogs includes the way of ascertaining the difference between a fake and genuine content. Aside from content analysis, the inclusion of meta-data and telltale behavior of questionable sources are being utilized (Chu et al., 2010). Political perception influences have recently used Twitter (Cook et al., 2013) is one example where specific data, namely the use of hyperlinks or associated network-based text analysis, represents the content of big sets of text by recognizing the most important words that link another word in the network. This is applied is to examine content patterns in posts about Egypt's elections in 2012 (Papacharissi & Oliveira, 2012). The combination of sentiment and behaviour studies have shown the content that sentiment-focused reviews from singleton contributors paramount affect online ranking (Wu et al., 2010), and an "shilling" indicator or achieving fake reviews to artificially manipulate a ranking.

3 DATA GATHERING

3.1 Input

There were two categories of input data sets that were used and manipulated across our methods. The first input data set comprises of the news articles pulled from Facebook. This dataset was gathered programmatically through the use of the Facebook Graph API. The articles were scraped from the posts of Thinking Pinoy in its Facebook account. Thinking Pinoy is a notorious account that comments, posts, about the different anomalies occurring in the current Philippine government. This specific input data set was the input to the reliability classifier. The researchers gathered a count of 245 news.

Moreover, the news articles from the top five news providers in the Philippines that have channels on-line comprise the second input dataset. The dataset was gathered using the RSS feeds of the said news providers. This dataset will be the source of the baseline sentiment. This was compared with the dataset gathered from Facebook.

3.2 RSS feed scraper

The top five news providers in the Philippines that have channels on-line were chosen. These news providers were not picked out of specific standards but purely on popularity and of availability of their RSS feed. The method to which the news from these sites was gathered was the Really Simple Syndication (RSS). RSS is the way a specific site gives service to its customers by providing formatted and light-weight data of its contents. RSS was used to gather the specific and formatted text of the news contents of the chosen news providers. Python was used to incorporate different modules such as "feedparser" that were readily available to scrape the news contents of the providers.

3.3 *Natural language processor*

To aid the scraping process, NLP worked as a complementary method. NLP is a processing method that could convert natural language to a specific format that is easily processed and that follows the standard of a specific system.

In the methodology, NLP was used to filter the news content to all English words and proper nouns and their occurrences in a specific news article. The available sentiment analyzers limit only to English words so the words used were only of the English language with the exception of proper nouns. Sentiment analysis is further discussed in the succeeding sections. In addition, noise words were also eradicated for further processing. Noise words are words that have no specific impact on the overall semantics of a sentence. These words are only used to add up form, color, and style on the construction of sentences. Words such as the articles – the, a, an; and other prepositions among others were considered as noise words. The primary reason is to provide a more reliable output since we are taking away words that only add up to the style but not the content.

4 DATA PROCESSING

For the data processing, the researchers used the technologies and concepts of Facebook Graph API, RSS, and NLP to create a data scraper and data processor.

4.1 *Scraping phase and processing phase*

There were two sets of input we needed to scrape. One input is from Facebook. This is the input being tested for their reliability. To scrape this data, the researcher had used Facebook Graph API. They gathered the posts posted by the Facebook user 'Thinking Pinoy'. The researcher decided to use Thinking Pinoy as the account to be tested since most of its posts were written in English. Since we are only able to get the sentiment for English words in our chosen method, it is just a good choice, for us to have a sensible output. After scraping using Facebook Graph API under the account of 'Thinking Pinoy' from *April 01* to *April 28, 2017*, we had successfully gathered **245** news posts. These posts were the base news the researchers tested.

After scraping and processing phase, we already have a set of formatted data and can already be added to the database for further processing and analysis.

5 TOPIC GENERATION

A great number of methods used to classify specific texts were in the literature. One of which is the Naive-Bayes classifier that needs a Ham or Spam bag of words as the prerequisite. This methodology was unfit because of the lack of a source of Ham. Meanwhile, k-means clustering uses clusters and heuristics in determining the classification of texts which also needs a data set for both classifications, legitimate and fake news, which in this case the data set for fake data was not available. Hence, the method deemed appropriate was the topic generation. This method makes use of the specific words discussed in specific news text to form a topic. N-grams multi frequencies are used to aid in the formation of the topic generation. Each news article was limited to be included in one topic.

A Topic from here on is defined as the collection of meaningful words. A Topic consists of Articles News. Each Topic contains the words in it. Using the n-gram multi-frequencies, two algorithms were performed to generate topics from the scraped article news data.

- *All English Words* The first algorithm uses the most frequent words as the basis of the topic generation. Most commonly used words in the language were excluded to focus on the words

Table 1. Summary of the Topic Generation Phase result using the All English Words, and Proper Nouns and Numbers algorithms

	All English Words	Proper Nouns and Numbers
Topic generated	270 Topics	493 Topics
One News Topic	93 Topics	464 Topics
Multiple News Topic	177 Topics	29 Topics
Average News count	3.07 News/topic	1.29 News/Topic

that are meaningful. The goal of this is to group the news in the concept of a Topic into a collection of Article News that uses the most frequent words. It was an assumption that the news with common most frequently used words are most likely to fall in the same news category.

- *Proper Nouns and Numbers* Upon inspection of the first generated a set of topics, a different approach was looked into because of the less coherent Article News under the same Topic. This second approach only looks into specific words. Still, using the n-gram multi-frequencies, the words checked to form Topics are the proper nouns and the numbers. With these, the expected topics only contain the proper nouns in news article.

Special characterization of a news article that separates it apart from different context analysis is that news articles from a short range of time are more likely to be related to each other. Another interesting point about news articles is that their scope of the topic is promoted by the proper nouns and numbers in the content. These characteristics were taken advantages of and used in the topic generation of this study.

Published news from the list of chosen news providers were scraped from their official websites with publish dates ranging from *November 2, 2016* until *April 26, 2017*. The database has been revamped that resulted in minimal outlier input data from late 2016. The result of the topic generation using the recently discussed two algorithms generated was summarized in Table 1.

Six hundred thirty-nine (639) rows of Article News were gathered. Using All English Words algorithm, 270 Topics were generated. Out of the 270 Topics, **93** only contains a single News. The implication of this is that 14% of the News scraped were unique, as long as this algorithm is concerned. The average News Topic count is **3.07** News/Topic, the better data input in the Sentiment Analysis Phase.

On the other hand, using the Proper Nouns and Number algorithm, **493** topics were produced, which is 223 more compared to the All English Words. This implies that some of the matches in the All English Words are non-proper nouns and non-number word strings. Four hundred sixty-four **(464)** of the Topics generated were single News which lead to a more accurate topic generation but the average of **1.29** News/Topic is not that suitable for Sentiment Analysis phase because of the importance of the average sentiment per Topic. With these, the result of All English Words was used in the proceeding phases.

Using the Topics produced using the Article News, assignment of Topic for the Input News was also performed. As for the Input News, the Facebook page Thinking Pinoy, a notorious page that promotes black propaganda against the Vice President, and of the opposition to the administration was also scrapped.

6 SENTIMENT ANALYSIS

In this process, a news article was computed a sentiment rating from the words contained in each legitimate news article. There are three approaches to sentiment analysis: knowledge-based techniques, statistical methods, and hybrid approaches. The knowledge-based technique is used in this case. The approach is to use unambiguous affect words that can be classified as a positive or negative word. Affect words are words that express undeniable emotions such as happy, sad, etc.

Initially, a data set of English words rated as positive or negative was acquired from a https://www.github.com/wso2/demos with **2,006** positive words and **4,784** negative words. Positive words were given a sentiment of +1 while negative words were assigned -1 sentiment. The words consisting an Article News were matched with this list. The sentiment of a News whether it was an Article News or an Input News was computed as the sum of all the matching positive words and negative words. The sentiment of a News either Input or Article is computed as,

$$S_{\text{News}} = \sum (S_{pa}) + \sum (S_{na})$$

where
S_{pa}: sentiment value of positive affect word
S_{na}: sentiment value of negative affect word

For demonstration purpose, let's take an example Article News Article 1. Article 1 contains 1000 words in its content. Out of the 1000 words, 200 affected words. Out of the 200 affect words, the negative word count was 50. The sum of the negative words -50 and positive words +150 is +100. The final sentiment rating of Article 1 is +100. The negativity of the article was cancelled out by the positive effect words. This result supports the psychological behavior theory of the common usage of negative words if the intention is deception.

Moreover, a sentiment rating was also computed per Topic. To compute for the Topic sentiment, the average sentiment of the News Articles in that Topic was calculated. The average sentiment of all the News Articles computed as **+0.6538** while the mode is **1.0** and **0.0**. The mean +0.6538 was used as the baseline of the "reliable" news. Using the scraped posts from Thinking Pinoy Facebook page, *59 out of 245* Input News have sentiment greater than +0.6538, the baseline set earlier. On the other hand, **186** news are rated below 0.6538. Moreover, around **76 percent** of the Input News from Thinking Pinoy Facebook page had a sentiment rating below or equal to zero.

7 RELIABILITY CLASSIFICATION

Once the Topics were generated and the corresponding sentiments and a Topic was assigned to the Input News which is in our case, scraped from Thinking Pinoy Facebook page, reliability classification is ready to be performed. All Input News that have not been classified under a specific Topic during the Topic Generation Phase were discarded for reliability classification because it is not qualified due to the lack of basis. The algorithm for Input News reliability classification is as follows.

1. Check if the Input News has a topic. If yes, proceed to the next step. Otherwise, stop at this step and declare that it is not classifiable.
2. Compare the sentiment of the Input News to the average Topic sentiment. If the sentiment of the Input News is greater than or equal to the average Topic sentiment, the Input News is said to be "reliable". Otherwise, it is considered to be "unreliable".

Moreover, the Topic sentiment is computed as,

$$S_{\text{Topic}} = \frac{\sum (S_{\text{News}})}{N_{\text{News}}}$$

where
S_{News}: sentiment of News under a particular Topic
N_{News}: count of News under a particular Topic

Using this algorithm, 35 out of 245 or 14.28% Thinking Pinoy posts were rated above its Topic average sentiment for reliability while 210 posts or 85.71% of the overall posts were rated below the baseline. Moreover, 225 out of 245 or 92% Thinking Pinoy posts were classified below the set baseline.

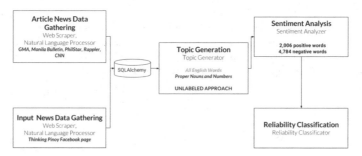

Figure 1.   The summary flow of the system.

8   CONCLUSION

After performing the data gathering and the analysis through the phases Scraping and Processing, Topic Generation, Sentiment Analysis, and Reliability Classification. The following statements can be concluded:

- The Article News scraped from the top news providers in the Philippines through their respective RSS feeds had a positive statistical mean and positive/neutral statistical mode with regards to the sentiment rating.
- The majority of the Input News from Thinking Pinoy Facebook page fell below the average Topic sentiment it belongs to. This means that the news of Thinking Pinoy under the same topic as of the Article News have unmatched sentiments as to their counterparts in the Article News.
- Most of the posts in the Thinking Pinoy Facebook page were classified as unreliable news.

However, this study did not confirm a direct correlation between the use of negative words in deception in News, neither in general but strengthened the said psychological behavior theory.

Also, the baseline as dcfincd in the previous paragraphs as the average sentiment of the Article News are arbitrary and changing depending on the values and count of the Article News. The higher the number of Articles, the more accurate the baseline sentiment we can get.

In addition, while our algorithm had successfully generated a value to quantify the reliability, there are still factors that need yet to be considered in order to arrive in more accurate and unbiased reliability ratings of news articles.

REFERENCES

Chu, Z. et al. 2010. *Who is tweeting on twitter: Human, bot, or cyborg?*, Proceedings of the 26th AnnualComputer Security Applications Conference, ACSAC '10.

Ciampaglia, G. L. et al. 2015. *Computational fact-checking from knowledge networks*, Proceedings of NAACLHLT.

Conroy, N.J. & Rubin, V.L. & Chen, Y. 2015. *Automatic deception detection:Methods for finding fake news*,ASIST.

Cook, D. M. et al. 2013. *Twitter deception and influence: Issues of identity, slacktivism, and puppetry*.

Feng V. W., & Hirst, G. 2013. *Detecting deceptive opinion with profile compatibility*.

Larcker, D. F. & Zakolyukina, A. A.2012. *Detecting deceptive discussions in conference calls*, Journal of Accounting Research, 50(2).

Markowitz, D. M. & Hancock, J. T., 2014. *Linguistic traces of a scientific fraud: The case of diederik stapel*, PLoS ONE, p. 9(8).

Mihalcea, R. & Strapparava, C. 2009. *The lie detector: Explorations in the automatic recognition of deceptive language*, Proceedings of the ACL-IJCNLP Conference Short Paper, 309.

Mosserri, A. April 2017. *Working to stop misinformation and false news* [Online; posted 06-April-2017].

Oraby, S. et al. 2015. *And that's a fact: Distinguishing factual and emotional argumentation in online dialogue.*

Oremus, W., December 2016. *Only you can stop the spread of fake news*, [Online; posted 13-December-2016].

Ott, M. & Cardie, C. & Hancock, J. T., 2013. *Negative deceptive opinion spam*, Proceedings of NAACLHLT, 497.

Pang, B. & Lee,L. 2008. *Opinion mining and sentiment analysis, Foundations and Trends in Information Retrieval.*

Papacharissi, Z. & de Fatima Oliveira, M. 012. *Affective news and networked publics: The rhythms of news storytelling on egypt*, Journal of Communication. 62.

Rubin, V. & Lukoianova, T. 2014. *Truth and deception at the rhetorical structure level*, Journal of the American Society for Information Science and Technology, p. 66(5).

Strehl, A. & Ghosh, J. & Mooney, R. 2000. *Impact of similarity measures on webpage clustering*, Journal of Networks.

Wu,G. et al., 2010. *Distortion as a validation criterion in the identification of suspicious reviews*,1st Workshop on Social Media Analytics.

Zhang, H. & Fan, Z. & Zheng J. & Liu, Q. 2012. *An improving deception detection method in computer-mediated communication*, Journal of Networks, p. 7(11).

Theory and Practice of Computation – Nishizaki et al. (eds)
© 2019 Taylor & Francis Group, London, ISBN 978-0-367-20417-4

Wireless sensor and actuator network: Self-healing and ad-hoc routing protocol with load balancing

R.K. Medel, L.A. Payofelin, P.G. Tee, J.E. Valle & F.K. Flores
De La Salle University, Manila, Philippines

ABSTRACT: Internet of Things (IoT) intends to connect everyday objects and appliances with the Internet in the aims of providing integrated services and applications geared towards the improvement of different aspects of human life. IoT applications are typically implemented through wireless sensor network (WSN) or wireless sensor and actuator network (WSAN). The research aims to design and implement a self-healing and ad-hoc routing protocol with load balancing for WSAN environments. This was consequently validated via performance and application which included testing for network convergence time, packet sending, ad-hoc time, self-healing time, and load-balancing capability. SHARP is proven to be usable as it achieved its intended function in the areas of routing, ad-hoc, self-healing, and load balancing. However, load balancing has no clear advantage in topologies with a single sink architecture.

1 INTRODUCTION

The Internet of things (IoT) is a growing area of technology where addressable devices are interconnected through a medium such as the cloud, in which such implementations are Wireless Sensor Networks (WSN) or Wireless Sensor and Actuator Networks (WSAN). WSN is comprised of spatially distributed environmental sensing devices called nodes; which possess limited processing capabilities and transmit information wirelessly. Since these nodes communicate together via wireless, the need to have an effective communication is one important area that smart environments demand.

Communication in WSAN are predominantly between wireless sensor nodes. The wireless sensor nodes in WSN detect activities and gather information in its environment which will be forwarded to a sink. WSAN features an actuator which paved the way for bidirectional communication for two-way interaction contrary to WSN where it is constrained by unidirectional transmission amongst the nodes [2]. In order to have a central processing unit in a WSAN application, a sink node is also used to act as a focal point of all nodes which could receive and process data, or even communicate with a host computer. However, mainly due to WSAN's relatively recent development, it still lacks implementation standards and protocols. Existing communication protocols such as IEEE 802.15.4 and ZigBee are widely used in WSN applications with each of them having their own limitations. IEEE 802.15.4 does not perform any network and traffic handling like routing and load balancing, while ZigBee has high overhead, limited coverage, line-of-sight, one-way communication, and is non-backwards compatible [3, 4, 5, 6].

To address the limitations of existing communication protocols like ZigBee and allow a bidirectional end-to-end communication between nodes, this research aims to provide a reactive protocol capable of self-healing and ad-hoc routing with load balancing in the form of Self-Healing and Ad-Hoc Routing Protocol with Load Balancing or SHARP. The core capabilities of a routing protocol are the ability to transmit data to its respective destination via message passing from one device to another and sustain itself in case a node is newly added or has gone down. The developed protocol emphasizes the first capability through the utilization of the best path possible, and the second capability through continuous detection in the network for new and inactive nodes by using hello and keepalive packets to achieve its effectivity.

The proposed protocol is utilized in a WSAN environment and is built on top of the IEEE 802.15.4, which is a low power and low data rate wireless connectivity standard on the physical and data link layers of a network. It transmits data packets with little overhead making it is fast and reliable and has a frequency band of 2.4 GHz which can be obstructed by Bluetooth and WiFi. IEEE 802.15.4 is used as the protocol of the XBee transceiver which is attached to a microcontroller similar to an Arduino Uno. Additionally, the XBee module is responsible for transmitting and receiving packets as it is ideal for low latency and predictable communication [7, 8, 9]

2   SELF-HEALING AND AD-HOC ROUTING PROTOCOL WITH LOAD BALANCING

The predominant functions of SHARP are to route data packets sent by the sink node to reach a certain destination, detect new and inactive nodes in the network and share the network resources by load balancing. To achieve this, the environment is implemented wherein the seven nodes have static configurations for their MAC address to identify whether it is a sink, sensor, actuator, or generic routing node. Each node has an adjacency table containing information on the node's neighbors, and a routing table containing information on how the node could reach a destination.

2.1   *Routing process*

The routing process discusses the fundamental methods involved as they highlight its overall functionalities and are broken down into three parts which handle the different phases of the network from startup until the duration of its runtime. The nodes begin initialization when they are powered up and become functional. The node address is checked if it is similar to the SHARP packet footer or the terminating character. The node is set to active if it is not, while it is set to inactive if otherwise. After initialization of the network the building of the topology occurs. This is where the sink initiates the building of topology by broadcasting a hello packet to its neighboring nodes and the neighboring nodes continue the broadcast. After a node receives a hello packet in this phase, it retains the source address of the packet in its adjacency and routing table, and proceeds to the running environment stage. The running environment is the condition of the system after the topology has been built. At this point, the network is functioning and being maintained through the environment, route, and topology handling. Depending on the message sent by the nodes, certain types of packets will be forwarded to specific modules accordingly.

During the running environment stage, it would be implementing three phases; for environment handling, route handling, and topology handling. The environment handling phase is a continuous process for event detection and processing. The node address is initially checked if it is a sensor or actuator node. If it is a sensor node, the output from the sensor is read once an activity is identified and if the value is equal to the threshold, a data packet is created to be forwarded to the sink. If it is an actuator node and a data packet is received from the sink, the packet is parsed and read. The obtained payload from the data can be used to actuate a part of the environment.

During route handling phase, there would be three types of packets: data packet, query route packet, and data node unreachable packet. The data packet is used by the sensors, actuators, and the sink node to forward informational messages to one another. Query route packets are used by the nodes to search for potential routes to the specified destination. Data node unreachable packets are used to inform the source node that there is no active route to the destination node. A corresponding packet is replied by the destination node for each type of packet received, which could be a data acknowledgement packet, query route reply packet, or data node unreachable acknowledgement packet. This phase also considers the actual routing process of the protocol. When a packet is received, the keepalive timer of the outgoing node is immediately reset before the packet type is determined to signify that the node is still active. If a data packet needs to be routed, the best path to the destination node is selected as long as there are no multiple paths. On the event of multiple paths with equal cost, round robin is performed. After the data packet is sent and no data acknowledgement is received after three tries, this means that the next hop has gone down and a data node unreachable packet is forwarded to the source node before the data packet is dropped. The query route packet is sent by the sink node if there are no existing paths to the destination node. This packet is broadcasted by each node until the destination address matches the address of the node. If it is a match, a query route reply would be broadcasted back to the sink node. The sink node and the nodes along the path update their routing table once a query route reply is received. The data node unreachable packet is sent to the sink node whenever the route to the destination node is unavailable. A data node unreachable acknowledgement packet is sent as a reply for the data node unreachable queue to be cleared.

Lastly is the topology handling phase, where three types of packets also circulate in topology handling phase: hello packet, keepalive packet, and inactivity packet. Hello packets are used to identify the neighbors of the nodes and is broadcasted during the network startup. Keepalive packets are packets that guarantee the active state of the neighboring nodes by implementing acknowledgements. Inactivity packets are used to inform the adjacent nodes that a certain node is down. The topology handling phase handles the state of the topology, which includes detection of inactive updates, hello packets for new nodes, and keepalive packets for active connections. If a node receives an inactive update, its adjacency and routing tables are updated for the inactive node entry and this inactivity is also broadcasted to the other nodes within its radius. Broadcasts are only done once per node to prevent continuous broadcast updates. If hello packets are received, it signifies that there is a newly active node in the network; hence, the node is added to the adjacency and routing table of its neighbors. On the other hand, if keepalive packets are obtained, the keepalive timer of the source node is updated and a keepalive acknowledgement is sent to ensure that existing node connection is still active

3 IMPLEMENTATION

3.1 *Routing*

SHARP has three key features: ad-hoc, self-healing, and load balancing capabilities. These features would allow a reliable and suitable communication process in a WSAN application. Firstly is routing, which is the assurance that a packet reaches the right destination rests on the routing ability of the protocol. Routing in this research is defined as how a packet from one node reaches its destination node through the use of the available information in the routing and adjacency tables. When a node is about to send a unicast of a packet to a destination node, it first tries to search for the best route to the destination node in its routing table. If only one best path to the destination node exists, the node immediately forwards the packet to the next hop address. Otherwise, it performs load balancing. The pseudo-code for getting the best path is shown in Fig. 1.

3.1.1 *Ad-hoc*

The ad-hoc characteristic provides the nodes the ability to self-discover single or multiple paths to route packets in the network on its own. New nodes have no prior knowledge of the network topology though would still be able to communicate with their neighbors in order to create topological information. This feature would allow the nodes to determine the routes to forward the packets to either the sink or to the destination node. The newly added nodes will broadcast a hello packet, announcing its presence in the network. Its neighbors will get the newly added node's essential details and add it to its adjacent and routing table.

When a new node is added to the network, it waits for a packet. Once it receives a packet and sees that it is still in the build topology stage, it broadcasts a new hello packet with a time-to-live (TTL) value of 31. A hello packet with a TTL of 31 indicates that the packet came from a new node and it is looking for its neighbors. When the neighbors of the new node receive the hello packet, they will broadcast a hello packet with their respective hop count values. The hop count value is the distance of the node from the sink which ranges from 0 to 30 hops. Upon receiving hello packets from its neighbors, the new node will add them to its adjacency and routing tables

Algorithm 1 Get Best Path (Destination Node Address)
1. //minHopCount is set to 32 which is greater than any possible hop count value a node could have
2. int ctr, bestHopIndex = 0, minHopCount = 32;
3. int numBestPath = 0;
4. boolean found = false, inactive = false, multipleBestPath = false;
5. destNode = Destination Node Address
6. //Searches active routing table entries with minimum hop count in the routing table
7. for (ctr = 0; ctr < size of routing table; ctr++) {
8. //RT_DESTNODE[] consists of the destination nodes of the routing entries in the routing table
9. if (RT_DESTNODE[ctr] == destNode) {
10. //Checks if the route is not inactive and if the hop count is less than the current minimum hop count
11. //RT_HOPCOUNT[] consists of the hop counts of the routing entries in the routing table
12. if (RT_HOPCOUNT[ctr] != 31 && RT_HOPCOUNT < minHopCount) {
13. bestHopIndex = ctr;
14. minHopCount = RT_HOPCOUNT[ctr];
15. found = true;
16. numBestPath = 1;
17. multipleBestPath = false;
18. } else if (RT_HOPCOUNT[ctr] == minHopCount) {
19. //If true, it means that there are multiple best paths to the destination node
20. numBestPath += 1;
21. multipleBestPath = true;
22. } else if (RT_HOPCOUNT[ctr] == 31) {
23. //If true, it means that the route is inactive
24. inactive = true;
25. }}}
26. if (found && !inactive)
27. //Returns the index of the best path in the routing table
28. return bestHopIndex;
29. return -1;

Figure 1.   Obtaining the best patch pseudo-code.

Algorithm 2 Ad-Hoc (Received Hello Packet)
1. ADDRESS = get previous hop address from hello packet;
2. ttl = get time-to-live value from hello packet;
3. //Checks if the hello packet is from a newly added node
4. if (ttl == 31) {
5. boolean found = false;
6. //Searches for node's own hop count in its adjacency table
7. for (ctr = 0; ctr < size of adjacency table; ctr++) {
8. //AT_ADDRESS[] consists of the neighbor address entries in the adjacency table
9. if (AT_ADDRESS[ctr] == own address) {
10. Broadcast hello packet with own hop count;
11. found = true;
12. break;
13. }}} else if (ttl < 31){
14. if (ADDRESS is not in adjacency table) {
15. Add ADDRESS to adjacency table with its own TTL value;
16. Add ADDRESS to routing table;
17. }}

Figure 2.   Ad-hoc pseudo-code.

and it will broadcast a hello packet with its own hop count. When the node's neighbors receive the hello packet from the new node, they will add the new node to their respective adjacency and routing tables. The pseudo-code for when a new node is added in the network is shown in Fig. 2.

3.1.2 *Self-healing*

The self-healing feature provides the nodes the ability to maintain and recover its connection to the sink when a node along its communication path unexpectedly goes down. Once a node detects that a neighboring node has gone down, it will broadcast an inactivity packet to its other adjacent nodes saying that one of its neighbors has gone inactive. Afterwards, its adjacent nodes will update their own routing table and broadcast the same inactivity packet to its neighboring nodes. This process will repeat until all the nodes have updated their routing table.

	Algorithm 3 Self-Healing (Received Hello Packet)
1.	ADDRESS = get previous hop address from hello packet;
2.	ttl = get time-to-live value from hello packet;
3.	//Checks if the hello packet is from a newly added node
4.	if (ttl == 31) {
5.	boolean found = false;
6.	//Searches for node's own hop count in its adjacency table
7.	for (ctr = 0; ctr < size of adjacency table; ctr++) {
8.	if (AT_ADDRESS[ctr] == own address) {
9.	Broadcast hello packet with own hop count;
10.	found = true;
11.	break;
12.	}}} else if (ttl < 31) {
13.	if (ADDRESS is in adjacency table and its TTL value is 31){
14.	//If true, this means that ADDRESS is currently inactive in the node's adjacency and routing tables
15.	Update hop count of ADDRESS in adjacency table with its new TTL value
16.	Update hop count of ADDRESS in routing table with its new TTL value
17.	}}

Figure 3.   Self healing pseudo-code.

	Algorithm 4 Perform Load Balancing (Destinaton Node Address)
1.	int ctr, bestHopIndex = -1, numBestPath = 0;
2.	int BESTPATHINDICES_SIZE = 0;
3.	//BEST_PATH_INDICES[] consists of the indices of the best paths in the routing table
4.	int BEST_PATH_INDICES[];
5.	destNode = Destination Node Address
6.	//Searches multiple routing table entries with minimum hop count in the routing table
7.	for (ctr = 0; ctr < size of routing table; ctr++) {
8.	if (RT_DESTNODE[ctr] == destNode) {
9.	if (bestHopIndex == -1)
10.	bestHopIndex = ctr;
11.	if (RT_HOPCOUNT[ctr] < RT_HOPCOUNT[bestHopIndex]) {
12.	bestHopIndex = ctr;
13.	BESTPATHINDICES_SIZE = 0;
14.	Add route index to BEST_PATH_INDICES array
15.	BESTPATHINDICES_SIZE += 1;
16.	} else if (RT_HOPCOUNT[ctr] == RT_HOPCOUNT[bestHopIndex]) {
17.	Add route index to BEST_PATH_INDICES array
18.	BESTPATHINDICES_SIZE += 1;
19.	}}}

Figure 4.   Load balancing pseudo-code.

When the node has gone inactive, its neighbors change its hop count to 31 in their adjacency and routing tables. A hop count of 31 indicates that the node is inactive. When the inactive node suddenly recovers, it appears like a new node is added to the network. Hence, the process is identical to adhoc feature wherein a hello packet with TTL value of 31 is used to indicate that the node is looking for its neighbors. However, rather than adding a new entry in the adjacency and routing tables of the node's neighbors, they only update the hop count of the node in their respective adjacency and routing tables. The pseudo-code for the self-healing process is shown in Fig. 3.

3.2 *Load balancing*

The load balancing attribute presents the network with the ability to maximize its network resources by sharing the traffic load between multiple nodes provided that there are multiple paths with equal cost to reach the destination. It follows the round robin algorithm wherein each node progressively balances the network load by taking turns in handling packet forwarding.

Moreover, the order of the nodes is essentially cyclic in nature as it will return to the first node once all the eligible nodes have been used in load balancing for packet forwarding. When a node is about to send a unicast of a packet to a destination node, it first tries to search for the best route to the destination node in its routing table. If multiple best paths to the destination node exist, the node performs load balancing. Otherwise, it immediately forwards the packet to the next hop address. The pseudo-code for performing load balancing is shown in Fig. 4.

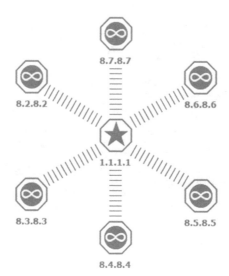

Figure 5.   Best case topology.

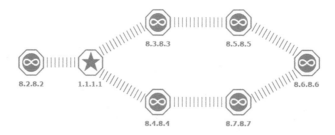

Figure 6.   Intermediate case topology.

Figure 7.   Worst case topology.

4   RESULTS AND ANALYSIS

The performance of the protocol is evaluated through several tests such as network convergence time, packet sending, ad-hoc time, self-healing time, and load balancing capability. All tests are done in three trials and using a network consisting of seven nodes. Depending on the test executed, the network is set up as one or two of the three main topologies shown in Fig. 5, 6, and 7: star topology as the best case, multipath multi-hop topology as the intermediate case, and linear topology as the worst case. The load balancing and application tests have different topologies that best suited their respective environments. The tests were conducted in varying locations in the Gokongwei building of De La Salle University.

4.1   *Network convergence time*

The network convergence time test aims to measure the time it takes for the network to converge from start up. A converged network is the state where all the nodes are in their running environment.

Table 1. Results of convergence time test.

	Best	Intermediate	Worst
2 nodes	260 ms	260 ms	260 ms
3 nodes	626 ms	626 ms	260 ms
4 nodes	1144 ms	1144 ms	648 ms
5 nodes	1814 ms	1144 ms	762 ms
6 nodes	2635 ms	1144 ms	741 ms
7 nodes	3608 ms	2603 ms	2534 ms

This is the state where the topology is built and complete, along with its respective and proper routing and adjacency tables. The test was conducted by setting up networks with different number of nodes gradually increasing in the number of nodes from two nodes, including the sink node, up to a total of seven nodes. When all the nodes were set, the sink node initiated the building of topology by broadcasting a hello packet. The activities including sending hello packet, proceeding to running environment stage, and adding of the adjacency and routing table entries were logged all throughout the process.

$$Convergence\ Time = T_C - T_H \tag{1}$$

where T_C is the time when the last node converged and T_H is the time when sink broadcasted hello packet. The convergence time, as seen in Eq. (1), is computed by subtracting the time when sink broadcasted hello packet from the time when the last node transitioned to the running environment stage and had complete adjacency and routing table. The results of the test are seen in Table 1.

The outcome of the tests shows that the network converged faster when the network topology is the worst case topology than the best case topology. In the best case topology, when the sink node broadcasts a hello packet, its neighbors would receive and reply with a hello packet consecutively. However, a node can only process one packet at a time; hence, when the sink node receives the hello packet from its adjacent nodes, it checks the packet type of the incoming packet, takes the previous hop address, and adds the information in the adjacency and routing tables one by one, which causes the network to converge slowly. In the worst case topology, each node could only have a maximum of two neighbors; therefore, the network converged faster than the other network topology cases. Thus, it can be concluded that the number of nodes processing the hello packets in the network is a primary factor that affects the time it takes for the network to reach the converged state.

4.2 Packet sending

The packet sending test aims to determine the capacity of the protocol to forward packets. This is evaluated using metrics such as latency, throughput, goodput, and packet loss rate in an environment where it has increasing hop count for one data to reach its destination.

The test was conducted by sending 10, 100, and 1000 packets over a different number of hop counts. The number of hop counts ranged from zero to five hops. In other words, from using two to seven nodes considering that it takes zero hops between directly connected nodes. Fig. 7 shows the worst case topology used during the tests. For all sets of tests, the sink performed the sending of data packet only when the network has converged.

$$Latency = T_R - T_S \tag{2}$$

where T_R is the time the packet was received and T_S is the time when the packet was sent.

$$Throughput = (N_R \times S_P \times 8) \div 60 \tag{3}$$

where N_R is the number of packets received, S_P is size of the packet, 8 is the number of bits, and 60 is the number of seconds in a minute.

$$Goodput = (N_R \times S_L \times 8) \div 60 \tag{4}$$

Table 2. Results of sending variable packets.

		Latency (ms)	Throughput (bits/sec)	Goodput (bits/sec)	Packet Loss Rate
Sending 10 Packets	0 hop	42	18.667	1.333	0.00%
	1 hop	242	18.667	1.333	0.00%
	2 hops	447	18.667	1.333	0.00%
	3 hops	654	18.044	1.289	3.33%
	4 hops	791	16.178	1.156	13.33%
	5 hops	1069	16.178	1.156	13.33%
Sending 100 Packets	0 hop	43	186.667	13.333	0.00%
	1 hop	245	183.556	13.111	1.67%
	2 hops	452	185.442	13.244	0.67%
	3 hops	866	28.000	2.000	85.00%
	4 hops	1047	15.556	1.111	91.67%
	5 hops	1445	8.089	0.578	95.67%
Sending 1000 Packets	0 hop	43	1896.533	135.467	0.39%
	1 hop	248	1866.667	133.333	1.96%
	2 hops	479	1861.067	132.933	2.25%
	3 hops	871	11.200	0.800	99.41%
	4 hops	1198	11.200	0.800	99.35%
	5 hops	1286	4.667	0.333	99.71%

where N_R is the number of packets received, SL is size of the payload, 8 is the number of bits, and 60 is the number of seconds in a minute.

$$Packet\ Loss\ Rate = (N_R - N_N) \times 100 \qquad (5)$$

where NR is the number of packets received, NN is number of packets not received, and 100 is for the percentage.

Eq. (2), (3), (4) and (5) shows the formula for latency, throughput, goodput, and packet loss rate, respectively. Latency is calculated by the time the data packet was sent from the time the packet took to arrive at the destination. Throughput is obtained by dividing the product of the number of packets received, the size of packet, and 8 bits, with 60 seconds. Goodput is computed by dividing the product of the number of packets received, the payload size, and 8 bits, with 60 seconds. Packet loss rate is calculated by subtracting the number of packets not received from the number of packets sent, and multiplied by 100 percent. Test results are shown in Table 2.

The results of the metrics in the packet sending test present a consistent increase of latency values, and a decreasing trend for the throughput, goodput values and packet loss rate. The increase in latency levels shows the consistency of the protocol in terms of packet delivery time as hop count changes when routing to the destination. The decreasing trend of the goodput, throughput, and packet loss rate reflects the declining number of packets which arrives to the destination node as the number of hops to the destination increases.

4.3 Ad-hoc time

The ad-hoc time test aims to measure the time it takes for the network to re-achieve a converged network state after a new node or nodes have been added. The network has reached convergence when all nodes are in the running environment and contains the proper routing and adjacency tables. This test represents the condition where a new node has been included to the network. The test was conducted by setting up a network with a fixed number of nodes and has an incrementing number of additional nodes from one to five nodes. The three different topology cases shown in Fig. 6, 7, and 8 were used in the test.

$$Ad\text{-}Hoc\ Time = T_N - T_H \qquad (6)$$

Table 3.   Results of ad-hoc time test.

	Best	Intermediate	Worst
1 node	4929 ms	4929 ms	3526 ms
2 nodes	6617 ms	6617 ms	7130 ms
3 nodes	9753 ms	13852 ms	8633 ms
4 nodes	9509 ms	17574 ms	13673 ms
5 nodes	9343 ms	17561 ms	16931 ms

where T_N is the time when the new node was included in the neighbor's tables and T_H is the time when the neighboring node broadcasted a hello packet. The ad-hoc time, as seen in Eq. (6), is computed by subtracting the time when the neighbor node broadcasts a hello packet after it has completed the routing and adjacency tables with the initial nodes from the time when the neighboring node has completed the routing and adjacency tables when the new node was included. The results are seen in Table 3.

As observed, the ad-hoc time in the best case topology is increasing until the three hops mark and has stabilized for the succeeding tests. The ad-hoc time stabilization in the best case topology is due to the algorithm of the protocol that when a non-hello packet is received, a node then sends a hello packet. With the new nodes receiving a packet at roughly similar intervals with milliseconds in difference due to varying time a packet is received between transceivers, this gave the sink node an ample time to process each hello packet which led to the similar ad-hoc times for the best case.

For the intermediate and worst case topology, the ad-hoc time progressed as the hop count increased. The increase in the worst case topology is a result of the processing time delay brought by the environment of the topology where traffic has to pass several nodes and with each node requiring time to receive and process each packet before forwarding to the destination. Another factor is that nodes may only forward traffic if they are in the running environment which means that if, for example, a new node is added at the edge of the topology and the node before the last node is still in the process of entering the running environment, the last node has to wait for that node in order to properly communicate and update its routing and adjacency tables. The increase in ad-hoc time in the intermediate case topology is similar to the reasons of increase of both the worst case and best case topology.

4.4   Self-healing time

The self-healing time test aims to measure the time taken by the network to regain a converged network state after a node or nodes have been inactive. The network is said to have reached convergence when all nodes are in the running environment and contains the proper routing and adjacency tables. This test represents the condition where a node within the network has become inactive or down. The test was conducted by setting up an initial network of seven nodes with an incrementing number of nodes, from one to five nodes, to be made inactive and later reactivated. There were three topologies being followed which can be seen in Fig. 6, 7, and 8.

$$Self\text{-}Healing\ Time = T_R - T_I \qquad (7)$$

where T_R is the time when the reactivated node was included in the neighbor's table and T_I is the time when the neighbor processed the inactivity packet. The self-healing time, as seen in Eq. (7), is computed by subtracting the time when the neighboring node processes an inactivity packet containing the address of the inactive node from the time the neighboring node has completed the routing and adjacency tables with the reactivated node. The results are seen in Table 4.

The overall result shows that the self-healing capability of the protocol performs best when the network topology is similar to either the intermediate or worst-case topologies. The self-healing time in the topologies only slightly increases to around 9000 milliseconds as the number of nodes removed and added back increases. On the other hand, when the network topology is similar to

Table 4. Results of self-healing time test.

	Best	Intermediate	Worst
1 node	54605.33 ms	64321.33 ms	77388.67 ms
2 nodes	76862.33 ms	72522.00 ms	84728.67 ms
3 nodes	88219.00 ms	89264.00 ms	86717.50 ms
4 nodes	109943.67 ms	90449.67 ms	96902.33 ms
5 nodes	197136.00 ms	80354.50 ms	81069.00 ms

Table 5. Performance of load balancing test.

	No Load Balancing	With Load Balancing
Latency	385 ms	408 ms
Packet success rate	91%	70%
Packet loss rate	9%	30%

the best-case topology, the self-healing time increases to around 35000 milliseconds as the number of nodes removed and added increases. This is due to the number of nodes handling the packets coming from the reactivated nodes. A node can only process one packet at a time; therefore, when a node receives several packets simultaneously, it takes an extended amount of time for it to go through each of the packets it received. In the best-case topology, only the sink node handles all the hello packets coming from the reactivated nodes; hence, the slower performance.

4.5 *Load balancing*

The load balancing test aims to evaluate the performance of the protocol when implemented with the round robin load balancing algorithm. This test examines whether the protocol achieves a better outcome with or without the round robin algorithm. This test was conducted in two different scenarios: when no load balancing occurs and when two nodes are used in load balancing with an assumption that the network has already converged and the have finished building their adjacency and routing tables. The sink node sends a packet to a destination node every 500 milliseconds.

$$Packet\ Success\ Rate = NTR \div NTS \tag{8}$$

where NTR is the total number of packets received and NTS is the total number of packets sent.

$$Packet\ Loss\ Rate = 1 - Packet\ Success\ Rate \tag{9}$$

Latency is computed by subtracting the time the sink sent the data packet from the time node 8.6.8.6 received the packet. The packet success rate, as seen in Eq. (8), is calculated by dividing the total number of packets received by node 8.6.8.6 with the total number of packets sent by the sink node. The packet loss rate, as seen in Eq. (9), is calculated by one minus the packet success rate. The results are shown in Table 5.

Table 5 shows the performance of the protocol in the two different scenarios. The result shows that SHARP performed better when no load balancing occurs as it only has a latency of 385 milliseconds, 91% packet success rate, and only 9% packet loss rate. This is due to the presence of only one sink node in the network that communicates with all the other nodes. A node is unable to process multiple packets simultaneously which means that it can only communicate with other nodes one at a time, making load balancing inconclusive for environments and setups with a single central node. Hence, rather than utilizing multiple routes to a destination node for load balancing, they can be used to increase the reliability of the protocol by having backup routes. The outcome also shows that as the number of nodes in the network increases, the performance of the protocol decreases due to the packets that are lost or dropped among the nodes in the route.

5 CONCLUSION

This paper has presented SHARP which allows a bidirectional communication between the sink and the nodes. Although the protocol is functional in its key features, it is observed from the analyses above that as the number of nodes used increases, its overall performance decreases. This could be due to several reasons such as the network congestion brought by the proximity of the nodes during testing and its broadcasted transmissions, and the limitations of the Arduino node or IEEE 802.15.4 XBee transceiver which could cause some packet loss in the network. This means that the protocol still has room for improvement for all of its features in the future.

The routing feature is the ability to deliver a packet or data from a source to the intended destination. The outcome of latency, goodput, throughput, and packet loss exhibit a certain prevalent trend instigated by the number of hops in the topologies used, as well as the environment where these tests were executed. The ad-hoc feature is the ability to regain a converged network state after a node or nodes have been newly added where all affected nodes should have a complete routing and adjacency table. The ad-hoc time is shown to be increasing as more nodes are added to the network. These results exemplify a degree of consistency of the protocol where ad-hoc time is increasing as the network adds more nodes. The self-healing feature provides the nodes the ability to maintain and recover its connection to the sink when a node along its communication path unexpectedly goes down. The results present a varying trend in self-healing time as more nodes were set to inactive depending on the topology. This is promising since it shows that a consistent self-healing time may be achieved as evident in the intermediate and worst case topologies, though it still produces a relatively high self- healing time overhead.

The load balancing feature provides the network with the ability to maximize its network resources by sharing the traffic load between multiple nodes in the event that there are multiple paths with equal cost to reach the destination. The load balancing test versus the no load balancing test indicates that no load balancing is favorable in topologies where there is only a single central node as it provided less packet loss and latency. The load balancing implementation in the protocol is unfavorable in this setting; however, it provided route reliability by using backup routes.

REFERENCES

Alliance, Z. 2011, *ZigBee Smart Energy Profile Document 075356r16ZB*, 15th ed. 2011, pp. 1–304.

Atzori, L., Iera, A. & Morabito, G. 2010. *The Internet of Things: A survey.* Computer Networks, vol. 54, no. 15, pp. 2787–2805, 2010.

Flores, F.K. and Cu, G., 2017. *WSAN: Node Network Communication Protocol through Coordination Messaging.* In Theory and Practice of Computation: Proceedings of Workshop on Computation: Theory and Practice WCTP2015 (pp. 122–135). Digi, XBee S1 802.15.4 RF Modules Datasheet, 1st ed. 2016.

Lee, J., Su, Y. & Shen, C. 2007. *A Comparative Study of Wireless Protocols: Bluetooth, UWB, ZigBee, and Wi-Fi*, IECON 2007 – 33rd Annual Conference of the IEEE Industrial Electronics Society, 2007.

Mainetti, L., Patrono L. & Vilei A. 2011. *Evolution of wireless sensor networks towards the Internet of Things: A survey.* SoftCOM 2011, 19th International Conference on Software, Telecommunications and Computer Networks, Split, pp. 1–6, 2011.

Park, J.Y., Cha, Y.T., Kang, S.H., Jin, K.C. and Hwang, J.A., 2010, August. *Interoperation of wired and wireless sensor networks over CATV network in hospitals.* In Mechanical and Electronics Engineering (ICMEE), 2010 2nd International Conference on (Vol. 1, pp. V1-420). IEEE.

Sheng, Z., Yang, S., Yu, Y., Vasilakos, A., Mccann, J., & Leung, K. 2013. *A survey on the ietf protocol suite for the internet of things: standards, challenges, and opportunities*, IEEE Wireless Communications, vol. 20, no. 6, pp. 91–98, 2013.

Verdone, R., Dardari, D., Mazzini, G. & Conti, A. 2008. *Wireless Sensor and Actuator Networks: Technologies, Analysis and Design*, 1st ed. Elsevier, 2008.

Theory and Practice of Computation – Nishizaki et al. (eds)
© 2019 Taylor & Francis Group, London, ISBN 978-0-367-20417-4

TRICEP: Technologies of RFID and image recognition in a checkout enhancement platform

F.K. Flores, D.C. Baldemor, A. Espiritu, P.A. Galang & M.C. Toleran
De La Salle University, Manila, Philippines

ABSTRACT: The presence of the Internet, Machine Learning, as well as the Internet of Things, have greatly improved many aspects of various industries globally. One of the main benefactors of these technological advancements in the industry, is with retail stores. Beginning from informative websites, online transactions, user-friendly retail applications, and recently, intelligent mobile applications; these have paved the way for retail industries, to improve in various aspects such as process improvement, transaction speed, data accuracy, inventory tracking, customer experience, and others. Organization such as Amazon Go makes use of deep learning, computer vision, and various sensors to provide a "Just Walk Out" shopping experience, allowing for the currently most advanced shopping technology. TPiSHOP, FutureProof Grocery, Future Store, and Regi-Robo Robotic Checkout and Bagging System focuses on allowing self-scanning of items via RFID or QR codes, with some of them having additional self-checkout capabilities. Although these technologies are already available in many countries and many retail industries have started to use them, they are typically known to be very costly to implement and use proprietary technologies, while some of them have not been fully tested nor integrated for use in production. The research investigates an approach to improve retail industries by developing a cost-effective and integrated checkout enhancement platform that implements RFID and image recognition using deep learning, a smart shopping basket, and a real-time integrated tool to improve the customer transaction process.

1 BACKGROUND

The presence of the Internet, Machine Learning, as well as the Internet of Things, have greatly improved many aspects of various industries globally. One of the main benefactors of these technological advancements in the industry, is with retail stores. These organization must continuously satisfy their customers by providing them with the best products, services, and experiences. In the traditional retail stores nowadays, cashiers at the checkout have to manually scan each and every item that the customer is going to purchase.

There are also instances when cashiers incorrectly scan the items wherein items are either scanned twice or sometimes they are not scanned at all. This results to customers experiencing a longer waiting time than expected because of the slow queue and slow checkout [1]. Since customer satisfaction is considered to be critical for customer behavior, customers become dissatisfied with the company's services thus, this causes the company long term problems in terms of profit and sales. In order to aid the said problem, several organizations geared towards implementing informative websites, online transactions, user-friendly retail applications, and recently, intelligent mobile applications in order to improve various aspects such as process improvement, transaction speed, data accuracy, inventory tracking, customer experience, and others. With these, several companies tend to rely on the use of technology such as Radio Frequency Identification and Computer Vision separately to solve the different problems that customers experience.

Radio Frequency Identification or RFID uses radio waves to read and capture the information that is stored on the RFID tag. This information is read by the RFID reader and these tags must be attached to all of the items in order to have a RFID based technology in retail stores [2]. Computer Vision on the other hand deals with the analysis and understanding of an information from an image [5]. Even if this is a relatively new technology, there are several tools that available in order for the image to be detected and classified accordingly. Since the RFID and Computer Vision technologies are implemented separately, customers still experience dissatisfaction when shopping because of the different limitations that each technology have.

In the RFID Technology, these limitations include being too costly and tedious to be implemented while in the Computer Vision Technology, the camera used can be prone to occlusion, the inability to see something because of the set-up and having a low accuracy in detecting and classifying items.

2 RELATED WORKS

2.1 *Mobile application in retail*

One of the initial implementations of technology integration with retail is through mobile applications. Organizations develop these applications to help provide users with better customer experience. Most technology integrated retail implementations offer either a proprietary equipment being provided to users; such as scanners, tablets, and other gadgets; in-store kiosks; or even publicly downloadable mobile applications and other such implementations to provide better customer experience. One such organization is FutureProof Grocery [4], which focuses on implementing a faster and cheaper way to shop via a company provided mobile app to help keep track of items, get notifications of promotions, keep track of receipts and transactions.

2.2 *RFID and QR code implementations*

Many have implemented RFID and QR Code technologies for use in identifying users as well as products. Organizations such as TPiSHOP [3] focuses on allowing users to self-scan items either using the store's device or a mobile phone, together with a mobile wallet and TPiSCAN app for an easier goods tagging and checkout.

Future Store LLC[3] is a partnership between three groups of company that namely: X5 Retail Group, Russia's largest food retailer, Rusnano, a Russian nanotechnology company, and Sitronics, a Russian technology firm. The joint venture focuses on developing an item-level RFID solutions and self-checkout for supermarkets in Russia, whose objective is to improve the supply chain. They have implemented smart shelves which detects items, smart point of sales terminals to immediately capture all goods in a basket, and automated payment via a RFID scanner at the store exits.

Regi-Robo Robotic Checkout and Bagging System Panasonic, one of the major electronic companies in Japan partnered with Lawson, a convenience store franchise in 2016 to develop and implement a robotic system for self-checkout. As stated by Fukushima [13], each item has its corresponding barcode sticker where customer manually scans the item on the robotic basket before placing it inside. The smart basket also automatically calculates the total bill and participates in the automatic packing of the items during checkout. In 2017 Panasonic improved the implementation by using RFID Tags instead of barcode stickers, where customer would now simply place their items in the basket instead of manually scanning each of the items to be included in the cart[9].

One major difficulty in using RFID Tags is during scanning with multiple tags present, where there are times that items are not read due to the presence of multiple tags congesting the reading process. There are many techniques such as implementing active scanners, or providing delays when reading tags, however many are limited due to delays in reading as well as congestion. Although these technologies are already available in many countries and many retail industries have started to use them, they are typically known to be very costly to implement and use proprietary technologies. while some of them have not been fully tested not fully integrated as the implementations are quite new.

Wallmart[10] implemented the use of RFID back in 2004 reported that their implementation on using Low Frequencey RFID tags resulted in having a costly implementation due to the tags not working on water bottles and metal products. Future Store is also reported to be costly, thus is not able to be deployed on all small scale stores. Others such as that of Standard Cognition System[8], uses machine vision-powered checkout, at the cost of five million dollars. While implementations such as Tesco Checkout-Free Supermarket System[1], are currently in their last phases of development thus there are still no figures of their results.

2.3 *Hybrid implementations*

One such organization that implements computer vision, deep learning algorithms, and sensor fusions as well as RGB cameras, depth sensing cameras, and infrared sensors is Amazon Go[12], recently launched in January 2018, providing customers the "Just Walk Out" technology. A "Just Walk Out" shopping experience, one of the currently most advanced shopping technologies, allowing the customers to simply grab the products from the shelf and leave the store and the products brought would automatically be charged to the credit card on the Amazon account and the receipt will be sent to the customer's mobile phone.

The process starts as soon as a customer enters the store, scans a QR code from the Amazon Go app, and passes through the transition area, which identifies the customer using facial recognition. Item purchases are detected through "a series of images of a user's hand before and after the hand crosses a plane into the inventory location" [13]. These images, together with sensor devices from scale, pressure sensor, and load cell, as well as a customer's past purchase help the software identify if the item is returned or placed into the cart. Combining these data allows Amazon Go to have a higher confidence score to be generated.

Although Amazon Go is at the leading edge of technology integration for retail, the technology and algorithms used are proprietary and very expensive to implement. During March 2017, Amazon released a statement that Amazon Go experiences technical complications whenever there are more than twenty customers at the store due to the difficulty in keeping track of customers and items, as well as when customers move too fast for the system [14].

3   DESIGN AND IMPLEMENTATION

Even though these technologies are already available in many countries and many retail industries have started to use them, they are typically known to be very costly to implement and use proprietary technologies. Current implementations focus on using RFID for tagging with an accompanying mobile application, only few integrates their implementation with Image Recognition, such as Amazon Go, which aids in improving accuracy and decreasing cost of tags and sensors that are deployed in the shelves. The research investigates an approach to improve retail industries by developing a cost-effective and integrated checkout enhancement platform that implements RFID

Figure 1.   Conceptual framework.

and image recognition using deep learning, a smart shopping basket, and a real-time integrated tool to improve the customer transaction process in an accompanying web-based application.

The implementation would focus on the three main users of a retail business; the customer, cashier, and the owner or manager. Each type of user have specific roles in the retail businesses. The customers are the ones to use the system to add items to the cart, purchase, and overall be provided with better customer experience. The cashiers are the ones responsible for approving and handling the transaction of the customers; while the owner or manager is the one responsible for replenishing inventory or stock, voiding products, and managing the overall users and activities of the system.

Similar to the related works, the implementation would focus on using an integration of RFID, Image Recognition, and a web-based application to allow usage for both desktop and mobile devices. The RFID would be used to uniquely identify an item while the Image Recognition would be used as a supplement to the RFID scanner in the event that a product is not scanned due to the speed of a user in putting the items in the cart. A smart basket would also be implemented in order to hold the RFID scanner and the camera to be used for Image Recognition. Lastly the web-based application would contain functionalities for authentication, authorization, shopping list, budget assistance, transaction history, checkout, inventory management, and others.

The architecture of the implementation would be separated into four segments; a shopping cart or basket, the web-based application, a database, and a user device. The shopping cart would contain a QR Code to allow identification of cart number; a camera connected to a Raspberry Pi or RPi, which would obtain continuous images of the basket, sending them to a server to be processed for image recognition; an RFID scanner, connected to an Arduino module which reads the scanned items' tag and sends the data to the basket's RPi in order to be routed to the server for tagging of basket items.

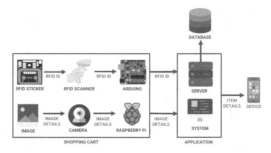

Figure 2.   Architecture design.

Connected to the basket is the application, which is both deployed in a central server at the retail store as well as a REST API based application in the RPi. This is used to allow communication between the cart or basket and the central server. The central server is connected to a centralized database where the customers' mobile devices, cashier's point of sales systems, and manager's management dashboard are connected to. This is to ensure that information of the retail store are centralized and synchronized at all times.

Figure 3.   Smart basket prototypes with QR code, concealed RFID scanner, and a camera.

The web-based application is built using Python Django Web Framework, due to Python's extensive library database together with its ease in development. The image recognition application used stars with OpenCV to obtain the images and are send to a DeepLearning server where TensorFlow was used with ImageNet and a retrained InceptionV3 model for image classification.

Connected to the basket is the application, which is both deployed in a central server at the retail store as well as a REST API based application in the RPi. This is used to allow communication between the cart or basket and the central server. The central server is connected to a centralized database where the customers' mobile devices, cashier's point of sales systems, and manager's management dashboard are connected to. This is to ensure that information of the retail store are centralized and synchronized at all times.

The web-based application is built using Python Django Web Framework, due to Python's extensive library database together with its ease in development. The image recognition application used stars with OpenCV to obtain the images and are send to a DeepLearning server where TensorFlow was used with ImageNet and a retrained InceptionV3 model for image classification.

4 TESTING AND RESULTS

The implementation of the test is based on a typical grocery store, with products that can normally be bought. At least fifty (50) different products that are typically present in a grocery store are used for testing. Item size and shape variety were considered when selecting items, some with varying shaped and colors, while others are typically only differentiated by the amount of liters or grams.

4.1 RFID test

For this test, the researchers checked whether all of the sides of the items (front, back, top, and bottom) can be scanned by the 125 kHz RFID or not. This is due to the fact that the material used for the different sides of an item, on each item, are not the same. Some of which are made of thick Tetra Pack carton package, some have small contents of metal, while others are made of thick plastic.

Table 1. RFID reading test snippet 1 – fast scanning results.

Product Details			Placement of RFID on Products				RFID Reading Performance	
Name and Description	Container	Content	Front	Back	Top	Bottom	Average Time to Read Tag	Comments
Close Up Fire Freeze 66g	Box	None	✓	✓	✓	✓	0.60	Slow Scanning
Cloud 9 Overload 50g	Plastic	Chocolate	✓	✓	✓	✓	0.63	Fast Scanning
Colgate Charcoal 2x 2x150g	Box	None	✓	✓	✓	✓	0.62	Fast Scanning
Colgate Plax 60mL.	Hard Plastic	None	✓	✓	✓	✓	0.57	Fast Scanning
Colgate Triple Action 126g	Box	None	✓	✓	N/A	✓	0.64	Fast Scanning

In order to determine the average reading time of RFID per item, the researchers conducted five trials for each item. In this testing, the sticker was placed at the back of the items. The results of the testing of the RFID shows that the average reading time and the comments about the reading performance of the RIFD. The legends used for the comments are as follows: Very Fast Scanning: Scanning Time $<= 0.50$ s, Slow Scanning: Scanning Time > 1.0 s and Scanning Time < 1.5 s, Fast Scanning: Scanning Time > 0.50 s and Scanning Time < 1.0 s, and Very Slow Scanning: Scanning Time > 1.5 s.

Table 2.   RFID reading test snippet 2 – slow scanning results.

Product Details			Placement of RFID on Products				RFID Reading Performance	
Name and Description	Container	Content	Front	Back	Top	Bottom	Average Time to Read Tag	Comments
Pantene Root Lift 100mL	Hard plastic	Liquid	✓	✓	N/A	✓	1.94	Slow Scanning
Pepero White Cookie 32g	Box	None	✓	✓	✓	✓	1.86	Very Slow Scanning
PikNik Shoestring Orig 255g	Hard Plastic with few materials of metal	None	✓	✓	✓	✓	1.93	Very Slow Scanning
PikNik Cheese Curls 240g	Hard Plastic with few materials of metal	None	✓	✓	✓	✓	1.05	Slow Scanning
Pringles Cheese 158g	Cardboard with few materials of metal	None	✓	✓	✓	✓	0.58	Very Slow Scanning, Inconsistent

It can be observed that each item is very different in terms of scanning speed, however products with large or dense containers, metallic surfaces, and liquid contents tend to have a slower reading time. This may be due to the fact that density and conductivity of a material affects the ability of an RFID scanner since radio waves are used, which are susceptible to these effects.

4.2   Image recognition test

For this test, the researchers tried to determine the confidence level and the rank number of the products when it is detected by the Image Recognition module. The image recognition module was implemented using TensorFlow with InceptionV3 model. The camera capture module is continuously capturing images and feeding them to the RPi, while the RPi is continuously sending the images to the DeepLearning server for tagging. For every image sent, it is processed and classified, resulting into a top 3 confidence rating of what the item might be.

However due to the number of classification, minimal training time, images being processed without products, similarity of the product items, and overhead cost of transmission when the RPi sends the image to the DeepLearning server for classification, the results of the Image Recognition test is not at all ideal. The highest confidence rating that was achieved was about 30–33% confidence.

As seen in the results of the Table 3. Image Recognition Test Snippet 1, products such as the A4Tech Zero Delay Mouse received top 3 classifications with a confidence level of only about 0.08, which means that the image classification is not confident at all, as well as that the product itself did not appear as one of the top 3 classified items. A similar output resulted with Baygon Kidlat Katol, where the top 3 did not include the actual product, however for this one, the confidence level reached up to 0.17. This is because shape of the Baygon and the top 1 classified output of Eden Cheese is similar in terms of being box-shaped, also that they share the same color blue.

Also in Table 3, Absolute, Aquafresh, and Breeze shows that the items are included in their top 3 classified outputs by the image classifier, with the top 1 results being from Absolute and Breeze. As for the results of Absolute Water, it is evident that the misclassified items, Sprite and Rhea Isopropyl, are similar to Absolute Water in a way that all three items are liquid based and have the same green color. As for the results of Aquafresh, the top 3 classified items of Zonrox, Aquafresh, and Safeguard share the same color of white.

For the rest of the items in the list their general results were about 0.05 to 0.12 confidence levels, which just means that the image recognitions is not yet ready to perform by itself, but only act

Table 3. Image recognition test snippet 1.

Product Details			Placement of RFID on Products				RFID Reading Performance	
Name and Description	Container	Content	Front	Back	Top	Bottom	Average Time to Read Tag	Comments
Pantene Root Lift 100mL	Hard plastic	Liquid	✓	✓	N/A	✓	1.94	Slow Scanning
Pepero White Cookie 32g	Box	None	✓	✓	✓	✓	1.86	Very Slow Scanning
PikNik Shoestring Orig 255g	Hard Plastic with few materials of metal	None	✓	✓	✓	✓	1.93	Very Slow Scanning
PikNik Cheese Curls 240g	Hard Plastic with few materials of metal	None	✓	✓	✓	✓	1.05	Slow Scanning
Pringles Cheese 158g	Cardboard with few materials of metal	None	✓	✓	✓	✓	0.58	Very Slow Scanning, Inconsistent

as a compliment to the RFID in the event that an item was not scanned. These results do indicate that the image recognition can generally pickup similarities of the products be it in shape or in color, however since majority of the products in a grocery or retail setting are very similar to each other, there is very little differences that the image recognition must be able to determine in order to provide a better classification. As for the study, since speed was more favored than accuracy due to its nature of being real-time, as well as that the DeepLearning server used by the study is not as powerful, the image recognition model was not trained to a more desirable extent.

4.3 *User acceptance test*

For this test, nineteen random students, faculty, and university personnel were asked to use the system. Participants start by creating their account, shop in the grocery store that the researchers have setup, and complete their transaction with the cashier. In their shopping experience, participants were to scan the QR Code to identify the basket ID being used, add and remove items from the cart, add and remove items from their shopping list, view their transactions, edit their account, and reset their password. Lastly survey was given to the participants to rate their satisfaction and usage of the system.

5 CONCLUSION AND RECOMMENDATION

The researchers were able to develop an Internet of Things solution that integrates both RFID and Image Recognition technologies in order to create a smart basket, which is cheaper and uses open source equipment and libraries, however resulted only as a prototype. In here, the researchers made use of RFID and existing tools for Image Recognition in order to classify the different products that the camera captures that goes through the scanner. The researchers also developed a real time integrated tool that caters to the needs to both the administrative side of retail stores as well as the customers.

A low frequency RFID tag may be appropriate for this type of implementation, such as the 125 kHz RFID tags used by the researchers because of a read range of up to 10 cm as to not scan

Table 4.   User acceptance test survey results.

Criteria	Strongly Disagree	Somewhat Disagree	Neutral	Somewhat Agree	Strongly Agree
The Sign Up process was convenient	0	0	0	2	17
I did not experience problems when getting a basket and scanning the QR code	0	0	0	5	14
I had no troubles in placing items inside my basket	0	1	0	6	12
I had no troubles removing items from my basket	0	0	0	3	16
There were no extra items placed inside by basket upon checkout	0	0	0	1	18
I can easily determine if the total cost of the items is within my budget	0	0	0	1	18
I can easily add items to my shopping list	0	0	0	2	17
I can easily remove items from my shopping list	0	0	0	2	17
I can easily access my shopping list even before or after shopping	0	0	0	1	18
I had no troubles when updating my account details	0	1	0	1	17
I am satisfied with my shopping experience	0	0	0	3	16

products that are not within the vicinity of the basket. The material of the packaging have also been proved to affect the read time of the RFID reader, which usually takes around three to five seconds for the reader to scan the tag and send its details to the server of the application.

For the Image Recognition, the researchers made use of TensorFlow in order to recognize and classify the images of the products accordingly. This was selected because of it being opensource. Here, the researchers have conducted several training iterations in order to improve the accuracy when the product is being detected. However, after conducting thousands of iterations and testing them accordingly, the researchers discovered that the accuracy of the TensorFlow goes down whenever there are more products that are being added to the application. This is because the tool is having difficulties when it comes to differentiating products from one another especially if the products have similar attributes.

In order to identify if TRICEP can handle real world scenarios, a user acceptance testing was conducted with random students, faculty, and personnel from De La Salle University. Their shopping experience and feedback when shopping with TRICEP were gathered and used as a basis to further improve the platform.

Based on the results of the development of TRICEP, the researchers has a number of recommendations for future researchers who would conduct a similar study or who will use this study as a reference. First, when creating a smart basket, other placements of the RFID reader should be considered. This is because there is a chance that there will be a faster reading time for the RFID tags and the placement of the RFID reader – whether it is placed outside the basket, at the side, and the like can also affect the user experience of the customers using TRICEP.

In addition to this, a better camera can also be used because the pictures that were taken by the camera will be used by the Image Recognition, thus, the quality of the pictures can also affect how TensorFlow recognizes and classifies the products. Second, future researchers can also consider using other existing tools for the Image Recognition. This will allow the future researchers to explore the different capabilities of the available Image Recognition tools and select which is the most applicable tool to use for their respective project. In addition, future researchers can also conduct a more extensive training for the models of the Image Recognition. With this, the accuracy when it comes to detecting and classifying the objects can increase thus, it will become more accurate.

Additional features and modules can be added to the platform such as inventory, sales, cashless payments, and addressing the possible problem of item switching. These will further enhance the platform developed and it will cover the whole process of shopping in retail stores.

REFERENCES

Amazon (n.d.). *Amazon Go Frequently Asked Questions*. [Online], Available: https://www.amazon.com/b?node=16008589011&tag=bisafetynet2-2011

BMVA (n.d.). *What is Computer Vision?*. [Online]. Available: www.bmva.org/visionoverview2

Carroll, J. (n.d.). *Computer Vision and Deep Learning Technology at the heart of Amazon Go*, Vision Systems, January 13, 2017. [Online], Available: http://www.visionsystems.com/articles/2017/01/computer-vision-and-deep-learning-technology-atthe-heart-of-amazon-go.html12

Diebold Nixdorf (n.d.). *TPiShop*. [Online], Available: http://www.dieboldnixdorf.com/en-us/software/retail/customer-touchpointsolutions/tpishop4

Fukushima, K. 2016. *Panasonic Introduces Robotic Checkout at a Grocery Store in Osaka*, CNBC International, December 14, 2016. [Online], Available: http://www.cnbc.com/2016/12/14/panasonic-introduces-robotic-checkout-at-agrocery-store-in-osaka.html6

Futureproof (n.d.). *About Us*. [Online], Available: https://futureproofretail.com/company3

Gutierrez, B.P.B. and Jegasothy, K., 2010. *Identifying Shopping Problems and Improving Retail Patronage Among Urban Filipino Customers*. Philippine Management Review, 17, pp. 66–79.

Omni-ID. (n.d.). *RFID Tag On Metal Technology White Paper*. [Online]. Available: https://www.omni-id.com/pdfs/RFID_Tag_OnMetal_Technology_WhitePaper.pdf1

Holden, R. 2017. *Amazon Go Is Not a Go After All At Least Not Yet*. March 27, 2017, [Online], Available: https://www.forbes.com/sites/ronaldholden/2017/03/27/amazon-go-is-not-a-go-after-all-at-least-not-yet13

Lynley, M. 2017. *Standard Cognition Gets $5M to Build a Machine Vision-Powered Checkout*. [Online]. Available: https://techcrunch.com/2017/10/10/standard-cognition-gets-5m-to-build-a-machine-vision-powered-checkout/9

Parsons, J. 2017. *Tesco Trials Checkout-Free supermarkets where your shopping is processed by artificial intelligence*. [Online]. Available: http://www.mirror.co.uk/tech/tesco-trials-checkout-free-supermarkets-1131386410

Roberti, M. *Wal-Mart, Suppliers Affirm RFID Benefits*, RFID Journal, February 22, 2007. [Online], Available: http://www.rfidjournal.com/articles/view?30598

Shayon, S. 2017 *Panasonic Trials 'Regi-Robo' Robotic Checkout and Bagging System* brandchannel.com, February 28, 2017. [Online]. Available: http://www.brandchannel.com/2017/02/28/panasonic-regi-robo-0228177

Swedberg, C. 2013. *Russia's Future Store Seeks a Supermarket for its RFID Solution*, RFID Journal, April 2, 2013. [Online], Available: http://www.rfidjournal.com/articles/view?10559/5

Theory and Practice of Computation – Nishizaki et al. (eds)
© 2019 Taylor & Francis Group, London, ISBN 978-0-367-20417-4

Image classification of Philippine bird species using deep learning

C.R. Raquel, K.M.A. Alarcon & L.L. Figueroa
University of the Philippines Diliman, Quezon City, Philippines

ABSTRACT: This paper presents an approach for Philippine bird species classification using Deep Learning specifically Transfer Learning. We have developed a Philippine bird species dataset since most existing bird species dataset are limited to birds from certain regions such as Northern America. The performance of Convolutional Neural Network (CNN) on image classification has been shown to be very efficient but requires a very large dataset and a significant amount of training time in order to generate a very high accuracy in its classification. In Transfer Learning, the pre-trained model output of the CNN can be further fine-tuned in order to classify image datasets that could possibly be different from the original dataset. In this paper, the pre-trained model of Google's Inception-v3 having 1000 different categories is retrained to classify 50 Philippine bird species using the TensorFlow library. Our approach achieved an accuracy of 94% for the Philippine bird species classification.

1 INTRODUCTION

The Philippines has more than 600 species of resident and migratory birds where more than 200 of them are endemic (Lepage n.d.). With this diversity of birds in our country, bird watching has become a hobby for many Filipinos. There are organizations such as the Wild Bird Club of the Philippines (WBCP) which promotes responsible appreciation of nature specifically on collecting and providing information about birds of the Philippines. Bird watching activities are also organized by these organizations or even a group of individuals where they would observe the birds in their natural habitat, capture their images and identify the name or species of the birds. Bird identification would be based on the expertise of the people involved, or they could consult books and other reference materials about the birds.

Several mobile applications have been developed to aid in the task of identifying bird species. For example, the Merlin Bird ID application (Merlin Bird ID by Cornell Lab of Ornithology n.d.) would allow the user to take a picture of bird and it would identify the species of the bird. One of the limitations of this mobile application is that the bird species for classification are only limited to certain countries such as the US, Canada and parts of Europe where these birds could be found. Asian countries like the Philippines are not included in their dataset. This is true for other mobile applications like IBird (iBird Pro Guide to Birds n.d.) and Morcombe (Morcombe's Birds of Australia n.d.). In the Philippines, the organization Haribon (BirdLife in the Philippines) has developed an iPhone application that displays images of Philippine birds captured by members of the organization (Haribon embraces the iPhone 2010). Information about the birds are also provided by the mobile application but it has no capability to automatically identify the bird specie given a picture provided by the user.

Mobile applications such as the Merlin Bird ID classifies birds were developed by data mining techniques and used a dataset of bird images in a particular area or region. An example of this dataset is the Caltech-UCSD Birds 200 (CUB200) which contains 200 bird species mostly from the North American region (Welinder et al. 2010). As of today, there is no published dataset of Philippine bird species which means there is no study yet on image classification of Philippine bird species. In this research, we developed a dataset consisting of 50 Philippine bird species.

Deep Learning is a type of machine learning that utilizes deep neural networks in training a machine to perform human tasks such as recognizing images or speech. It has recently achieved massive achievement on image classification tasks. It has shown excellent results as they generate models based on the training and test sets having the data distribution. But a change in data distribution would require the generation of a new model which is both expensive and difficult to do.

Reusing the pre-trained model could prove to be useful and possibly speed up the task of producing new models of new datasets. Knowledge transfer or Transfer Learning can achieve this by extracting knowledge from a source dataset and using this to another target task.

In this paper, we show how Transfer Learning can be used to classify 50 Philippine bird species by retraining the model generated by Google's Inception-v2.

In the remainder of this paper, we will first provide some review of related literature in Section II. Then, our methodology is presented in Section III. Section IV provides the details of our experimental results. Finally, Section V concludes this paper and provides some future directions.

2 LITERATURE REVIEW

According to Avibase (Lepage n.d.), a world bird database, there are 686 bird species found in the Philippines and 224 of them are endemic. There is a total of 95 globally threatened bird species in the Philippines. Bird watching as an activity can serve both as a hobby and a way to monitor the existence of different bird species in an area. Aside from manual bird identification using experts and consulting reference materials on bird species, it is a valuable idea to perform bird classification automatically using a software or application.

There has been a growing interest in bird classification research. A bird dataset called CUB 200 have been developed having 200 bird species which are mostly from the North American region (Welinder et al. 2010). Van Horn et al. discussed the difficulty of building a bird dataset in terms of collecting images and annotating them (Van Horn et al. 2015). They were able to produce a large dataset called NABirds containing 48,653 images of North American birds with 555 categories. They have worked not only with domain experts but made used of crowdsourcing with citizen scientist (non-professional scientists or enthusiasts) to come up with the dataset. They also developed the Merlin Photo ID mobile application which is a publicly available tool for bird species classification where a user can upload an image of a bird and the tool with a computer vision capability would identify the bird specie.

Huang et al. proposed a saliency based graphical model (GMS) that can precisely annotate the object on the pixel level (Huang et al. 2014). They have used Support Vector Machine (SVM) to classify the images in the CUB-200 dataset based on the features of the annotated birds. Marini et al. performed bird species classification based on color features extracted from images in the CUB-200 dataset while Lucio et al. used the textural content of spectrogram images using SVM (Marini et al. 2013; Lucio et al. 2015). Nanni et al. Combined both visual and acoustic features for bird specifies classification using SVM (Nanni et al. 2016). Yoshihashi et al. used deep learning algorithm in classifying bird species from images taken from the wind farm, which is the target location of their research (Yoshihashi et al. 2017).

Deep Learning techniques has achieved a higher accuracy than human vision on many computer vision tasks due to the use of Convolutional Neural Network (CNN) such as the Inception-v4 which has a 3.08% error rate when trained on the ImageNet dataset. This model has 75 trainable layers but requires a long training time.

Convolutional Neural Network (CNN) has multiple layers of receptive fields where each layer consists of a number of neurons that process the input image. The output of one layer is usually fed as input to the next layer in order to produce a representation of the input images. CNN could have different layers such as convolutional, pooling, Rectified Linear Unit and Full Connected Layers (A guide to TF layers: Building a convolutional neural networks n.d.).

Convolutional layers are used as feature detectors as they extract the features from the input image dataset. This type of layer is designed to find suitable filters of the image by modifying its weights during training.

Since the convolutional layer undergoes a linear operation, a non-linear Rectified Linear Unit or ReLU is usually introduced to provide non-linearity in the network. The task of pooling or sub-subsampling is to reduce the dimensionality of each feature map but retains the most important information of the input data. Examples if pooling operations could be max, average or sum (A guide to TF layers: Building a convolutional neural networks n.d.).

The last part of the network is usually a fully connected layer of neurons which handles the high-level reasoning of the neural network. This is where classification or detection usually happens.

There are usually more available images for popular or more common birds compared to unpopular bird species. Since CNNs require very large datasets for training, it would be difficult to acquire a bird species dataset that could satisfy this requirement. But Transfer Learning can be used for image classification of bird species by using the pre-trained model which used a large dataset. An example of this is Google's Inception-v2 which was trained on the ImageNet dataset having 100,000 images with 1,000 classes.

3 METHODOLOGY

In this section, we describe the Philippine bird species dataset that we developed and how we used a deep learning technique specifically transfer learning in performing bird species classification.

3.1 *Philippine bird species dataset*

Since all available bird species datasets consists of birds in United States or in Europe, we developed a dataset for Philippine bird species. Due to the interest of time, the dataset consists of 50 out of 686 bird species in the Philippines. The list of bird species can be found in Appendix A.

Each bird specie has 100 images each. The bird images have been obtained from bird related websites such as Oriental Bird Images (Oriental Bird Images n.d.), Handbook of the Birds of the World (HBW) (Handbook of the Birds of the World n.d.) and NABirds (Van Horn et al. 2015). Images also came from social media websites such as Flickr (Flickr n.d.), personal websites of bird enthusiasts and other websites. Some Philippine bird species such as the Purple Needletail has limited number of images on the Internet and we decided not to include it in the dataset. The downloaded images were used only for research purposes and the authors do not mean to infringe any copyright of the images.

3.2 *Transfer learning*

The classification of the Philippine bird species has been done through transfer learning which makes use of a CNN pre-trained on the ImageNet dataset. The output of the CNN consists of low-level and high-level features learned from the input datasets. These could be used to augment learning in a different classification or detection task. In Inception-v2, we can extract the data feature from the next-to-last layer. The last layer is where classification is usually performed (How to Retrain Inception's Final Layer for New Categories n.d.).

When a new dataset is different from the dataset used by the pre-trained model, the last layer of the model is not suitable for use. We can modify this last layer to make it applicable to the new classification needs while still using the generic features learned the CNN having a large dataset (How to Retrain Inception's Final Layer for New Categories n.d.).

We used the Philippine Bird Species dataset which consists of 50 bird species containing 100 images each. The total number of images in the data set is 5000 images. The dataset is divided into 70% for the training set and 30% for the test set. The image dataset was transformed into standard TensorFlow binary files.

The reason why we can learn with a new dataset using the pre-trained model is that the layer before classification already provides substantial summary of features for the new classification problem. These features are often generic to the original problem of classifying 1000 categories in an image such as edge and color blob detector. One could simply use the pre-trained Inception-v2 and augment a repurposed classification layer. Though these can be done with relatively little time without even the need for GPU, it might suffer a bit in performance (Oriental Bird Images n.d.). This work instead fine-tunes the pre-trained model. We repurposed a transfer learning Python code from (A guide to TF layers: Building a convolutional neural networks n.d.) and use TensorFlow models for Inception-v2 (Szegedy et al. 2015). With a good starting point for the weights, training can be done in acceptable time. We fine-tuned the model with a batch size of 8 in 30 epochs. The learning rate is set to decay after running on one epoch for better stability.

4   EXPERIMENTAL RESULTS

The computational neural network (CNN) was trained and tested using the Philippine bird species dataset. The training time ran for approximately 24 hours. The network was run on a Hewlett-Packard Envy Notebook having an Intel Core i76500U CPU, 8GB memory with an NVIDIA GEFORCE GTX graphics processing unit (GPU). The model achieved an accuracy of 93% in the train set with a loss score of 0.54. The test set accuracy is 94%. The confusion matrix (see Appendix) shows that majority of the bird species in the test set have been classified correctly. For example, all the images of the bird specie Philippine Scops-Owl have been correctly classified (27 out of 27 images found on the 32nd row of the confusion matrix). This is possibly due to its unique features such as having a round red eye and unique head shape compared to other birds.

According to the matrix, the bird specie with the worst classification (77.4% accuracy) is the Philippine Hawk Eagle where 7 out of 31 test images were misclassified. It has been mistaken to be an Osprey, Brown Shrike, Brush Cuckoo, Mallard or a Philippine Hawk-Cuckoo. Intuitively, the model would have been mistaken in discriminating similar looking birds.

The bird specie with the second lowest classification rate (78.2% accuracy) is Great Cormorant where 5 out of our 37 test images were misclassified. It has been mistaken to be an Eared Grebe, Eurasian Tree Sparrow or an Osprey. The third bird specie with the lowest accuracy (80.7%) is Mallard. And the fourth bird specie is the lowest accuracy (81%) is the Gadwall where it was incorrectly classified 7 out of 37 test images. It has been incorrectly classified as a Green-Winged Teal, Mallard, Northern Pintail, White-Browed Crake or a Yellow Bittern. The model incorrectly classified the bird specie of Mallard 5 out of 26 test images while the bird specie Great Cormorant was misclassified 5 out of 23 test images. Images of birds where the birds are clear or focused are easier to classify compared to bird images where the birds are small or partly obstructed by other objects in the image such as branches or leaves.

We have compared the performance of our model to that of the Google Images search engine (Google Images n.d.). We used 30 images each for the four bird species with the lowest accuracy in the test set namely: Philippine Hawk-Eagle, Gadwall, Mallard and Great Cormorant. We also included the bird specie Philippine Scops-Owl which has a 100 percent accuracy in the test set for comparison purposes. For example, we uploaded each of the 30 test images from the bird specie Philippine Hawk-Eagle to Google for identification. Google only correctly identified 13 out of the 30 images uploaded. Table 1 shows the bird species together with their accuracy generated by Google. Among the 5 birds species tested, Philippine Scops-Owl produced the highest accuracy but much lower than the accuracy produced by our model (100% accuracy). Google incorrectly classified one of the Philippine Scops-Owl image to be an "eastern screech owl". Other incorrect label produced by Google for this bird specie is "madagascar red owl". It also produced the labels "philippine owl", "kinds of owl in the philippines" and "owls in the philippines". Another common incorrect label produced by Google search for the other four bird species is "beak" which is actually a body part of the bird. This shows that Google is a general image search engine and is not always really suitable for identifying the specific bird specie of an image.

We further tested Google Image search engine by comparing the first thirty images produced by Google when uploading an image from our test set. The objective of this test is to see how many of the images produced by Google belong to that bird specie. The average accuracy ranged from 23% to 40% but never even above 50% accuracy. Therefore, if we want to classify the bird specie of a particular image of a bird, a general search engine such as Google Image might not be the

Table 1. Accuracy results produced by Google Image search engine.

Bird Species	Accuracy
Philippine Scops-Owl	66%
Philippine Hawk-Eagle	43%
Great Cormorant	66%
Mallard	26%
Gadwall	63%

most suitable option to use. The accuracy of our model is way higher than that produced by Google Image which shows that a model developed to identify bird species given an image could perform better for this particular image classification task of Philippine bird species.

5 CONCLUSION

In this paper, we have shown how a deep learning approach using transfer learning was able to classify images of bird species. We have shown how a pre-trained model generated by Inception-v2 on the ImageNet dataset can be used to augment the learning of a network to correctly classify the Philippine bird species dataset that we have developed. This dataset is small and different compared to the large ImageNet dataset having 1,000 object classes. The experimental results showed that using this method, a network can classify Philippine bird species with a high accuracy despite some birds having similar features. In future work, it is recommended to extend the size of the dataset of Philippine bird species and explore how to further improve the accuracy of the network model. Also, a mobile application should also be developed to make the results useful and test its applicability.

6 APPENDIX

Appendix A – Philippine Bird Species Dataset

#	Species	Diagonal
1	Arctic warbler	27
2	Black-bellied Plover	36
3	Black-naped oriole	27
4	Black-winged stilt	24
5	Blue breasted pitta	33
6	Blue rock-thrush	28
7	Brnst	32
8	Brown shrike	34
9	Brush cuckoo	25
10	Chestnut munia	27
11	Cinnamon bittern	24
12	Coppersmith barbet	34
13	Eared Grebe	28
14	Eurasian tree sparrow	32
15	Gadwall	30
16	Golden-bellied gerygone	26
17	Great Cormorant	18
18	Greater Scaup	26
19	Greater White-fronted Goose	27
20	Greater painted-snipe	37
21	Green-winged Teal	21
22	Java sparrow	31
23	Long-tailed shrike	24
24	Lowland White-eye	34
25	Mallard	21
26	Narcissus flycatcher	37
27	Northern Pintail	24
28	Northern Shoveler	34
29	Olive backed sunbird	30
30	Osprey	29
31	Pacific Swallow	31
32	Philippine Scops-Owl	27
33	Philippine hanging -parrot	26
34	Philippine hawk eagle	34
35	Philippine hawk-cuckoo	29
36	Philippine nightjar	30
37	Philippine pied-fantail	26
38	Philippine woodpecker	25
39	Pied Triller	31
40	Richard_s pipit	30
41	Spotted kingfisher	25
42	Striated Grassbird	27
43	Swinhoe_s snipe	23
44	Tundra Swan	27
45	White-breasted waterhen	29
46	White-browed crake	38
47	Yellow bittern	34
48	Yellow-vented bulbul	23
49	Zebra dove	36
50	Zitting cisticola	26

REFERENCES

A guide to TF layers: Building a convolutional neural networks. https://www.tensorflow.org/tutorials/layers.

Flickr. https://www.flickr.com/.

Google Images. https://images.google.com.

Handbook of the Birds of the World. https://www.hbw.com/.

Haribon embraces the iPhone. 2015. https://www.birdlife.org/asia/news/haribon-embraces-iphone.

How to Retrain Inception's Final Layer for New Categories. https://www.tensorflow.org/tutorials/image_retraining.

Huang, C., Meng, F., Luo, W., Zhu, S. 2014. Bird breed classification and annotation using saliency based graphical model. *Journal of Visual Communication and Image Representation* (25)6: 1299–1307.

iBird Pro Guide to Birds. https://itunes.apple.com/us/app/ibird-pro-guide-to-birds/id308018823?mt=8.

Lepage, D. *Avibase – Bird Checklists of the World Philippines.* https://avibase.bsc-eoc.org/checklist.jsp?region=PH.

Lucio, D. R., Maldonado, Y., da Costa, G. 2015. Bird species classification using spectrograms. *2015 Latin American Computing Conference (CLEI).* Arequipa, Peru.

Marini, A., Facon, J., Koerich, A. L. 2013. Bird Species Classification Based on Color Features. *2013 IEEE International Conference on Systems, Man, and Cybernetics.* Manchester, UK.

Merlin Bird ID by Cornell Lab of Ornithology. https://play.google.com/store/apps/details?id=com.labs.merlinbirdid.app&hl=en.

Morcombe's Birds of Australia. https://play.google.com/store/apps/details?id=com.coolideas.eproducts.ausbirds&hl=en.

Nanni, L., Costa, Y. M. G., Lucio, D. R., Silla, C. N., Brahnam, S. 2016. Combining Visual and Acoustic Features for Bird Species Classification. *2016 IEEE 28th International Conference on Tools with Artificial Intelligence (ICTAI).* San Jose, CA, USA.

Oriental Bird Images. http://orientalbirdimages.org/.

Szegedy, C., Liu, W., Jia, Y., Sermanet, P., Reed, S., Anguelov, D., Erhan, D., Vanhoucke, V., Rabinovich, A. 2015. Going deeper with convolutions. *2015 IEEE Conference on Computer Vision and Pattern Recognition (CVPR).* Boston, MA, USA.

Van Horn, G. et al. 2015. Building a bird recognition app and large scale dataset with citizen scientists: The fine print in fine-grained dataset collection. 2015 *IEEE Conference on Computer Vision and Pattern Recognition (CVPR).* Boston, MA, USA.

Welinder, P., Branson, S., Mita, T., Wah, C., Schroff, F., Belongie, S., Perona, P. 2010. *Caltech-UCSD Birds 200.* http://www.vision.caltech.edu/visipedia/CUB-200.html.

Yoshihashi, R., Kawakani R., Iida, M., Naemura, T. 2017. Bird detection and species classification with time-lapse images around a wind farm: Dataset construction and evaluation. *Wind Energy.* 1983–1995.

Theory and Practice of Computation – Nishizaki et al. (eds)
© 2019 Taylor & Francis Group, London, ISBN 978-0-367-20417-4

Recognition of emotions towards commercial ads based on EEG and facial landmarks

E.V. Empaynado, H.W. Francisco, N.K. Gardose & J.J. Azcarraga
De La Salle University, Malate, Metro Manila, Philippines

ABSTRACT: Emotions play a significant role to an individual's social interaction and response to his/her environment. Emotions may be observed and expressed through one's facial expressions and physiological manifestations. As such, emotions may play a big role in advertisements as customers may be attracted to a product if they can relate with what is being shown in the advertisement. Video segments that elicit some emotional reactions may be identified by capturing facial expressions and physiological signals such as the brainwaves signals. With proper implementation of advertisements, the popularity, desirability and impact of a product to the viewers may be increased. This research aims to determine the appropriate machine learning models for emotion recognition using EEG and Facial Landmarks that can be used to create a system that can recognize emotions of an individual while watching commercial advertisements.

1   INTRODUCTION

1.1   *What is advertising?*

Advertising and marketing are commercially driven with the goal of informing the public about goods and services, persuading people to buy, building and maintaining brands as well as maximizing profits for the organization (Terkan 2014). Video advertisements (video ads) have grown bigger over the past years due to the rapidly evolving technology. In relation to that, more and more companies are creating a significant amount of video ads due to its effectiveness in attracting customers/consumers. Most people nowadays use social media applications such as Facebook, Instagram, Twitter, and YouTube on their devices on a daily basis. The companies of these social media applications usually include advertisements in their applications for it is one of their methods in gaining revenue since all of the said applications can be used for free. The statistics of distribution of advertising by media states that digital advertising is linearly growing while other distributions such as radio, magazines, newspapers, directories, and television are slowly declining over the years (Statistica 2018). It is also common to see content producers in the said social media platforms monetize their contents by inserting video ads on some portions of the video.

To guarantee that companies attract consumers with their video ads, the video should be able to capture the interest of the targeted users. Also, the video ads must be built with considerations. For example, shorter ads are more likely to be finished by viewers than longer ones which are also the case to ads that are placed in the middle instead of the beginning of the video (Krishnan and Sitaraman 2013). One of the methodologies that may increase probability of attracting consumers is advertisement testing wherein it aims to increase marketing effectiveness. It is also stated that the first reaction of a consumer on seeing a new product is an important factor in determining the success of the product (Abhishek et. al, 2016). By this, designing an application that can identify emotions of viewers of the advertisements that uses facial landmarks and electroencephalogram (EEG) can help companies in improving their advertisements. Affective characterization in multimedia can be used to improve multimedia retrieval and recommendation. In addition, emotion detection is an effective way to unobtrusively identify emotional traces of videos or other content without interrupting viewers. Lastly, collected emotional trace is more reliable since we do not have to rely on emotional self-reports that can be influenced by different social and personality factions (Asghari-Esfeden et. al, 2015). As such, having software that will identify emotions can provide more consistent results since the testers are not distracted during the process of watching the video ads. In addition, it can also provide a foolproof testing since collected emotional traces by EEG cannot be faked nor modified, thus providing a more authentic result.

1.2 *The goal of this research*

This research aims to create different models in order to design an application that will assist companies in determining emotions of advertisement testers by using facial landmarks and EEG. This can help companies design better advertisements since they can use the application to determine the emotions that the testers felt during the video or at specific time frames to see whether the video succeeded in eliciting the right emotion from the viewer. Then, the companies can then redesign their advertisements to fit the audience better.

2 DATA COLLECTION

2.1 *Data collection procedure*

A total of 20 right-handed students aged from 18 to 21 years old participated in this study with equal number of male and female participants.

Eleven (11) advertisement videos are chosen as a way to elicit emotions from the participants. These advertisements are chosen based on the emotions it can induce from the participants. The emotions are Interested, Happiness, Sadness, and Surprise. Also, the advertisements are foreign and new to the participants in order to assure real and genuine reactions from the participants. The data gathering procedure is held in a controlled environment to minimize the amount of distractions to the participant to ensure the consistency of the data. A 5-channel Emotiv Insight headset is worn by the participants. The headset is used to record the EEG signals during the session which is able translate it into a meaningful data that can be processed (Emotiv 2018). Aside from capturing the brainwaves signals, facial expression are also recorded with the use of a webcam. The recordings are used to extract the facial landmarks of the participant during the session.

Every session starts with recording the baseline EEG signals of the participants. Each participant is asked to wear earphones and to close their eyes in order for the participants to calm and reach a neutral/baseline state. Recording the baseline of the participants takes for about 2 minutes. After which, participants are asked to watch the advertisements. During this session, the participants are asked to report their emotion, after each advertisement video. A program is used that allows them to check all of the emotions they felt while watching the advertisement using the radio buttons and checkboxes provided. Participants are provided with 8 emotions (Interested, Indifferent, Happiness, Sadness, Fear, Anger, Surprise, and Disgust) to choose from while reporting. A special case has been implemented with the emotions *interested* and *indifferent* where participants need to choose between the two emotions. After watching all of the videos, the participants are asked to indicate the specific time frame to tag every emotion they felt while watching the videos. Only *interested* and *indifferent* emotions are tagged for the whole duration of the video. In the end, we decide to only keep the emotions, *interested, indifferent, happiness, sadness, and surprise.* The *interested* and *indifferent* are later transformed to binominal class where *interested* being the positive (1) and *indifferent* being the negative (0). Other emotions are omitted from this research since they are rarely picked by the participants thus resulting in low frequency of such emotions in the dataset.

3 DATA PRE-PROCESSING

3.1 *Data pre-processing procedure*

EEG signals and facial landmarks at every frame of the videos are pre-processed and prepared that involve cleaning and syncing the timestamps of the data for EEG and facial landmarks.

The preprocessing procedure employed on the EEG dataset follows the methodology in the paper by Azcarraga, Azcarraga, & Talavera (2016) in which the dataset is segmented into 2-second window samples with a 1-second overlap between segments. The Fast Fourier Transform (FFT) technique is applied on the segments to remove artifacts in the EEG data. Brainwave frequencies are then extracted by using low-pass and high-pass filters. Mean Spectral Power (MSP) and Peak Magnitude (PM) are the signals extracted from the *Alpha*, *Beta Low*, *Beta High*, and *Gamma* waves of the brain. Based on these frequencies, several features are formed during the calm/baseline state and during the session when participants are watching videos. The baseline state produces only a single vector from which all the session samples are subtracted. The resulting values are normalized from -3 to 3 to eliminate any extremities in the data.

For the facial landmarks, the approach of Rosebrock (2017) in detecting facial landmarks is used. X and Y coordinates of 68 facial points in each frame are identified from facial videos. Other factors to consider when recording the data from the participant's video include cleaning and synchronizing with EEG data.

Cleaning the datasets include the removal of data segments that are blank. Three (3) different categories are used for sorting the data sets: EEG data only, facial landmarks data only, and combined EEG and facial landmarks. The method of cleaning the data sets is performed depending on which of the categories they will be used in. For the two uncombined categories, blank segments and parts when the participants are reporting are all removed. In the combined EEG and facial landmarks category, if at least one of them has a blank segment, that segment and its corresponding segment in the other data set will be removed even if the corresponding segment is not blank. This is to ensure that the EEG and facial landmark data sets are properly synced using the timestamps.

EEG and facial landmark data are synchronized based on their timestamps. However, the EEG and facial landmark have different recorded rate per second. Some adjustments are performed in order to synchronize the two modalities. Since the recorded data from EEG have much faster record rate per second as compared to facial landmark, data from facial landmark are duplicated multiple times until it matches the timestamp of the EEG data. This process is repeated until all files are read.

4 DATA PROCESSING

4.1 *Data processing procedure*

The tool used for data processing and classification is the Rapidminer software. A total of four machine learning models are applied to test their performance in predicting emotions in the context of commercial videos. These were the Decision Tree (DT), Naive Bayes (NB), Support Vector Machine (SVM), and Multilayer Perceptron (MLP). Oversampling is applied in order to balance out the distribution of classes in the dataset, to prevent biases in the data. Student-level cross validation was also applied after oversampling as the cross-validation method. In student-level cross validation, each fold has samples only of a particular student. For example, if there are 10 students, there are 10 folds with one fold per student and that the folds are mutually exclusive. This is to ensure that samples of the same student should not appear in both train and test set.

Twelve (12) models of the same type are trained since there are three (3) datasets (EEG data only, facial landmark data only, and combined data of EEG and facial landmarks) and for each, one model is built for each of the four (4) emotions (happiness, sadness, surprise, and interest). Since there are four (4) machine learning algorithms, a total of 48 learning models are compared in terms of prediction performance.

5 RESULTS AND DISCUSSION

5.1 *Table legends*

Performance in predicting happiness, sadness, surprise, and interest where accuracy, f-measure, sensitivity, and specificity are used as performance measures, on three modality sets (EEG only,

Table 1. Results of the models using the interested emotion.

	Facial Landmark data only					EEG data only				
	Acc	Pre	F1	TP	TN	Acc	Pre	F1	TP	TN
A	54.60	54.30	56.14	58.10	51.10	34.25	35.51	36.99	37.60	29.90
B	44.60	46.05	53.17	62.90	26.30	38.25	39.15	40.71	42.40	32.10
C	44.90	45.53	48.55	52	37.80	37.45	38.22	39.42	40.70	34.20
D	46.35	46.85	50.25	54.70	38.50	45	47.19	60.40	83.90	6.10
E	41.35	45.18	58.00	81	1.7	34.50	36.16	38.21	40.50	28.50

	Combined EEG and Facial Landmark data				
	Accuracy	Precision	F-Measure	Sensitivity	Specificity
A	47.55	48.03	53.23	59.70	35.40
B	44.70	46.09	53.06	62.50	26.90
C	41.20	43.15	48.51	55.40	27
D	45.95	46.03	46.46	46.90	45
E	41.35	45.18	58.00	81.00	1.70

Facial Landmarks Only, Combined EEG and Facial Landmarks), are shown in Tables 1–4. The leftmost column of each table represents the models used, *A* represents *decision tree*, *B* is *naive bayes*, *C* is *SVM*, D is MLP, and E is decision stump. The values in the table are percentages.

5.2 Interested

For the *interested* emotion, using the facial landmarks features, the accuracy and F-measure range from 41–54% and 48–58%, respectively. When EEG features are used, the accuracy and F-measure range from 34–45% and 36–60%, respectively. When face and EEG features are combined, the performance did not improve, with accuracy and F-measure that range from 41–47% and 46–58%, respectively. Sensitivity of the three modalities ranges from 37% to 83% while the specificity ranges from 1% to 54%. The trained models are more likely to detect if the emotion is present over detecting if it is not present.

The distribution of data for the *interested* emotion has more positive samples (9496) than negative samples (3633). With a ratio of 3:1 between the two classifications, it may be the reason for the models in the *interested* emotion to predict more towards the positive classifier despite the oversampling to balance the data.

5.3 Happiness

For the *happiness* emotion, the performance in predicting such emotion is low (see Table 2). Using facial landmarks as features, the accuracy and F-measure range from 34–47% and 40–54%, respectively. When EEG features are used, the accuracy and F-measure range from 29–60% and 33–61%, respectively. When SVM is employed. Performance has not improved even when face and EEG features are combined. The accuracy and F-measure only range from 34–51% and 40–56%, respectively. Unlike the *interested* dataset, the *happiness* dataset are not as highly imbalanced in which there are a total of 7236 samples for the negative while 5893 samples for the positive class.

5.4 Sadness

For the *sadness* emotion, using the facial landmarks features, the accuracy and F-measure range from 51–63% and 64–77%, respectively. When EEG features are used, the accuracy and F-measure

Table 2. Results of the models using the happiness emotion.

	Facial Landmark data only					EEG data only				
	Acc	Pre	F1	TP	TN	Acc	Pre	F1	TP	TN
A	36.80	38.24	40.03	30.70	42.90	29.60	31.56	33.14	24.30	34.90
B	46.85	47.62	54.20	30.80	62.90	60.60	60.11	61.52	58.20	63.00
C	42.55	43.00	44.36	39.30	45.80	50.55	50.51	52.99	40.90	54.20
D	45.75	45.88	46.56	44.20	47.30	43.80	45.09	50.35	30.60	52.00
E	34.75	38.99	45.91	12.70	55.80	29.65	31.65	33.29	24.20	35.10

	Combined EEG and Facial Landmark data				
	Accuracy	Precision	F-Measure	Sensitivity	Specificity
A	37.95	38.81	40.75	34.10	41.80
B	51.12	50.97	56.24	39.50	62.71
C	46.75	47.06	44.41	41.50	52.00
D	43.95	44.37	45.98	40.20	47.70
E	34.25	38.99	45.91	12.70	55.80

Table 3. Results of the models using the sadness emotion.

	Facial Landmark data only					EEG data only				
	Acc	Pre	F1	TP	TN	Acc	Pre	F1	TP	TN
A	62.81	65.72	76.74	92.70	4.37	62.54	65.16	76.94	93.90	0.2
B	51.03	62.48	64.24	66.10	21.07	60.81	92.32	65.37	55.60	71.17
C	61.81	64.87	76.40	92.90	0	55.22	62.88	70.34	79.80	6.36
D	59.75	64.03	73.66	86.20	3.18	52.16	61.53	67.60	75	6.76
E	58.55	64.72	72.69	82.90	10.14	59.55	64.39	74.26	87.70	3.58

	Combined EEG and Facial Landmark data				
	Accuracy	Precision	F-Measure	Sensitivity	Specificity
A	64.87	66.01	78.66	97.30	0.40
B	51.70	62.34	65.59	69.20	16.90
C	59.48	64.73	73.83	85.90	6.96
D	60.01	64.38	74.82	89.30	1.79
E	51.50	61.88	65.95	70.60	13.53

range from 52–62% and 65–78%, respectively. And when face and EEG features are combined, the performance does not improve and has a worse performance than the facial landmark modal. The accuracy and F-measure range from 51–65% and 65–79%, respectively. With the sensitivity between the three modalities ranges from 55% to 97%, and the specificity ranges from 0% to 21%.

The difference between sensitivity and specificity is quite large with the sensitivity close to 100 and the specificity closer to 0. This may be attributed to imbalance data distribution, with it having a ratio close to 1:11 between the two classifiers. With the positive classifier only having a total of 1191 tags, and the negative classifier having a large total of 11938 tags.

5.5 *Surprise*

For the *surprise* emotion, using the facial landmarks features, the accuracy and F-measure range from 60–74% and 73–85%, respectively. When EEG features are used, the accuracy and F-measure

Table 4. Results of the models using the surprise emotion.

	Facial Landmark data only					EEG data only				
	Acc	Pre	F1	TP	TN	Acc	Pre	F1	TP	TN
A	73.54	73.65	84.76	99.80	0	69.79	73.01	82.03	93.60	3.50
B	60.50	72.26	73.76	75.30	19.05	49.08	70.57	60.54	53	38.10
C	73.69	73.69	84.85	100	0	73.69	73.69	84.85	100	0
D	63.82	72.07	77.19	83.10	9.80	72.59	73.43	84.10	98.40	0.28
E	73.69	73.69	84.85	100	0	69.79	73.01	82.03	93.60	03.05

	Combined EEG and Facial Landmark data				
	Accuracy	Precision	F-Measure	Sensitivity	Specificity
A	69.57	72.95	81.88	93.30	03.08
B	58.81	71.53	72.06	72.60	19.05
C	73.69	73.69	84.85	100	0
D	68.61	73.49	80.83	89.80	09.24
E	73.69	73.69	84.85	100	0

range from 49–74% and 60–85%, respectively. And when face and EEG features are combined, the performance did not improve having the same performance with the other modalities. The accuracy and F-measure range from 58–74% and 72–85%, respectively. With the sensitivity between the three modalities ranges from 69% to 100%, and the specificity ranges from 0% to 19%.

Compared to the *sadness* emotion, *surprise* had a slightly worse distribution of the positive (1191) and negative (11938) samples. As such, all models such as SVM, some Decision tree and Decision Stump have shown the same confusion matrix for all the modalities, specifically, 998, 357, 2, and 0 for its true negative, false negative, false positive, and true positive, respectively where all the models predicted the test samples as *not surprise*. This can be observed by looking to the specificity values, with majority of it being at 0%.

5.6 *Discussion*

Most models in predicting *sadness* and *surprised*, predicted all test samples as *not sad* and *not surprised*. This may be attributed to the small number of videos that successfully elicited these emotions. Only a few videos were able to successfully make the students feel *sad* and/or *surprised*. Also in the videos that succeeded in eliciting these emotions, such as the Doritos commercial for *surprise* and the P&G commercial for *sadness*, not all the participants reported that they felt such emotion since only a little more than half of them have reported that they felt *surprised* and *sad* for those respective videos. Due to the low number of tags for both *surprise* and *sadness*, the system predicts the more common tags that it sees which is *not surprise* and *not sad*.

As explained the way the emotions class are tagged in the datasets may also have contributed on the accuracies of the models for each emotions. *Interested* and *happiness* are emotions that are tagged in long time segments, mainly because the participants indicating that they felt these emotions for a significant time in an advertisement. While the *sadness* and *surprise* emotions are tagged with short time segments, with them being identified for a short time in an advertisement. And the difference between the time segments may have affected the performance of the models with these emotions. Because of a noticeable margin of difference between the accuracies of the models in the *interested* and *happiness* emotions compared to *sadness* and *surprise*. With the accuracies between *interested* and *happiness* only range from a low 29% to 60%, while the accuracies between *sadness* and *surprise* ranges from 49% to 74%.

To evaluate the accuracy rates of the various models, the previous work of Azcarraga et. al, (2015) was used as a reference. In their study, they used EEG to predict the emotions of students solving math problems. The emotions that were used are interested, frustrated, bored, and confused. In their study, they achieved accuracies of 18% for interested, 74% for frustrated, 75% for confused, and 66% for bored. With regard to the highest accuracy achieved, both studies got a similar highest accuracy rate at 75% in models for *confused* emotion. In this study however, SVM models for all three modalities and Decision Stump in facial landmarks only and the combined data set, achieved the highest accuracy. However, Decision Tree in *surprise* did achieve 73.54% using facial landmarks only, its accuracy in EEG only and the combined data set is slightly lower at 69%.

6   CONCLUSION AND FUTURE WORKS

6.1   *Conclusion*

This study has explored the use of the electroencephalogram (EEG) signal and facial landmark data to recognize the emotions of a participant while watching a series of commercial videos. The emotions include *interested, indifferent, happiness, sadness,* and *surprise*. Three different data sets particularly, EEG data only, facial landmark data only, and combined EEG and facial landmark data are used to build machine learning models such as Multi-layered Perceptron, Decision Trees, SVM and Naive Bayes, and Decision Stump.

None of the models are able to achieve high accuracy rates that range only from 29% to 73%. The *sadness* emotion achieved the highest accuracies for all three modalities. Best results are achieved in predicting *interest* when only facial landmarks are used. For the *happiness* emotion, the combined EEG and facial landmarks, and the EEG only, have very similar accuracy rates. The combined modality for *surprise* produced the highest average accuracy at 69% but like the other emotions, the accuracy of the other modalities are not far behind, with a difference of less than 3%. For other emotions such as *surprise* and *sadness*, the models tend to predict in most cases *not surprise* and *not sad*. This may be attributed to the imbalance dataset. Only a few samples were tagged as s*urprise* and *sad*.

6.2   *Future works*

For future works, different commercial videos may be used. Commercial videos with more scenes that could elicit strong emotions, such as shock or surprise, spontaneously rather than over a long period of time, may be explored. Selecting strong feelings or emotions that can be triggered spontaneously can also help in gathering data since these emotions can easily be triggered or elicited as long as the scene or event is appropriate. Examples of such emotions are like the aforementioned shock or surprise, and also disgust. Using these kinds of commercial videos along with strong spontaneous emotions might make the participants be more accurate in identifying which part(s) of the video they have experienced those emotions. This may solve the low accuracies acquired from this research, and may provide a better performance of the classifiers for each of the emotions. Based on the results of this research, it is recommended that only facial landmark data is used in future works due to the minimal increase in performance that combining EEG data and facial landmark brings. Using EEG data can also make the participant uncomfortable due to the headset attached to their head which normally placed on the head for long period of time. Next, reported emotions could have an additional parameter wherein a participant is requested to report the intensity of emotions at a certain time frame. For our experiment, the participants are just asked on which time frame they felt the emotion on the video. With the addition of the intensity, they can specify at which specific time frame they became the most emotional at the given range. For example, a user can report that he/she felt happy starting from fifth to thirtieth second of the video. With intensity, the participant can now specify where she felt most happy or so happy between the given ranges. It is also recommended to get an expert in emotion annotation because experts are more knowledgeable about the different tendencies and characteristics regarding these emotions. Lastly, facial action unit (AU) could be used in place of facial landmark because it is difficult for models since raw facial landmark innately differ from each individual. AU is the movements of muscle groups in an action and these movements remain consistent for different individual thus making AU the more appropriate facial expression feature.

REFERENCES

Abhishek, D., Chaugule V., Koolagudi, S. G., Ramteke, P. B., & Vijayakumar, A. 2016. Product review based on optimized facial expression detection. *2016 Ninth International Conference on Contemporary Computing (IC3).*

Asghari-Esfeden, S., Fu, Y., Pantic, M., & Soleymani, M., 2015. Continuous emotion detection using EEG signals and facial expressions. *2014 IEEE International Conference on Multimedia and Expo (ICME).*

Azcarraga, A. P., Azcarraga, J. J., Hayashi, Y., & Marcos, N. 2015. Selective Prediction of Student Emotions based on Unusually Strong EEG Signals. *In Ogata, H. et al. (Eds.) 23rd International Conference on Computers in Education. (pp. 79–84). Hangzhou, China. (ISBN: 978-4-9908014-7-2).*

Azcarraga A. P., Azcarraga, J. J., & Talavera, A. 2016. Gender-Specific Classifiers in Phoneme Recognition and Academic Emotion Detection. *Neural Information Processing Lecture Notes in Computer Science (2016), 497–504.*

Azcarraga, J. J., Kalaw, K., & Ong, E. 2017. Prospects in Modeling Reader's Affect Based on EEG Signals. *25th International Conference on Computers in Education. (pp. 98–100). New Zealand*

Krishnan, S. S., & Sitaraman, R. K. 2013. Understanding the effectiveness of video ads: a measurement study. *Internet Measurement Conference (2013).*

Rosebrock, A. 2017. Real-time facial landmark detection with OpenCV, Python, and dlib. *Retrieved from https://www.pyimagesearch.com/2017/04/17/real-time-facial-landmark-detection-opencv-python-dlib/*

Terkan, R. 2014. Importance of Creative Advertising and Marketing According to University Students' Perspective. *International Review of Management and Marketing (2014).*

Emotive Insight Headset 2018. *http://www.emotiv.com*

Statistica 2018. Distribution of advertising spending in the United States from 2010 to 2020. *https://www.statista.com/statistics/272316/advertising-spending-share-in-the-us-by-media/*

Theory and Practice of Computation – Nishizaki et al. (eds)
© 2019 Taylor & Francis Group, London, ISBN 978-0-367-20417-4

Digital joint ROM measurement tool for geriatric rehabilitation assessment

C.Y. Ong, M.M. Paragas & B.C. Huang
De La Salle University, Manila, NCR, Philippines

ABSTRACT: Physical rehabilitation assessments are usually accomplished using direct observation with the aid of a measurement tool such as a goniometer. However, reliability, misalignment, and poor stabilization of the tool may cause inconsistent data during successive measurements. A prototype system was developed using a shaft encoder and inertial sensors to consistently measure the range of motion and track the speed of a patient while performing a specific exercise. With the supervision of a licensed physical therapist (PT), a test was conducted to collect data from the device which was transmitted to an Android-based application using a microcontroller unit and a Bluetooth module. Testing was done by assessing five healthy participants performing specific simple exercises, measured by the PT to get the range of motion and joint movement speed of each participant.

1 INTRODUCTION

By the end of 2018, it is projected that 8.2 percent of the Philippine population will be comprised of senior citizens aged 60 years old and older (Commission on Population, 2018). It is projected to increase dramatically in years as the population also increases, in which it may double by the year 2030 (Crisostomo, 2017, He et al. 2016). The aging population are at high risk of having chronic and disabling conditions which leads to the inability of performing normal tasks. They may become restricted in movements or physically impaired (Studenski et al. 1999). Rehabilitation is fundamental in geriatric care as it helps the older patients improve their joint functions. Physical therapists (PT) provide care to patients suffering from impairments, limitation in mobility, neurological disorders and musculoskeletal disorders (Brown & Flood, 2013). Therapeutic exercises are performed to correct and prevent impairments such as deficits in flexibility, strength, balance, and endurance (Studenski et al. 1999). Current methods for assessing or evaluating movement disorders and evaluating physical therapy sessions are through clinical workups where the patient is asked to perform certain movements while a specialist observes (Rampp et al. 2015).

Goniometry is an important part in joint examinations in which measures and records the amount of active and passive joint motion of a patient. The obtained goniometric data can provide basis for diagnosis of impairments modification of physical rehabilitation treatments, and progress evaluation. Range of Motion (ROM), the arc of motion in degrees occurring in a single or series of joints, is one of the parameters being observed and measured in goniometry (Norkin & White, 2003). Currently, ROM is typically recorded and measured manually using a handheld device called a goniometer. Goniometers obtain the patient's quantifiable baseline range of motion measurement around a specific joint (Chen et al. 2015). Humans are subject to errors, thus there are a lot of criteria that may affect goniometric measurements, one of which is reliability—refers to consistency of the gathered measurements. Other factors would also come into play such as improper alignment, misidentification of bony landmarks, and variations in manual force that would contribute to goniometric error. Thus, a standardized method should be followed to get a minimal error in measurement.

Although a universal goniometer is the most widely used tool used by physical therapists for Range of Motion (ROM) measurements, it has been found that intra and inter-rater assessments vary, putting in question the reliability and precision of measurements. Additional information during the exercise such as the orientation of the patient's joints, movement speed of the patient, and alignment of the goniometer towards the patients' joints might give the physical therapist a better picture on how every session of the patient is conducted.

The proposed system uses an electromechanical device which generates angular data for the Range of Motion. An inertial sensor is used to obtain the additional parameters included in the system. The study aims to use the devices for an easier transmission of data to an application.

2 DIGIROM SYSTEM

The DigiROM system, Figure 1, aims to make physical rehabilitation assessment more convenient and consistent in measuring the joint range of motion (ROM) of a patient while performing simple exercises. Additional parameters were included in the system to help the physical therapist (PT) in analyzing the quality of movement of the patient. Usually, the ROM measurements are only estimated by the PT while using the goniometer—giving a subjective assessment. The system can aid the PT in measuring and tracking the improvement of the patient in the succeeding rehabilitation sessions. The system followed the standard procedure of the goniometric measurement.

2.1 *Handheld device*

The handheld device, illustrated in Figure 2, is composed of a shaft encoder, and two (2) inertial measurement units (IMU). Its physical design was based on the goniometer itself.

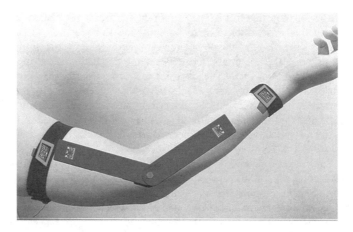

Figure 1. The DigiROM system.

Figure 2. Handheld device prototype.

The prototype of the device was 3D printed using a Poly Lactic Acid (PLA) filament as it was said to be used in prototype medical devices (Rogers, 2015). The two arms in the device serve as the proximal and distal arms of the goniometer. A ball bearing with a 6mm inner radius was fixed into the proximal arm, and a shaft encoder with 500 pulses per revolution (PPR) was attached on the back of the same of the device. A metal shaft was attached in the center of both arms connecting to the code wheel of the shaft encoder as it serves as the pivot of the handheld device.

To capture the orientation of the arms of the device, two IMUs were attached at both ends of the distal and proximal arms of the device. An Arduino Nano microcontroller was used to interface the shaft encoder and IMUs to the Bluetooth module which will transmit the readings to an Android device.

2.2 Shaft encoders

Electromechanical devices convert electrical energy into mechanical movements. Shaft encoders are electromechanical devices which can detect position and speed based on the rotational mechanical displacements converted and processed into electrical signals. It measures the number of rotations, rotational angle, and rotational position. The shaft encoder that was used in the system is an incremental encoder, which generates square wave outputs. The encoder resolution is measured in pulses per revolution (PPR).

A HEDS-5540 dual-channel incremental encoder was used in this study which, at 500 pulses per revolution (PPR), provides a 0.72 degree resolution. This betters the handheld universal goniometer which has one-degree graduations imprinted, giving an equivalent 360 "PPR".

2.3 Inertial measurement unit

An inertial measurement unit or IMU is an electronic device that is used to measure specific forces and angular rate. A common IMU is usually composed of accelerometers and gyroscopes. The accelerometer is responsible for capturing linear forces while the gyroscope is responsible for angular force measurement.

Since accelerometers can capture and detect linear accelerations like gravity, the sensor can be used as a tilt sensor, but aside from gravity, the sensor can also capture other outside forces thus making the signal from the sensor noisy. Gyroscopes on the other hand detect angular speed without relying on outside forces and by performing integration, the gyroscope can be used to estimate angular position or tilt. But over time the lack of a reference can cause the gyroscope data to drift rendering the data unusable.

A six-degree of freedom (6-DOF) IMU which comprises of a 3-axis accelerometer and a 3-axis gyroscope was used in order to read the joint orientation and alignment in 3 dimensions. InvenSense's MPU-6050 is a common 6-DOF IMU due to the availability of a breakout board in the market and as a result makes it easier to interface with a microcontroller. The MPU-6050 uses I2C to interface with an MCU.

The inertial sensor has a built-in digital motion processor (DMP) that performs the fusion inside the chip, rather than adding up the computational load in the MCU. The data can be accessed through the chip's built-in registers.

2.4 Wearable device

Similar with the handheld device, the orientation of the proximal joint and the distal joint of the patient will be recorded. The wearable device is responsible for capturing both orientation and movement speed of the patient. The wearable device consists of two IMUs. Velcro belts were tailored according to the average length of person's wrist, arm, hip, and thigh.

2.5 Data acquisition

Each device module was connected to a microcontroller unit (MCU) for data acquisition. An Android Nano was used as the MCU as it is portable and easy to be attached to both modules.

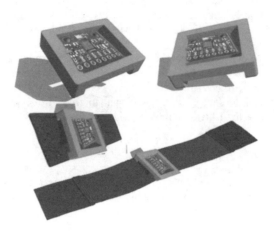

Figure 3. Wearable device prototype.

The microcontroller unit will interface the sensors and the Bluetooth module. The sensor data gathered by the microcontroller unit will be transmitted to the smartphone via Bluetooth communication. An Android-based application was developed to display the transmitted data from both handheld and wearable devices specifically, the Range of Motion in degrees, speed in degree/sec, and orientation.

3 METHODOLOGY

Five (5) healthy students aged 18 to 22 from De La Salle University were asked to participate during the data collection. The body structure of each subject who participated varies in which these may contribute on the variation of motion for each subject. One (1) licensed physical therapist served as the examiner, with one (1) student assistant manually recorded the readings. A third student operated the Android-based app while the PT examined the subject. The PT alternately used the goniometer and DigiROM during the assessment.

3.1 Range of motion exercises

The subjects' elbow flexion and straight leg raise ranges were examined. Each exercise was repeated ten (10) times as a set. The measurement was done for each repetition in which the examiner used the measurement tool alternately by using the DigiROM system first and followed by the goniometer– thus having 20 readings for each subject.

Initially, the subject lies in a supine anatomical position. The forearm also has to be in a supine position in order for the palms to face anteriorly, i.e. Figure 4(a). Before performing the exercise, the examiner must palpate the bony landmark in the specific joint being measured. In every repetition, the examiner asked the subject to hold their position for three (3) seconds before being measured for their joint ROM. A similar process is undertaken for determining the straight leg raise joint ROM, as shown in Figure 5 (Norkin, 2003).

3.2 Tests

The subject is asked to wear the wearable belts before proceeding to the testing. Once the subject is in proper position, the examiner attaches the wearable sensors to the sensor belt. Data collection was accomplished in a single phase, with the examiner measuring the range of motion using the DigiROM system as shown in Figure 6, followed by the universal goniometer as shown in Figure 7.

(a) Starting position of elbow flexion.

(b) Ending position of elbow flexion.

Figure 4.   Elbow flexion.

(a) Starting Position of Straight Leg Raise

(b) End Position of Straight Leg Raise

Figure 5.   Straight leg raise.

Figure 6.   Measuring elbow flexion using the DigiROM system.

The initial alignment data are first recorded. The subject performed the specific exercise, and the speed in terms of time and degrees per second (deg/s) of the movement were then recorded. The subject had to pause for three (3) seconds, and the examiner had to move the distal arm of the handheld device towards the distal joint of the subject. The ROM in degrees and the final alignment were then recorded. Once all data obtained from the DigiROM system were recorded, the subject had to stay in the same pose for the PT to obtain the ROM reading using the goniometer. The procedure is repeated until ten repetitions are performed by the subject for each exercise.

4   RESULTS AND DISCUSSION

4.1   *Goniometric data*

Tables 1 and 2 show data samples of the goniometric data obtained from the goniometer and the DigiROM system during the data collection. Elbow flexion and hip flexion were tested among the

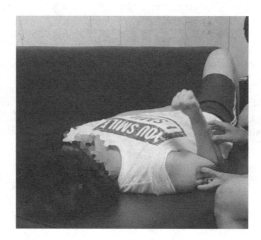

Figure 7.   Measuring elbow flexion using the universal goniometer.

Table 1.   Goniometric data of elbow flexion of Participant C.

Participant	Repetition	Goniometer	DigiROM
C	1	136	133.2
	2	140	141.84
	3	140	142.56
	4	136	135.36
	5	134	133.2
	6	136	135.36
	7	136	136.8
	8	138	137.52
	9	138	133.92
	10	130	129.6

Table 2.   Goniometric data of straight leg raise of Participant D.

Participant	Repetition	Goniometer	DigiROM
D	1	58	59.04
	2	58	57.6
	3	51	49.68
	4	52	49.68
	5	60	60.48
	6	48	46.8
	7	58	54.72
	8	56	53.28
	9	60	59.76
	10	58	61.2

ten participants. The notation system used in the measurement was 0-to-180 degree system since the exercise was flexion in which its ROM proceeds from the zero position through an arc of 180 degrees.

Verification of data was done by the Physical Therapists if the data obtained from the DigiROM system was acceptable to the "Normative Range of Motion Values". There are different guides that Physical Therapists refer to, and one of which is the American Association of Orthopaedic

Table 3. Descriptive and mean standard deviation for each subject performing hip flexion.

Subject	Mean	Standard Deviation	Minimum Range	Maximum Range	Covariance
A	66.89	2.69	63.15	70.63	4.01
B	62.11	7.09	58.37	65.85	11.4
C	62.22	2.39	58.48	65.96	3.85
D	55.67	4.06	51.92	59.41	7.28
E	54.78	2.48	51.04	58.52	4.54
Mean Standard Deviation			3.742390332		

Surgeon (AAOS). The Normative ROM of elbow flexion is 180 degrees, while the hip flexion is 120 degrees. The data obtained from both instruments were in the range of the Normative ROM.

An intra-rater reliability test was conducted to verify the consistency of the developed device between its successive repetitions for measurement by the same rater or examiner. An Intraclass Correlation Coefficient (ICC) statistical technique was used in this testing as it is used to measure the reliability of measurement or ratings. The ICC of the DigiROM tool for both elbow flexion and hip flexion are 0.716 and 0.550, respectively, which are interpreted in the ICC as a moderate reliability and acceptable measure in measuring the two exercises.

The PTs have verified that the discrepancy of the data obtained from the device is not clinically significant in the joint function since the measured joints have large ROM. Further tests were conducted to show the measurement error of the device. Standard deviation and coefficient of variation were the statistical methods used for intra-subject variation to get the measurement error of the goniometric data obtained from each subject.

The standard deviation indicating intra-subject variation, shown in Table 3, is equal to 3.74 degrees which is also in the range of the clinical acceptable 5-degree error. As compared to the measurement error of the tool used in measuring the elbow flexion, the measurement error of the tool when hip flexion was measured is 0.36 degree higher. The covariance for all subject has a range between 4.01% and 11.42% which is two (2) to six (6) times higher than the covariance range for all subjects when elbow flexion was measured. Based on the computation, the tool is reliable in terms of measuring the hip flexion of a subject.

Both goniometric data from different instruments show an inconsistency of data. The inconsistency may not be because of the instrument itself, but due to how the examiner holds the device and how the alignment was done during the measurement. There are several factors that may affect the consistency of the data. A change in the alignment of the tool with the bony landmark of the participant may reflect changes in the joint angles and may represent a joint ROM.

4.2 *Alignment*

The alignment data was examined to indicate the consistency of each repetition by comparing the orientation of the wearable device and the orientation of the handheld device. Alignment was derived by subtracting the wearable device proximal arm and distal arm orientation with the handheld device proximal arm and distal arm orientation. For each arm, the x-axis, y-axis and z-axis values in degrees were collected to indicate orientation. The values for each axis ranges from −180 degrees to 180 degrees. A sample of the recorded data, which includes the proximal and distal arm orientation for the wearable device, handheld device and alignment for one repetition is presented below in Table 4.

In order to compare the consistency over all the patients, the standard deviation of each axis of each arm per position was computed and compared with the other patients. The information is graphically presented in Figures 8a and 8b, for elbow ROM, and Figures 8c and 8d, for straight-leg ROM.

The elbow alignments had a larger variance in terms of alignment with standard deviations ranging from 0.6 to 35.9 degrees, while the hip alignments ranges from 0.6 to 15 degrees. Another finding within the data is that the axes with the highest values are usually the z-axis of the distal arm, z-axis of the proximal arm, x-axis of the distal arm, and y-axis of the distal arm only during hip flexion.

The data in the elbow starting position shows that the z-axis of the distal arm and z-axis of the proximal arm has the most spread out alignment values over all the repetitions which might indicate that the PT was aligned with both the x and y axis but had difficulty aligning in the z-axis. Factors that might affect z-axis discrepancy is the slight twists of the wrist by the examinee during measurement. Since when looking deeper in the data, some of the examinees has a repetition

Table 4. Alignment data in degrees.

WEARABLE	Proximal X (PX)	45.54
	Proximal Y (PY)	−174.14
	Proximal Z (PZ)	1.47
	Distal X (DX)	37.15
	Distal Y (DY)	167.4
	Distal Z (DZ)	54.72
HANDHELD	Proximal X	14.99
	Proximal Y	−177.55
	Proximal Z	26.28
	Distal X	152.33
	Distal Y	85.67
	Distal Z	43.05
ALIGNMENT	Proximal X	30.55
	Proximal Y	3.41
	Proximal Z	−24.81
	Distal X	−115.18
	Distal Y	81.73
	Distal Z	11.67

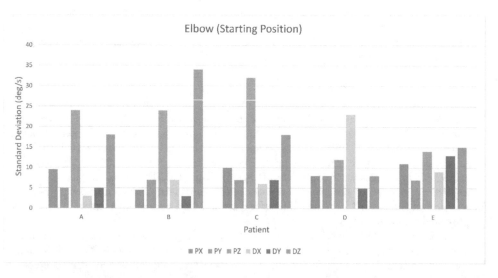

Figure 8a. Standard deviation of each axis for each participant, elbow starting position.

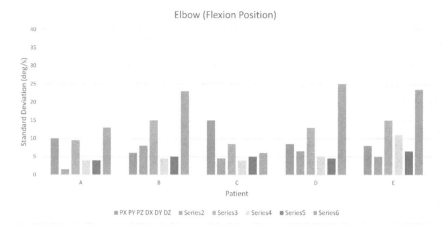

Figure 8b.   Standard deviation of each axis for each participant, elbow flexion position.

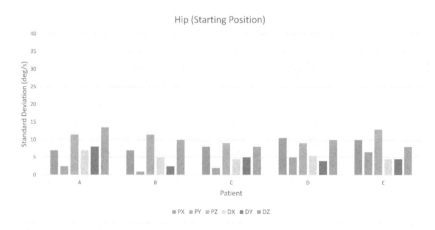

Figure 8c.   Standard deviation of each axis for each participant, hip starting position.

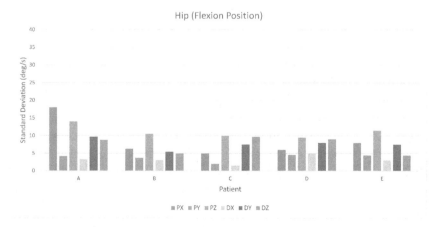

Figure 8d.   Standard deviation of each axis for each participant, hip flexion position.

115

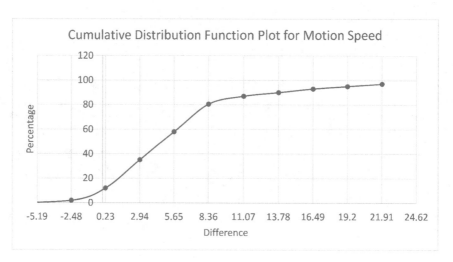

Figure 9.   Cumulative distribution frequency plot for motion speed.

wherein the wearable orientation is different from the previous repetition. Other factors might also include difficulty in using the tool by the examiner.

Transitioning the elbow from the starting position to the flexion position seems to make the distal arm's z-axis more consistent but spreads out the values of the distal arm in the x-axis. This might indicate that either the movement caused the wearable sensor to slightly move and misalign, or the aligning of the x-axis on that certain position was harder to compare on the initial position.

A similar behavior can also be seen on the hip alignment data wherein during the initial position, there exists an axis among the 6 axes that is more inconsistent. In this case, it is the x-axis of the distal arm. This indicates difficulty in alignment during the initial position.

The hip on flexion position seems to also change the consistency of some axes just like with the elbow measurements. For this case, the y-axis of the distal arm was more inconsistent compared with the starting position.

Overall, the gathered data shows that the estimated maximum standard deviation is around 500 degrees which makes the alignment data not too inconsistent from one another, and that majority of the time, the sessions were consistent since the standard deviations were just around 7% out of the maximum possible standard deviation.

4.3   Speed

A hundred samples were gathered from the data collection. The theoretical motion speed was computed and subtracted to the average captured angular velocity. The collected differences were then plotted on a cumulative distribution frequency (CDF) to visualize the collected difference, Figure 9. The figure below illustrates the generated CDF plot from the collected differences.

Four out of the 100 samples taken were unusable due to human errors during the data collection. 71.87% of the 96 samples fall under the difference range of 0.23 deg/s to 8.37 deg/s, while the remaining 28.12% falls under the difference ranges of −5.19 deg/s to 0.23 deg/s and 8.37 deg/s to 21.94 deg/s. Based on the data, the computed average angular speed can be used to measure motion speed majority of the time with the sensor being off by 0 deg/s to 8.37 deg/s most of the time.

4.4   Goniometric and alignment

The relationship between the ROM data obtained from the handheld module and the alignment data are observed. The alignment data were obtained by subtracting each gravity data of the handheld

Table 5. Coefficients obtained from multiple linear regression.

Coefficients

| Model | Standardized Coefficients | | | | Collinearity Statistics | |
	Beta	t−statistic	Significance	Correlation with ROM Data	Tolerance	Variance Inflation Factor
Proximal X	−0.436	−2.694	0.010	−0.748	0.230	4.347
Proximal Y	0.111	0.511	0.612	−0.533	0.128	7.801
Proximal Z	−0.369	−1.705	0.096	−0.435	0.128	7.798
Distal X	−0.629	−4.257	0.00013	−0.368	0.275	3.635
Distal Y	0.128	0.990	0.328	−0.176	0.360	2.778
Distal Z	0.383	3.148	0.003	0.353	0.407	2.459

module from each gravity data of the wearable module. This observation aims to show if the alignment error data affects the data being obtained from the handheld module. Given the null hypothesis that there is no significant distribution from the predictors or the independent variables, the null hypothesis has to be rejected since the significant value obtained from the ANOVA table is less than the alpha 0.05– therefore, there may be variables that may have significant contribution to the ROM data.

Correlation and multiple regression analyses were conducted to examine the relationship of the ROM data and the alignment data of pose 2; results in Table 5. Based on the co-linearity statistics, there is no multicollinearity between each independent variable since the variance inflation factor (VIF) of each variable is not greater than 10. Based on the correlation with the ROM data, there is strong negative correlation between the alignment of proximal X and Y and the ROM data. There is also a moderate negative correlation between Proximal Z, Distal X, Distal Z and ROM data. Lastly, there is a weak negative correlation between Distal Y and the ROM data.

Given the strong to weak negative correlation calculated from the independent variables, decreasing or increasing the alignment error between the handheld and wearable modules would mean that the ROM data vary on how the wearable and handheld modules are placed. Having these wearable and handheld data from inertial sensors entail an alignment between both modules. These alignment data contribute to the variation of the ROM data– thus these ROM data cannot be equal with each other in successive measurements.

5 FEEDBACK AND ACCEPTANCE

The Licensed Physical Therapists who were asked to test the new system have given feedback on the instruments they have used during the data collection. These are as follows:

– The system would be helpful during rehabilitation assessments in that it makes the process more efficient;
– It may lessen the difficulty that health professionals experience as they will no longer rely on reading the calibration which takes a lot of time during range of motion assessment,
– Additional parameters, like speed of movement and alignment, are helpful in rehabilitation as these functions may help in achieving functional ability of a body segment or a joint,
– In addition to it, tracking the speed of movement has clinical relevance as it guides the clinician in determining the quality of movement in a specific range, and
– This may be helpful for patients as well during their rehabilitation program as it may help them track their progress.

6 CONCLUSION

The DigiROM system is able to digitally measure Range of Motion (ROM) similarly to how a goniometer measures ROM, while wirelessly transmitting this to a mobile phone application for electronic recording. According to the results, the DigiROM system is able to produce reliable range of motion measurements while at the same time providing additional information such as joint speed and alignment. The reliable range of motion measurements indicated that the system is able to match readings from a manual universal goniometer.

The additional information from the system can provide the physical therapist with deeper insight on not just the position of the client's anatomy but also the speed of joint movements of the patient. The system is also able to present alignment and orientation information – this might be useful for rater reliability which could be of help in future sessions. The included Android application was able to record readings in real-time. The digitized records could help physical therapists easily and speedily reproduce and analyze the data, as well as more readily compare patient performance over previous sessions.

7 FUTURE WORK

The electronic goniometer can be further improved by use of a better-secured arm rotational joint to reduce encoder-wheel wobble. Additional recorded parameters may be added in the system to have a quantifiable data of the quality of movement of a patient. Development of the system as a tele-rehabilitation for geriatric patients is also plausible.

REFERENCES

Brown, C. & Flood, K. 2013. Mobility limitation in the older patient. JAMA, vol. 310, no. 11, p. 1168.

Chen, Y.C. Lee, H.J. & Lin, K. 2015. Measurement of body joint angles for physical therapy based on mean shift tracking using two low cost Kinect images", *37th Annual International Conference of the IEEE Engineering in Medicine and Biology Society (EMBC).*

Commission on Population. 2018. 107 million Filipinos by end- 2018. [Online]. Available: http://www.popcom.gov.ph/10-press-releases/578-107-million-filipinos-by-end-2018 [Accessed Sept. 8, 2018].

Crisostomo, S., 2017. PopCom worried over rising population of the elderly; in *The Philippine Star*, para. 5, November 18, 2017. [Online]. Available: www.philstar.com. [Accessed Sept. 10, 2018]

Elmenreich, W. 2001. An introduction to sensor fusion. Available: https://www.researchgate.net/publication/267771481_An_Introduction_to_Sensor_Fusion

He, W., Goodkind, D. & Kowal, P. 2016. An aging world: 2015. U.S. Census Bureau, International Population Reports, P95/16-1.

Norkin, C. & White, D. 2003. Measurement of joint motion: a guide to goniometry. Philadelphia: F. A. Davis

Rampp, A., Barth, J., Schuelein, S., Gassmann, K., Klucken, J., & Eskofier, B. 2015. Inertial sensor-based stride parameter calculation from gait sequences in geriatric patients. *IEEE transactions on biomedical engineering*; vol. 62, no. 4, pp. 1089–1097.

Rogers, T. 2015. "Everything You Need To Know About Polylactic Acid (PLA)," CM | Engineering Mechanisms and Prototype Design (Gears). [Online]. Available: https://www.creativemechanisms.com/blog/learn-about-polylactic-acid-pla-prototypes.

Studenski, S., Duncan P., & Maino J. Principles of rehabilitation in older patients. In Hazzard WR, Blass JP, Ettinger WH, Halter JB, Ouslander JG, editors. *Principles of geriatric medicine and gerontology*. 4th ed., New York: McGraw Hill; 1999. p. 435–55.

Theory and Practice of Computation – Nishizaki et al. (eds)
© 2019 Taylor & Francis Group, London, ISBN 978-0-367-20417-4

Simple type system for call-by-value calculus with first-class continuations and environments

Shin-ya Nishizaki

Tokyo Institute of Technology, Tokyo, Japan

ABSTRACT: In this paper, we propose a simple type system for the call-by-value lambda calculus with first-class continuations and environments. We give typing rules of the simple type system and show subject reduction theorem of the type system, which means that a typing of a term is preserved during reduction.

1 INTRODUCTION

A *continuation* is an abstract notion of the programming language processor, that represents a rest of computation at some point in time. In the implementation of the programming language processor, a call-stack of a runtime system is considered as a continuation. For example, consider the following program:

```
f(g(h(k(1.14))))
```

During computation, the subexpression `h(k(1.14))` is computed and its result is supposed to be `5.14`:

```
f(g(5.14))
```

At this point, the current continuation is considered as `f(g( ))`, which corresponds to the call-stack storing return addresses of `g` and `f`.

If you utilize first-class continuations, you can save an image of the call-stack at some point and recover the saved image later. In programming language Scheme, you can implement global jumps, exception handling, and coroutines (C. T. Haynes 1984) using the first-class continuation.

A *first-class object* is an entity that can be passed to a function and returned from a function as a resulting value. For example, an integer is a first-class entity in many programming languages. However, in C programming language, a pointer to a function is first-class but a function itself is not. In functional programming languages such as Scheme and Haskell, a function is considered as a first-class object.

In the framework of the lambda calculus (Plotkin 1975) (Felleisen, Friedman, Kohlbecker, & Duba 1986) (Felleisen, Friedman, Kohlbecker, & Duba 1987), the continuation is formalized as an *evaluation context*, which is a mechanism for pointing a sub-expression which to be reduced. For example, consider the following reduction sequence of an arithmetic expression.

$$(\underline{1+2}) * 3 \to 3 * 3$$

In the left-hand side $(1 + 2) * 3$, $1 + 2$ is the sub-expression to be reduced. The underlining can be represented as an evaluation context $E[\ ]$ such as

$$E[\ ] = [\ ] * 3,$$

which is a expression with a hole [ ]. The reduction is written as

$$E[1 + 2] \rightarrow E[3].$$

We studied the first-class continuation from the viewpoint of Girard's linear logic (Nishizaki 1994b).

An *environment* is a data structure in the programming language semantics that represents a mapping of variable names to bound values. In the lambda calculus (Abadi, Cardelli, Curien, & Lévy 1991), the environment is formalized as a substitution. For example, consider a lambda-term $\lambda x.\lambda y.(x + x + y)$. If you give actual parameters 1 and 2, then we have

$$\big(\lambda x.\lambda y.(x + x + y)\big)\,1\,2 \rightarrow \big(\lambda y.(x + x + y)[x:=1]\big)\,2 \rightarrow (x + x + y)[x:=1,\ y:=2].$$

The last term can be considered a term $(x + x + y)$ to which a substitution $[x:=1,\ y:=2]$ of 1 and 2 for x and y, respectively. The substition $[x:=1,\ y:=2]$ can be interpreted as an environment which assigns 1 and 2 to the variables x and y, respectively. In the $\lambda\sigma$-calculus (Abadi, Cardelli, Curien, & Lévy 1991) proposed by Abadi et al., an environment is formalized as a substitution not defined in the object-level. Nishizaki (Nishizaki 1995) (Nishizaki 1994a) (Nishizaki & Fujii 2012) (Nishizaki 2017a) studied the first-class environment in the framework of the lambda calculus and the $\lambda\sigma$-calculus. In his calculus, he formalized the first-class environment by handling the lambda terms and the substitution uniformly.

Furthermore, we proposed an untyped lambda calculus with first-class continuations and environments, λ_{CE}, in our previous work (Nishizaki 2017b). In the research, we introduced both continuation and environments as first-class objects into the untyped lambda calculus. We gave a translation of the calculus into the untyped lambda calculus with records (i.e. labelled products) and first-class continuations, λ_{CRec}, as a translation semantics.

Research motivation

In this paper, we give a simple type system $\lambda_{CE}^{\rightarrow}$ to the lambda calculus λ_{CE} with first-class continuations and environments. The simple type system has function types and environment types, which is an extension of the simply-typed lambda calculus with first-class environments. Similarly to the lambda calculus with first-class continuations, our calculus is given a call-by-value reduction as an operational semantics, which is a small-step semantics based on call-by-value evaluation strategy. In the reduction rule to the first-class continuation construct such as `call/cc` ($\mathcal{K}$ in the terminology in the style of Felleisen), it generates a new variable binding:

$$E[\mathcal{K}(M)] \rightarrow E[(M\ \lambda x.\mathcal{A}(E[x]))]$$

However, such generation of new redices is problematic in the calculus with first-class environments, because a new variable name affects the computational mechanism of the first-class environments. In our calculus, we avoid such variable name generation during the reduction.

2 SIMPLY-TYPED CALL-BY-VALUE LAMBDA CALCULUS WITH FIRST-CLASS CONTINUATIONS AND ENVIRONMENTS

In this section, we propose a simply-typed call-by-value lambda calculus with first-class continuations and environments

2.1 *Untyped calculus*

Definition 1.1 (Terms, Values, Evaluation Contexts) *We define terms, values and evaluation of the calculus λ_{CE} recursively by the following grammar.*

We use $M, N, L, \ldots$ for terms, U, V, W for values, and $\mathcal{E}[\ ], \mathcal{E}'[\ ], \ldots$ for evaluation contexts.

$M ::= x \mid (\lambda x.M) \mid (M\,N) \mid id \mid (M/x) \cdot N \mid (M \circ N)$
$\quad \mid \mathcal{K}(M) \mid \mathfrak{A}(\mathcal{E}[\ ])$

$V ::= x \mid (\lambda x.M) \mid (\lambda x.M) \circ \mid id \mid (V/x) \cdot W \mid \mathfrak{A}(\mathcal{E}[\ ])$

$\mathcal{E}[\ ] ::= [\ ] \mid (\mathcal{E}[\ ]\,N) \mid (V\mathcal{E}[\ ]) \mid (\mathcal{E}[\ ]/x) \cdot N \mid (V/x) \cdot \mathcal{E}[\ ]$
$\quad \mid (M \circ \mathcal{E}[\ ])$

where the hole $[\ ]$ does not occur in M.

A variable x, a lambda abstraction $\lambda x.m$, and a function application (MN) have the same meaning as the traditional lambda calculus. A term id is called the *identity environment*, which returns the current environment as a value. An *environment extension* $(M/x) \cdot N$ is an envoronment N added to a binding of x to a value of M. *An environment composition* $(M \circ N)$ is a value of M under an environment N. A term $\mathcal{K}(M)$ is a construct for first-class continuation, which corresponds to Scheme's `call-with-current-continuation`. A term $\mathfrak{A}(E[\ ])$ is an abort primitive; if $\mathfrak{A}(E[\ ]))$ is called with an actual parameter V, i.e. $(\mathfrak{A}(E[\ ])\,V)$, then the current continuation is abandoned and $E[V]$ is newly evaluated.

2.2 Call-by-value reduction

An operational semantics of our calculus $\lambda_{\text{CE}}^{\rightarrow}$ is given as a call-by-value reduction, which represents the call-by-value evaluation strategy as a small-step semantics.

Definition 1.2 (Call-by-Value Reduction). *The* call-by-value reduction *is a binary relation $M \rightarrow N$ between terms M and N, defined by the following rules.*

$\quad$ **Beta** $\mathcal{E}[((\lambda x.M)V)] \rightarrow \mathcal{E}\big[(M \circ ((V/x) \cdot id))\big]$

$\quad$ **BetaClos** $\mathcal{E}[(((\lambda x.M) \circ W)\,V)] \rightarrow \mathcal{E}\big[(M \circ ((V/x) \cdot W))\big]$

$\quad$ **VarRef** $\mathcal{E}[x \circ ((V/x) \cdot W)] \rightarrow \mathcal{E}[V]$

$\quad$ **VarSkip** $\mathcal{E}[y \circ ((V/x) \cdot W)] \rightarrow \mathcal{E}[y \circ V]$

$\quad$ AppComp $\mathcal{E}[(MN) \circ W] \rightarrow \mathcal{E}[(M \circ W)(N \circ W)]$

$\quad$ **ExtnComp** $\mathcal{E}[((M/x) \cdot N) \circ W] \rightarrow \mathcal{E}[((M \circ W)/x) \cdot (N \circ W)]$

$\quad$ **CompAssoc** $\mathcal{E}[(M \circ N) \circ V] \rightarrow \mathcal{E}[M \circ (N \circ V)]$

$\quad$ **IdL** $\mathcal{E}[(id \circ V)] \rightarrow \mathcal{E}[V]$

$\quad$ **IdR** $\mathcal{E}[(M \circ id)] \rightarrow \mathcal{E}[M]$

$\quad$ **CallccComp** $\mathcal{E}[\mathcal{K}(M) \circ W] \rightarrow \mathcal{E}[(M \circ W)\,(\mathfrak{A}(\mathcal{E}[\ ]) \circ W)]$

$\quad$ **Callcc** $\mathcal{E}[\mathcal{K}(M)] \rightarrow \mathcal{E}[(M\,(\mathfrak{A}(\mathcal{E}[\ ])))]$

$\quad$ **Abort** $\mathcal{E}[(\mathfrak{A}(\mathcal{E}'[\ ])\,V)] \rightarrow \mathcal{E}'[V]$

$\quad$ **AbortComp** $\mathcal{E}[\mathfrak{A}(\mathcal{E}'[\ ]) \circ W] \rightarrow \mathcal{E}'[\mathfrak{A}(\mathcal{E}[\ ])]$

In the reduction rule Beta,

$$\mathcal{E}[((\lambda x.M)V)]$$

is a parameter passing of an actual parameter V to a formal parameter x. This is reducted to a term

$$\mathcal{E}\big[(M \circ ((V/x) \cdot id))\big],$$

which means that a term M should be evaluated under an environment $(V/x) \cdot id$. In the environment $(V/x) \cdot id$, a variable x is bound to a value V.

A subterm $((\lambda x.M) \circ W)$ in the left-hand side of the reduction rule

$$\mathcal{E}[(((\lambda x.M) \circ W)\ V)]$$

corresponds a *closure* of the functional programming language, that is a pair of a function and the bindings for the free variables appearing in the function body. The right-hand side $\mathcal{E}[(M \circ ((V/x) \cdot W))]$ means that M should be evaluated under the environment $(V/x) \cdot W$, which is derived by adding a binding of x to V is added to the environment W.

The semantics of the abort construct $\mathfrak{A}$ is given by the reduction rule Abort:

$$\mathcal{E}[(\mathfrak{A}(\mathcal{E}'[\,])\ V)] \rightarrow \mathcal{E}'[V]$$

For the Felleisen's abort construct $\mathcal{A}(M)$, the reduction rule was given as

$$\mathcal{E}[\mathcal{A}(M)] \rightarrow M$$

and this is used in the definition of $\mathcal{K}(M)$ as

$$\mathcal{E}[\mathcal{K}(M)] \rightarrow \mathcal{E}[(M\ \lambda x.\mathcal{A}(\mathcal{E}[x]))].$$

Our abort construct $\mathfrak{A}(\mathcal{E}[\,])$ has the same meaning as $\lambda x.\mathcal{A}(\mathcal{E}[x])$. In our calculus, the environment is formulated in the object level; we have to avoid new variable name and binding. Considering the hole $[\,]$ as a meta-level bound variable and $\mathfrak{A}(\mathcal{E}[\,])$ as a unary function, we can avoid generating new variable binder $\lambda x.$.

We show an example of reduction sequence.

$$(\lambda x.x)\Big(\mathcal{K}(\lambda f.((\lambda y.y)(f\ c)))\Big)$$

$$\rightarrow (\lambda x.x)\Big(\big(\lambda f.((\lambda y.y)(f\ c))\big)\ \big(\mathfrak{A}((\lambda x.x)[\,])\big)\Big)$$

$$\rightarrow (\lambda x.x)\Big(((\lambda y.y)(f\ c)) \circ \big((({\mathfrak{A}}((\lambda x.x)[\,]))/f)\cdot id\big)\Big)$$

$$\rightarrow (\lambda x.x)\Big(((\lambda y.y) \circ W)\ ((f\ c) \circ W)\Big)$$

$$\rightarrow (\lambda x.x)\Big(((\lambda y.y) \circ W)\ (((f \circ W)\ (c \circ W)))\Big)$$

$$\rightarrow (\lambda x.x)\Big(((\lambda y.y) \circ W)\ (((\mathfrak{A}((\lambda x.x)[\,]))\ (c \circ W)))\Big)$$

$$\rightarrow (\lambda x.x)\Big(((\lambda y.y) \circ W)\ (((\mathfrak{A}((\lambda x.x)[\,]))\ (c \circ id)))\Big)$$

$$\rightarrow (\lambda x.x)\Big(((\lambda y.y) \circ W)\ (((\mathfrak{A}((\lambda x.x)[\,]))\ c))\Big)$$

$$\rightarrow ((\lambda x.x)c)$$

$$\rightarrow c,$$

where W is $((\mathfrak{A}((\lambda x.x)[\,]))/f) \cdot id$.

3   SIMPLE TYPE SYSTEM FOR λ_{CE}

In this section, we propose a simple type system for the lambda calculus λ_{CE} with first-class continuations and environments. First, we give a syntax of types, and second we introduce typing rules.

Definition 1.3 (Types)   We define *types* $A, B, C, \ldots$ and *environment types* $E, H, \ldots$ of λ_{CE} by the following grammar.

$$A ::= \alpha \mid (A \to B) \mid E$$
$$E ::= \{x_1 : A_1\} \cdots \{x_n : A_n\}$$

where $x_i \neq x_j$ $(i \neq j)$.

Next, we give typing rules to the calculus λ_{CE}. Like the traditional lambda calculus, we introduce typing rules for the terms, and moreover, for the evaluation contexts, too.

Definition 1.4 (Typing Rules)   We define a typing judgement $E \vdash M : A$ for a term and $E \vdash \mathcal{E}[\,] : B$ for an evaluation context inductively by the following rules.

$$\frac{}{\{x : A\}E \vdash x : A} \; \text{Var}$$

$$\frac{\{x : A\}E \vdash M : B}{\{x : C\}E \vdash (\lambda x.M) : A \to B} \; \text{Lam}$$

$$\frac{E \vdash M : A \to B \quad E \vdash N : A}{E \vdash (MN) : B} \; \text{App}$$

$$\frac{}{E \vdash id : E} \; \text{Id}$$

$$\frac{E \vdash M : A \quad E \vdash N : \{x : C\}H}{E \vdash (M/x) \cdot N : \{x : A\}H} \; \text{Extn}$$

$$\frac{E \vdash N : H \quad H \vdash M : A}{E \vdash (M \circ N) : A} \; \text{Comp}$$

$$\frac{E \vdash M : A}{E \vdash \mathcal{K}(M) : (A \to B) \to A} \; \text{Callcc}$$

$$\frac{\Phi \vdash_A \mathcal{E}[\,] : \phi}{E \vdash \mathfrak{A}(\mathcal{E}[\,]) : A \to B} \; \text{Abort}$$

where Φ is the top-level environment type and ϕ the top-level type.

$$\frac{}{E \vdash_A [\,] : A} \; \text{Hole}$$

$$\frac{E \vdash_C \mathcal{E}[\,] : A \to B \quad E \vdash N : A}{E \vdash_C (\mathcal{E}[\,] N) : B} \; \text{LHoleApp}$$

$$\frac{E \vdash V : A \to B \quad E \vdash_C \mathcal{E}[\,] : A}{E \vdash_C (V \; \mathcal{E}[\,]) : B} \; \text{RHoleApp}$$

$$\frac{E \vdash_D \mathcal{E}[\,] : A \quad E \vdash N : \{x : C\}H}{E \vdash_D (\mathcal{E}[\,]/x) \cdot N : \{x : A\}H} \; \text{LHoleExtn}$$

In $E \vdash_C \mathcal{E}[\,] : A$, the subscript C of $\vdash_C$ means the type of the hole $[\,]$ appearing in the context $\mathcal{E}[\,]$. The following lemma means that you can replace the hole of type C in a context $\mathcal{E}[\,]$ as term M of the same type.

Lemma 1.1   *If $E \vdash M : C$ and $E \vdash_C \mathcal{E}[\,] : A$, then $E \vdash \mathcal{E}[M] : A$.*

Conversely, if $\mathcal{E}[M]$ is typed, then both $\mathcal{E}[\,]$ and M are also typed.

Lemma 1.2   *If $E \vdash \mathcal{E}[M] : A$, then there is a type C satisfying that $E \vdash_C \mathcal{E}[\,] : A$ and $E \vdash M : C$.*

4 SUBJECT REDUCTION

Theorem 1 (Subject Reduction Theorem).   If $M \to M'$ and $\Phi \vdash M : \phi$, then $\Phi \vdash M' : \phi$.

Proof. In this proof, Φ means the top-level environment type and ϕ the top-level type. We prove this theorem by induction on the size of a term M. We make case-analysis on reduction rules deriving $M \to M'$.

Case of Beta. Suppose that

$$\mathcal{E}[((\lambda x.M)\ V)] \to \mathcal{E}[M \circ ((V/x) \cdot id)]$$

and

$$\Phi \vdash \mathcal{E}[((\lambda x.M)\ V)] : \phi.$$

By Lemma **1.2**, we know that $\Phi \vdash_B \mathcal{E}[] : \phi$ and $\Phi \vdash ((\lambda x.M)\ V) : B$, for some type B. Using typing rules, we have the following typing derivation:

$$\frac{\dfrac{\vdots}{\{x : A\}\Phi' \vdash M : B}}{\dfrac{\Phi \vdash \lambda x.M : A \to B \quad \Phi \vdash V : A}{\Phi \vdash ((\lambda x.M)\ V) : B}}$$

where the top-level environment type Φ should be supposed as $\{x : C\}\Phi'$. Then, by Lemma **1.1**, we have the typing derivation for $\mathcal{E}[M \circ ((V/x) \cdot id)]$:

$$\frac{\dfrac{\Phi \vdash V : A \quad \overline{\Phi \vdash id : \Phi}}{\Phi \vdash (V/x) \cdot id : \{x : A\}\Phi' \quad \{x : A\}\Phi' \vdash M : B}}{\dfrac{\Phi \vdash M \circ ((V/x) \cdot id) : B}{\Phi \vdash \mathcal{E}[M \circ ((V/x) \cdot id)] : \phi}}$$

Case of BetaClos. Suppose that

$$\mathcal{E}[(((\lambda x.M) \circ W)\ V)] \to \mathcal{E}[M \circ ((V/x) \cdot W)].$$

and

$$\Phi \vdash E[(((\lambda x.M) \circ W)\ V)] : \phi.$$

By Lemma **1.2**, we know that $\Phi \vdash_B \mathcal{E}[\ ] : B$ and $\Phi \vdash (((\lambda x.M) \circ W)\ V) : B$, for some type B. We have

$$\frac{\dfrac{\Phi \vdash W : \{x : C\}E \quad \dfrac{\{x : A\}E \vdash M : B}{\{x : C\}E \vdash \lambda x.M : A \to B}}{\Phi \vdash (\lambda x.M) \circ W : A \to B} \quad \Phi \vdash V : A}{\dfrac{\Phi \vdash (((\lambda x.M) \circ W)\ V) : B}{\Phi \vdash \mathcal{E}[(((\lambda x.M) \circ W)\ V)] : \phi}}$$

Then, we have

$$\frac{\dfrac{\Phi \vdash V : A \quad \Phi \vdash W : \{x:C\}E}{\Phi \vdash (V/x) \cdot W : \{x:A\}E} \quad \{x:A\}\Phi' \vdash M : B}{\dfrac{\Phi \vdash M \circ ((V/x) \cdot W) : B}{\Phi \vdash \mathcal{E}[M \circ ((V/x) \cdot W)] : \phi}}$$

Case of VarRef. Suppose that

$$\mathcal{E}[x \circ ((V/x) \cdot W)] \to \mathcal{E}[V]$$

and

$$\Phi \vdash \mathcal{E}[x \circ ((V/x) \cdot W)] : \phi$$

By Lemma **1.2**, we know that $\Phi \vdash_A \mathcal{E}[\ ] : A$ and $\Phi \vdash x \circ ((V/x) \cdot W) : A$, for some type A. We know

$$\cfrac{\cfrac{\Phi \vdash \overset{\vdots}{V} : A \quad \Phi \vdash W : \{x{:}C\}E}{\Phi \vdash (V/x) \cdot W : \{x{:}A\}E} \quad \{x{:}A\}E \vdash \overset{\vdots}{x} : A}{\cfrac{\Phi \vdash x \circ ((V/x) \cdot W) : A}{\Phi \vdash \mathcal{E}[x \circ ((V/x) \cdot W)] : \phi}}$$

Then, we have

$$\cfrac{\Phi \vdash \overset{\vdots}{V} : A}{\Phi \vdash \mathcal{E}[V] : \phi}$$

Case of VarSkip. Suppose that

$$\mathcal{E}[y \circ ((V/x) \cdot W)] \to \mathcal{E}[y \circ V]$$

and $\Phi \vdash \mathcal{E}[y \circ ((V/x) \cdot W)] : \phi$. By Lemma **1.2**, we know that $\Phi \vdash_A \mathcal{E}[\ ] : \phi$ and $\Phi \vdash y \circ ((V/x) \cdot W) : A$.

We know that

$$\cfrac{\cfrac{\Phi \vdash \overset{\vdots}{V} : A \quad \Phi \vdash W : \{x{:}C\}\{y{:}A\}E}{\Phi \vdash (V/x) \cdot W : \{x{:}B\}\{y{:}A\}E} \quad \{x{:}B\}\{y{:}A\}E \vdash y : A}{\cfrac{\Phi \vdash y \circ ((V/x) \cdot W) : A}{\Phi \vdash \mathcal{E}[y \circ ((V/x) \cdot W)] : \phi}}$$

Then, we have

$$\cfrac{\Phi \vdash \overset{\vdots}{W} : \{x{:}C\}\{y{:}A\}E \quad \{x{:}C\}\{y{:}A\}E \vdash y : A}{\Phi \vdash y \circ W : A}$$

Case of AppComp. Suppose that

$$\mathcal{E}[(MN) \circ W] \to \mathcal{E}[(M \circ W)(N \circ W)].$$

and $\Phi \vdash \mathcal{E}[(MN) \circ W] : \phi$. By Lemma **1.2**, we know that $\Phi \vdash_B \mathcal{E}[\ ] : \phi$ and $\Phi \vdash (MN) \circ W : B$. We have

$$\cfrac{\Phi \vdash \overset{\vdots}{W} : E \quad \cfrac{E \vdash M : A \to B \quad E \vdash \overset{\vdots}{N} : A}{E \vdash (MN) : B}}{\cfrac{\Phi \vdash (MN) \circ W : B}{\Phi \vdash \mathcal{E}[(MN) \circ W] : \phi}}$$

Then we know

$$\cfrac{\cfrac{\vdots \qquad\qquad \vdots}{\cfrac{\Phi \vdash W : E \quad E \vdash M : A \to B}{\Phi \vdash M \circ W : A \to B}} \quad \cfrac{\vdots \qquad\qquad \vdots}{\cfrac{\Phi \vdash W : E \quad E \vdash N : A}{\Phi \vdash N \circ W : A}}}{\Phi \vdash (M \circ W)(N \circ W) : B}$$

$$\vdots$$

$$\Phi \vdash \mathcal{E}[(M \circ W)(N \circ W)] : \phi$$

Case of ExtnComp. Suppose that

$$\mathcal{E}[((M/x) \cdot N) \circ W] \to \mathcal{E}[((M \circ W)/x) \cdot (N \circ W)].$$

and

$$\Phi \vdash \mathcal{E}[((M/x) \cdot N) \circ W] : \phi.$$

By Lemma **1.2**, we know that $\Phi \vdash_{\{x:A\}E} \mathcal{E}[\,] : \phi$ and $\Phi \vdash ((M/x) \cdot N) \circ W : \{x{:}A\}E$. Then, we know

$$\cfrac{\cfrac{\vdots}{\Phi \vdash W : E} \quad \cfrac{\cfrac{\vdots}{E \vdash M : A} \quad \cfrac{\vdots}{E \vdash N : \{x{:}C\}H}}{(M/x) \cdot N : \{x{:}A\}H}}{\Phi \vdash ((M/x) \cdot N) \circ W : \{x{:}A\}H}$$

$$\vdots$$

$$\Phi \vdash \mathcal{E}[((M/x) \cdot N) \circ W] : \phi$$

Then, we have

$$\cfrac{\cfrac{\vdots \qquad \vdots}{\cfrac{\Phi \vdash W : E \quad E \vdash M : A}{\Phi \vdash M \circ W : A}} \quad \cfrac{\vdots \qquad \vdots}{\cfrac{\Phi \vdash W : E \quad E \vdash N : \{x{:}A\}H}{\Phi \vdash N \circ W : \{x{:}A\}H}}}{\Phi \vdash ((M \circ W)/x) \cdot (N \circ W) : \{x{:}A\}H}$$

$$\vdots$$

$$\Phi \vdash \mathcal{E}[((M \circ W)/x) \cdot (N \circ W)] : \phi$$

Case of CompAssoc. Suppose that

$$\mathcal{E}[(M \circ N) \circ V] \to \mathcal{E}[M \circ (N \circ V)]$$

and

$$\Phi \vdash \mathcal{E}[(M \circ N) \circ V] : \phi.$$

By Lemma **1.2**, we know that $\Phi \vdash_A \mathcal{E}[\,] : \phi$ and $\Phi \vdash (M \circ N) \circ V : A$. We obtain that

$$\cfrac{\cfrac{\vdots}{\Phi \vdash V : E} \quad \cfrac{\cfrac{\vdots}{E \vdash N : H} \quad \cfrac{\vdots}{H \vdash M : A}}{E \vdash M \circ N : A}}{\Phi \vdash (M \circ N) \circ V : A}$$

$$\vdots$$

$$\Phi \vdash \mathcal{E}[(M \circ N) \circ V] : \phi$$

Then, we have

$$
\cfrac{\Phi \vdash V : E \quad \cfrac{E \vdash N : H \quad H \vdash M : A}{E \vdash M \circ N : A}}{\Phi \vdash M \circ (N \circ V) : A}
$$
$$
\vdots
$$
$$
\Phi \vdash \mathcal{E}[M \circ (N \circ V)] : \phi
$$

Case of IdL. Suppose that

$$
\mathcal{E}[(id \circ V)] \rightarrow \mathcal{E}[V]
$$

and

$$
\Phi \vdash \mathcal{E}[(id \circ V)] : \phi.
$$

By Lemma **1.2**, we know that $\Phi \vdash_E \mathcal{E}[\ ] : \phi$ and $\Phi \vdash id \circ V : E$. We obtain

$$
\cfrac{\Phi \vdash V : E \quad E \vdash id : E}{\Phi \vdash id \circ V : E}
$$
$$
\vdots
$$
$$
\Phi \vdash \mathcal{E}[(id \circ V)] : \phi
$$

Then, we have

$$
\Phi \vdash V : E
$$
$$
\vdots
$$
$$
\Phi \vdash \mathcal{E}[V] : \phi
$$

Case of IdR. Suppose that

$$
\mathcal{E}[(M \circ id)] \rightarrow \mathcal{E}[M]
$$

and

$$
\Phi \vdash \mathcal{E}[(M \circ id)] : \phi
$$

By Lemma **1.2**, we know that $\Phi \vdash_A \mathcal{E}[\ ] : \phi$ and $\Phi \vdash (M \circ id) : A$. We obtain

$$
\cfrac{\Phi \vdash id : \Phi \quad \Phi \vdash M : A}{\Phi \vdash M \circ id : A}
$$
$$
\vdots
$$
$$
\Phi \vdash \mathcal{E}[M \circ id] : \phi
$$

Then, we have

$$
\Phi \vdash M : A
$$
$$
\vdots
$$
$$
\Phi \vdash \mathcal{E}[M] : \phi
$$

Case of CallccComp. Suppose that

$$\mathcal{E}[\mathcal{K}(M) \circ W] \to \mathcal{E}[(M \circ W)\,(\mathfrak{A}(\mathcal{E}[\,]) \circ W)]$$

and

$$\Phi \vdash \mathcal{E}[\mathcal{K}(M) \circ W] : \phi$$

By Lemma **1.2**, we know that

$$\Phi \vdash_A \mathcal{E}[\,] : \phi$$

and

$$\Phi \vdash \mathcal{K}(M) \circ W : A.$$

We obtain

$$
\cfrac{
\cfrac{\vdots}{\Phi \vdash W : E} \quad
\cfrac{\cfrac{\vdots}{E \vdash M : (A \to B) \to A}}{E \vdash \mathcal{K}(M) : A}
}{
\cfrac{\Phi \vdash \mathcal{K}(M) \circ W : A}{\vdots}
}
$$
$$\Phi \vdash \mathcal{E}[\mathcal{K}(M) \circ W] : \phi$$

Then, we have

$$
\cfrac{
\cfrac{\cfrac{\vdots}{\Phi \vdash W : E} \quad \cfrac{\vdots}{E \vdash M : (A \to B) \to A}}{\Phi \vdash M \circ W : (A \to B) \to A}
\quad
\cfrac{\cfrac{\vdots}{\Phi \vdash W : E} \quad \cfrac{\cfrac{\vdots}{\Phi \vdash_A \mathcal{E}[\,] : \phi}}{E \vdash \mathfrak{A}(\mathcal{E}[\,]) : A \to B}}{\Phi \vdash \mathfrak{A}(\mathcal{E}[\,]) \circ W : A \to B}
}{
\cfrac{\Phi \vdash (M \circ W)(\mathfrak{A}(\mathcal{E}[\,]) \circ W) : A}{\vdots}
}
$$
$$\Phi \vdash \mathcal{E}[(M \circ W)(\mathfrak{A}(\mathcal{E}[\,]) \circ W)] : \phi$$

Case of Callcc. Suppose that

$$\mathcal{E}[\mathcal{K}(M)] \to \mathcal{E}[(M\,(\mathfrak{A}(\mathcal{E}[\,])))]$$

and

$$\Phi \vdash \mathcal{E}[\mathcal{K}(M)] : \phi$$

By Lemma **1.2**, we know that $\Phi \vdash_A \mathcal{E}[\,] : \phi$ and $\Phi \vdash \mathcal{K}(M) : A$. Then, we obtain

$$
\cfrac{
\cfrac{\cfrac{\vdots}{\Phi \vdash M : (A \to B) \to A}}{\Phi \vdash \mathcal{K}(M) : A}
}{\vdots}
$$
$$\Phi \vdash \mathcal{E}[\mathcal{K}(M)] : \phi$$

Then, we have

$$
\cfrac{
  \Phi \vdash M : (A \to B) \to A
  \quad
  \cfrac{
    \vdots
    \quad
    \Phi \vdash_A \mathcal{E}[\,] : \phi
  }{
    \Phi \vdash \mathfrak{A}(\mathcal{E}[\,]) : A \to B
  }
}{
  \Phi \vdash M(\mathfrak{A}(\mathcal{E}[\,])) : A
}
$$

$$
\vdots
$$

$$
\Phi \vdash \mathcal{E}[M(\mathfrak{A}(\mathcal{E}[\,]))] : \phi
$$

Case of Abort. Suppose that

$$
\mathcal{E}[(\mathfrak{A}(\mathcal{E}'[\,])\,V)] \to \mathcal{E}'[V]
$$

and

$$
\Phi \vdash \mathcal{E}[(\mathfrak{A}(\mathcal{E}'[\,])\,V)] : \phi
$$

By Lemma **1.2**, we know that $\Phi \vdash_B \mathcal{E}[\,] : \phi$ and $\Phi \vdash (\mathfrak{A}(\mathcal{E}'[\,])\,V) : B$. Then, we obtain

$$
\cfrac{
  \cfrac{
    \Phi \vdash_A \mathcal{E}'[\,] : \phi
  }{
    \Phi \vdash \mathfrak{A}(\mathcal{E}'[\,]) : A \to B
  }
  \quad
  \cfrac{\vdots}{\Phi \vdash V : A}
}{
  \Phi \vdash (\mathfrak{A}(\mathcal{E}'[\,])\,V) : B
}
$$

$$
\vdots
$$

$$
\Phi \vdash \mathcal{E}[(\mathfrak{A}(\mathcal{E}'[\,])\,V)] : \phi
$$

Case of AbortComp. Suppose that

$$
\mathcal{E}[\mathfrak{A}(\mathcal{E}'[\,]) \circ W] \to \mathcal{E}'[\mathfrak{A}(\mathcal{E}[\,])]
$$

and

$$
\Phi \vdash \mathcal{E}[\mathfrak{A}(\mathcal{E}'[\,]) \circ W] : \phi
$$

By Lemma **1.2**, we know that $\Phi \vdash_{A \to B} \mathcal{E}[\,] : \phi$ and $\Phi \vdash \mathcal{A}(\mathcal{E}'[\,]) \circ W : A \to B$. We obtain

$$
\cfrac{
  \cfrac{\vdots}{\Phi \vdash W : E}
  \quad
  \cfrac{
    \Phi \vdash_A \mathcal{E}'[\,] : \phi
  }{
    E \vdash \mathfrak{A}(\mathcal{E}'[\,]) : A \to B
  }
}{
  \Phi \vdash \mathfrak{A}(\mathcal{E}'[\,]) \circ W : A \to B
}
$$

$$
\vdots
$$

$$
\Phi \vdash \mathcal{E}[\mathfrak{A}(\mathcal{E}'[\,]) \circ W] : \phi
$$

Then, we know

$$
\cfrac{
  \Phi \vdash_A \mathcal{E}'[\,] : \phi
}{
  \Phi \vdash \mathfrak{A}(\mathcal{E}'[\,]) : A \to B
}
$$

$$
\vdots
$$

$$
\Phi \vdash \mathcal{E}[\mathfrak{A}(\mathcal{E}'[\,])] : \phi
$$

5 CONCLUDING REMARKS

In this paper, we proposed a simply-typed lambda calculus with first-class continuations and environments, which is an extension of the untyped calculus λ_{CE} which was proposed in the previous paper, adding a simple type system to the calculus.

We gave a call-by-value reduction as an operational semantics in the small-step style. In the call-by-value reduction, the notion of continuation is formalized as an evaluation context. The first-class environment is based on the environment calculus proposed in the previous works (Nishizaki 1994b) (Nishizaki 1994a) (Nishizaki 1995). We showed the subject reduction theorem with respect to the type system and the call-by-value reduction.

As future works, there are several issues on theoretical study of our calculus. First, we should show the strong normalization theorem, which means that there is no infinite reduction path for every typed term. Second, we should study other kinds of reduction strategy, such as call-by-name and call-by-need. In the call-by-value evaluation strategy, the bound values in an environment are values, which makes the calculus simpler. However, call-by-name and call-by need evaluation strategies are the theoretical basis of the lazy funcitonal languages such as Haskell.

REFERENCES

Abadi, M., L. Cardelli, P.-L. Curien, & J.-J. Lévy (1991, October). Explicit substitutions. *Journal of Functional Programming 1*(4), 375–416.

C. T. Haynes, D. P. Friedman, M. W. (1984). Continuations and coroutines. In *Proceedings of the 1984 ACM Symposium on LISP and Functional Programming*, pp. 293–298.

Felleisen, M., D. P. Friedman, E. Kohlbecker, & B. Duba (1986). Reasoning with continuations. In *Proceedings of the Symposium on Logic in Computer Science*. IEEE Computer Society Press.

Felleisen, M., D. P. Friedman, E. Kohlbecker, & B. Duba (1987). A syntactic theory of sequential control. *Theoretical Computer Science*.

Nishizaki, S. (1994a). ML with first-class environments and its type inference algorith. In *Lecture Notes in Computer Science*, Volume 792, pp. 95–116. Springer-Verlag Berlin Heidelberg.

Nishizaki, S. (1994b). Programs with continuations and linear logic. *21*(2), 165–190.

Nishizaki, S. (1995). Simply typed lambda calculus with first-class environments. *Publications of Research Institute for Mathematical Sciences Kyoto University 30*(6), 1055–1121.

Nishizaki, S. (2017a). Second-order type theory for first-class environment. *AIP Conference Proceedings 1839*(1), 020143.

Nishizaki, S. (2017b). Untyped call-by-value calculus with first-class continuations and environments. Accepted.

Nishizaki, S. & M. Fujii (2012). Strong reduction for typed lambda calculus with first-class environments. In *Lecture Notes in Computer Science*, Volume 7473, pp. 632–639. Springer-Verlag Berlin Heidelberg.

Plotkin, G. (1975). Call-by-name, call-by-value, and the λ-calculus. *Theoretical Computer Science 1*, 125–159.

Theory and Practice of Computation – Nishizaki et al. (eds)
© 2019 Taylor & Francis Group, London, ISBN 978-0-367-20417-4

Secure computation outsourcing of genome-wide association studies using homomorphic encryption

Angelica Khryss Yvanne C. Ladisla
Department of Physical Sciences and Mathematics, University of the Philippines Manila, Manila, Philippines

Richard Bryann L. Chua
Department of Physical Sciences and Mathematics, University of the Philippines Manila, Manila, Philippines
Department of Computer Science, University of the Philippines Diliman, Quezon City, Philippines

ABSTRACT: One of the major problems in genomic research is the delivery of necessary computational power to process extremely large genomic datasets. While cloud computing provides the computing resources needed for such a scenario, the outsourcing of data processing raises a broad range of security and privacy issues as genomic data contain highly sensitive information. In our work, we explored the use of Paillier scheme, a partially homomorphic encryption algorithm to perform several GWAS computations, the Hardy-Weinberg equilibrium and χ^2 test, remotely in a third-party server. We also evaluated the performance of Paillier scheme in doing these GWAS computations.

Keywords: genomic data privacy, genome-wide association studies, homomorphic encryption, Paillier scheme

1   INTRODUCTION

The increasing demand to understand human biology has pushed many researchers to sequence the entire human genome (Trinidad et al., 2010; Brutlag, 1998). A genome is a complete set of DNA contained in every cell of an organism that holds the complete genetic instructions used to build, develop, and maintain the organism (*Genome: Unlocking Life's Code*, n.d.). These instructions are encoded in the form of four letters: A, C, T, G, which represent the four DNA bases Adenine, Cytosine, Thymine, and Guanine, respectively (*Genome: Unlocking Life's Code*, n.d.). Identifying the sequence of all the DNA base pairs (bp) in the human genome would provide one of the most useful tools to understand the biological concepts of human health and development.

To that end, the Human Genome Project (HGP) was launched in 1990 (Brutlag, 1998; *Genome: Unlocking Life's Code*, n.d.) and was completed in thirteen years with 3 billion bp in the human genome sequence (Naveed et al., 2015; Guttmacher & Collins, 2003). Scientists have taken steps towards decoding the instructions embedded within it (Collins, Green, Guttmacher, & Guyer, 2003; Guttmacher & Collins, 2003; Brutlag, 1998). Deriving meaningful information from the obtained sequence would pave the way for improved strategies for diagnosis, treatment, and prevention of diseases (Collins et al., 2003; Guttmacher & Collins, 2003). Genome-wide association study (GWAS) is the most common approach used in genomic research that involves rapid scanning of genetic markers across the whole genomes in a large-scale population in order to detect any significant clinical associations (e.g. disease, adverse drug reactions) (*Genome-Wide Association Studies, 2015; Genome-wide association studies*, n.d.). These studies have led to the development of diagnostic DNA probes and personalized medicine (*Genome-wide association studies*, n.d.; for Biomedical Communications, 2018).

New-generation sequencing platforms have allowed many research institutions to produce large amounts of genomic data that are distributed across many different institutions (Naveed et al., 2015;

Ayday, Cristofaro, Hubaux, & Tsudik, 2013). Hence, scientists are aiming to establish a cloud-based common infrastructure that would enable highly accessible shared datasets and computational resources among authorized research institutions worldwide (Yoshizawa et al., 2014; Lauter, López-Alt, & Naehrig, 2015; Zhao, Wang, & Tang, 2015). However, outsourcing the storage, sharing and processing of highly sensitive genomic data to a third-party cloud raises important privacy concerns (Naveed et al., 2015; Lauter et al., 2015; Zhao et al., 2015).

It is important to protect genome privacy as genomic data contain information about genetic conditions and predispositions to specific diseases (Guttmacher & Collins, 2003; Naveed et al., 2015; Ayday, Cristofaro, et al., 2013). Several studies have shown that the common practice of de-identification does not fully protect genome privacy (Naveed et al., 2015; Gymrek, McGuire, Golan, Halperin, & Erlich, 2013; Frederick, 2015). The use of cryptographic techniques can potentially address the privacy issue of genomic data but they transform genomic data into an encrypted, yet not functional format, unless decrypted (Naveed et al., 2015).

Homomorphic encryption (HE) is a cryptographic technique that allows computation to be performed directly on the encrypted data without the need of decrypting it (Tebaa, Hajji, & Ghazi, 2012). Hence, HE is one tool that can be used to outsource genomic computations. In section 2, we reviewed the different researches done on protecting genomic data and development of homomorphic encryption. We introduced genome-wide association studies (GWAS) in section 3 and homomorphic encryption in sections 4 and 5. In sections 6 and 7, we discussed how we used homomorphic encryption to implement some GWAS statistical tests.

2   LITERATURE REVIEW

Many participants in genome-based studies chose to participate in the studies with the assurance that their genomic data will be protected on public research databases (Kupersmith, 2013). A widely-used method for protecting health information is de-identification, where explicit identifying attributes are removed. However, studies have revealed that genomic data cannot be anonymized by simply removing identifying information (Naveed et al., 2015; Gymrek et al., 2013; Tanner, 2013). These numerous privacy risks have resulted to the shutting down of some publicly accessible genomic databases (Hayden, 2013). However, rapid advances in genomic research necessitate the development of common infrastructures and platforms for international collaboration and public participation (Lauter et al., 2015; Zhao et al., 2015; *Global Alliance for Genomics and Health*, n.d.). To address the privacy threats that hurdle research growth, several cryptographic techniques (Baldi, Baronio, De Cristofaro, Gasti, & Tsudik, 2011; Kumar, Navya, Swetha, Sindhusha, & Kalyan, 2012; Blanton, Atallah, Frikken, & Malluhi, 2012) have been developed.

In the recent years, homomorphic encryption (HE) has been gaining attention since it allows data to be encrypted in a way where meaningful computation can be performed in its encrypted form. Homomorphic encryption was first suggested by Rivest, Adleman, Dertouzos (Rivest, Adleman, & Dertouzos, 1978) in 1978. Early works on HE focused on partially homomorphic encryption schemes, where homomorphism is present only on one operation, which is either addition or multiplication. A homomorphic scheme that is homomorphic only over addition is called an additive homomorphic encryption scheme (e.g. Goldwasser-Micali cryptosystem (Tebaa et al., 2012), Paillier scheme (Paillier, 1999), Boneh-Goh-Nissim scheme (Boneh, Goh, & Nis-sim, 2005)), while the one that is homomorphic only over multiplication is called a multiplicative homomorphic encryption scheme (e.g. RSA cryptosystem (Rivest, Shamir, & Adleman, 1978) and ElGamal scheme (ElGamal, 1985)). It is only within the past decade that fully homomorphic encryption scheme, where homomorphism is present for both addition and multiplication, have been developed with the seminal work of Gentry (Gentry, 2009). Although the properties of fully homomorphic encryption is scheme are more interesting than partially homomorphic encryption, it is still not widely used because of its high computational cost (Gentry, 2010).

Homomorphic encryption is already being used in a number of applications including securing genomic privacy. Lauter et al. in (Lauter et al., 2015) used practical homomorphic encryption on basic genomic algorithms. Yasuda et al. in (Yasuda, Shimoyama, Kogure, Yokoyama, & Koshiba, 2013) used the LNV scheme to compute Hamming distances. Cheon et al. in (Cheon, Kim, & Lauter, 2015) used homomorphic encryption to compute edit distance. Kim et al. in (Kim & Lauter, 2015) performed secure computation of minor allele frequencies, χ^2 statistics, edit distance, and hamming distance using BGV and YASHE scheme. Ayday et al. in (Ayday, Raisaro, McLaren, Fellay, & Hubaux, 2013) presented a privacy-preserving susceptibility test using Paillier scheme and proxy-re-encryption.

3 GENOME-WIDE ASSOCIATION STUDY (GWAS)

Genome-wide association study (GWAS) is an approach that involves rapid scanning of genetic markers across the genomes of many people to find genetic variations associated with a particular phenotype (i.e. an individual's observable trait) *(Genome-Wide Association Studies,* 2015). In GWAS, genetic markers are DNA sequences with known physical locations on chromosomes that exhibit polymorphism due to insertion, deletion, and/or substitution of nucleotides (Steen, 2015). Single nucleotide polymorphisms (SNP) are the most commonly examined markers in GWAS (Steen, 2015).

In most cases, GWAS is based on a case-control design in which SNPs across the human genomes in a case and control groups are genotyped and subjected to statistical correlation analyses (Naveed et al., 2015; Steen, 2015). Prior to statistical association methods, genetic markers must undergo quality control procedures to avoid potential false-negative and false-positive associations (Tabangin, Woo, & Martin, 2009). Quality control is attained by computing for the minor allele frequency (MAF) *(New SNP Attribute,* n.d.) and Hardy-Weinberg equilibrium (HWE) (Lauter et al., 2015). After the quality control procedures, the selected SNPs will be tested for association using a statistical association test. Studies on qualitative traits can use χ^2-square test, Cochran-Armitage Trend test, or logistic regression, while linear regression can be used for quantitative traits (Smith & Newton-Cheh, 2009). The method for association testing could have series of replications and validations before an interpretation can be made (Steen, 2015).

To date, GWAS have already revealed numerous disease-associated loci including those which are related to complex diseases such as diabetes, heart abnormalities, Parkinson disease, and Crohn's disease (Naveed et al., 2015; *Genome-wide association studies,* n.d.; Ayday, Cristofaro, et al., 2013). These identified genetic associations are invaluable information in developing better strategies on disease diagnosis, treatment, and prevention.

4 HOMOMORPHIC ENCRYPTION

Homomorphic encryption (HE) describes a class of encryption algorithms which satisfy the homomorphic property: that is certain computations can be performed on ciphertexts directly so that upon decryption, the same result is obtained as computing on the plaintexts (Aslett, Esperanca, & Holmes, 2015). An encryption scheme is said to be homomorphic for some operations acting in message space (e.g. addition) if there are corresponding operations acting in ciphertext space (Note that we omitted the public/private key pair arguments in the encryption/decryption functions to make them shorter.) satisfying the property (Aslett et al., 2015):

$$Dec(Enc(m_1) \circ Enc(m_2)) = m_1 \diamond m_2$$

Several encryption schemes are partial homomorphic encryption; that is, users are allowed to perform some mathematical functions on encrypted data, either addition or multiplication, but not both. An additively homomorphic scheme is one with a ciphertext operation that results in the sum of the plaintexts (Gentry, 2010; Tebaa et al., 2012). On the other hand, a multiplicatively homomorphic scheme is one that has an operation on two ciphertexts that results in the product of the plaintexts (Gentry, 2010; Tebaa et al., 2012). An encryption scheme is fully homomorphic if it can handle both addition and multiplication operations (Tebaa et al., 2012; Gentry, 2010; Aslett et al., 2015).

5 PAILLIER SCHEME

The Paillier scheme (Paillier, 1999) is a public key encryption scheme created by Pascal Paillier in 1999. For the algorithms for key generation, encryption and decryption, we refer the readers to (Tebaa et al., 2012).

The Paillier scheme has the additive homomorphic properties where the product of two cipher-texts will decrypt to the sum of their corresponding plaintexts (Tebaa et al., 2012). That is,

$$Dec(Enc(m_1) \cdot Enc(m_2) \bmod n^2) = (m_1 + m_2) \bmod n$$

In our work, we used The Homomorphic Encryption Project (THEP) *(The Homomorphic Encrytion Project,* n.d.), a Java implementation of the Paillier scheme to support the necessary homomorphic operations.

6 HARDY-WEINBERG EQUILIBRIUM (HWE) COMPUTATION WITH ADDITIVE HOMOMORPHIC ENCRYPTION

The Hardy-Weinberg equilibrium (HWE) is a model in population genetics which states that under random sampling both allele and genotype frequencies in a population remain constant or stable if no disturbing factors are introduced (Zheng, Yang, Zhu, & Elston, 2012). Departure from the equilibrium can be indicative of potential genotyping errors (Steen, 2015). If no technical errors are detected then a number of biologically plausible explanations exist such as population stratification or assortative mating and inbreeding (Steen, 2015; *Quality Control for Genome Wide Association Studies,* n.d.). Hence, HWE is used to test for data quality. SNPs that significantly deviates from the equilibrium are discarded.

For HWE computation, consider a biallelic SNP with alleles A and B, and let N_{AA}, N_{AB}, N_{BB} denote the observed population counts for genotypes AA, AB, BB, respectively. Also, let N be the total number of people in the sample population; that is, $N = N_{AA} + N_{AB} + N_{BB}$. The corresponding frequencies of genotype AA, AB, BB are given by

$$p_{AA} = \frac{N_{AA}}{N}, p_{AB} = \frac{N_{AB}}{N}, p_{BB} = \frac{N_{BB}}{N}.$$

Moreover, the frequencies of the alleles A and B are given by

$$p_A = \frac{2N_{AA} + N_{AB}}{2N}, p_B = \frac{2N_{BB} + N_{AB}}{2N} = 1 - p_A$$

since each count of genotype AA contributes two A alleles, each count of genotype BB contributes two B alleles, each count of genotype AB contributes one A allele and one B allele, and the total number of alleles in a sample of N people is $2N$.

The population is said to be in HWE if these frequencies are independent. That is,

$$p_{AA} = (p_A)^2, p_{AB} = 2p_A p_B, p_{BB} = (p_B)^2.$$

Testing for deviations from HWE can be carried out using Pearson goodness-of-fit test (*Quality Control for Genome Wide Association Studies*, n.d). If allele frequencies are independent, then the observed counts can be expected to be

$$E_{AA} = N(p_A)^2, E_{AB} = 2Np_Ap_B, E_{BB} = N(p_B)^2.$$

Thus, the test statistic can be computed as follows:

$$\chi^2 = \sum \frac{(N_i - E_i)^2}{E_i}, \text{where } i \in \{AA, AB, BB\}.$$

The obtained test statistic value can be used to determine the p-value then decide whether or not to discard a particular SNP from the dataset.

For our homomorphic HWE computation, we used the technique used by Lauter et al. in (Lauter et al., 2015). Given a biallelic SNP with alleles A and B, the three possible genotypes AA, AB, BB are assigned $0, 1, 2$, respectively. The ith sample genotype of SNP at a site can be encoded through the encodings $e_0^{(i)}, e_1^{(i)}$, and $e_2^{(i)}$ which returns 1 if the entry value is the same as the value that the encoding represents, and 0 otherwise. More specifically, the three possible genotypes is encoded as follows:

$$AA \text{ (value 0):} \quad e_0^{(i)} \leftarrow 1 \quad e_1^{(i)} \leftarrow 0 \quad e_2^{(i)} \leftarrow 0$$
$$AB \text{ (value 1):} \quad e_0^{(i)} \leftarrow 0 \quad e_1^{(i)} \leftarrow 1 \quad e_2^{(i)} \leftarrow 0$$
$$BB \text{ (value 2):} \quad e_0^{(i)} \leftarrow 0 \quad e_1^{(i)} \leftarrow 0 \quad e_2^{(i)} \leftarrow 1$$

Let $c_k^{(i)}$ be the encrypted value of $e_k^{(i)}$, $k = 0, 1, 2$. The (encrypted) counts N_k of value-k genotype, $k = 0, 1, 2$ at a site can be obtained by summing all the ciphertexts $c_k^{(i)}$, that is,

$$N_0 = \sum c_0^{(i)}, N_1 = \sum c_1^{(i)}, N_2 = \sum c_2^{(i)}.$$

The (encrypted) total number $N^{(j)}$ can be computed by summing all the $N_k^{(j)}$, that is,

$$N = N_0 + N_1 + N_2.$$

The expected genotype count can be computed as

$$E_0 = N \left(\frac{2N_0 + N_1}{2N}\right)^2, E_1 = 2N \left(\frac{2N_0 + N_1}{2N}\right) \left(\frac{2N_2 + N_1}{2N}\right), E_2 = N \left(\frac{2N_2 + N_1}{2N}\right)^2,$$

which can be simplified to

$$E_0 = \frac{(2N_0 + N_1)^2}{4N}, E_1 = \frac{(2N_0 + N_1)(2N_2 + N_1)}{2N}, E_2 = \frac{(2N_2 + N_1)^2}{4N}.$$

The test statistic χ^2 can then be computed as

$$\chi^2 = \frac{(4N_0 N_2 - N_1^2)^2}{2N} \left(\frac{1}{2(2N_0 + N_1)^2} + \frac{1}{(2N_0 + N_1)(2N_2 + N_1)} + \frac{1}{2(2N_2 + N_1)^2} \right).$$

Since we cannot perform homomorphic divisions, the server returns the ciphertexts $N_0, N_1, N_2, \beta_1, \beta_2$ back to the client, where

$$\beta_1 = 2N_0 + N_1, \beta_2 = 2N_2 + N_1.$$

On the client side, the client decrypts all the ciphertexts and computes for

$$\chi^2 = \frac{(4N_0 N_2 - N_1^2)^2}{2N} \left(\frac{1}{2(\beta_1)^2} + \frac{1}{(\beta_1)(\beta_2)} + \frac{1}{2(\beta_2)^2} \right).$$

Table 1. Allelic contingency table.

	Allele type		
	A	*B*	Total
Case	N_A	N_B	$R = 2N$
Control	N'_A	N'_B	$S = 2N$
Total	$G = N_A + N'_A$	$K = N_B + N'_B$	$T = 4N$

7 χ^2 TEST STATISTIC COMPUTATION WITH ADDITIVE HOMOMORPHIC ENCRYPTION

One of the statistical methods that are commonly used to measure the genotype-phenotype association in GWAS is the χ^2 test (Karczewski, n.d.; Kim & Lauter, 2015). The χ^2 test statistic in case-control groups is computed based on the allelic contingency table shown in Table 1,

$$\chi^2 = \frac{T(N_A N'_B - N'_A N_B)^2}{R \cdot S \cdot G \cdot K}.$$

where N_A and N_B are the counts of allele types A and B in the case group, respectively, N'_A and N'_B are the counts of allele types A and B in the control group, respectively, and N is the total number of people in the sample population (Kim & Lauter, 2015).

It can be written as a function of N_A and N'_A only and be expressed as

$$\chi^2 = \frac{4N(N_A(2N - N'_A) - N'_A(2N - N_A))^2}{2N \cdot 2N \cdot (N_A + N'_A) \cdot (2N - N_A + 2N - N'_A)}$$

$$= \frac{4N(N_A - N'_A)^2}{(N_A + N'_A) \cdot (4N - (N_A + N'_A))}$$

For our homomorphic χ^2 test statistic computation, we used the technique used by Kim and Lauter in (Kim & Lauter, 2015). In the case and control datasets, given a biallelic SNP with alleles A and B, the three possible genotypes AA, AB, BB are encoded as: $AA \rightarrow 2, AB \rightarrow 1, BB \rightarrow 0$. Using this encoding method, the counts of the allele A in case (N_A) and control datasets (N'_A) by getting the sum of the genotype encodings homomorphically. Since it is not possible to perform multiplications and divisions homomorphically, the server returns the encryptions α_1 and α_2 back to the client, where

$$\alpha_1 = N_A - N'_A, \alpha_2 = N_A + N'_A.$$

From these, the test statistic can be computed on the client side as

$$\chi^2 = \frac{(4N(\alpha_1))^2}{(\alpha_1)(4N - \alpha_2)}.$$

8 PERFORMANCE EVALUATION

To assess the performance of our homomorphic statistical tests that uses the Paillier scheme, we measure their running times using the following environment: Intel Core i3-247 CPU @ 2.40 GHz, 8GB RAM, running 64-bit Windows 10.

Table 2. Running times of the algorithms of the Paillier scheme.

SNP counts	Key size	Key generation	Encryption	Decryption
150	16-bit	0.052s	0.528s	0.015s
	32-bit	0.08s	1.476s	0.16s
	64-bit	0.96s	1.656s	0.16s
300	16-bit	0.001s	1.079s	0.017s
	32-bit	0.001s	1.24s	0.031s
	64-bit	0.081s	2.471s	0.047s
600	16-bit	0.065s	3.693s	0.063s
	32-bit	0.065s	4.005s	0.063s
	64-bit	0.081s	4.016s	0.063s

Since the strength of the security of Paillier scheme depends on the key size (i.e. large key sizes provides stronger security), we measured the execution times key generation, encryption and decryption, respectively, over different key sizes (Table 2). It can be observed that a larger key size resulted to a larger execution time for all the operations. It can also be observed that larger number of SNPs resulted to a larger execution for all the operations.

The resulting performance in our work also shows that a partial homomorphic encryption scheme is more efficient than fully homomorphic and somewhat homomorphic encryption schemes, since the performance surpassed the reported performance of BGV and YASHE schemes in (Kim & Lauter, 2015). Although most researches in secure genomic computation use somewhat homomorphic encryption schemes, our work shows that partial homomorphic encryption schemes can also be used in secure genomic computations. However, due to the limitations in the number of operations that can be performed homomorphically, some computations have to be performed on the client side.

9 CONCLUSIONS AND FUTURE WORK

In our work, we showed that it is possible to use a partially homomorphic encryption algorithm to perform several GWAS statistical tests. Partially homomorphic encryption is one viable alternative to fully homomorphic and somewhat homomorphic encryptions since it has a better performance albeit some parts of the computations have to be performed on the client side. Our work mainly focused on whether it is possible to use partially homomorphic computation for secure genomic computations. We plan to perform security analysis of the Paillier scheme and secure genomic computation techniques we have used.

We also plan to explore the use of other partially homomorphic encryption algorithms like the ElGamal scheme to perform GWAS tests and compare its performance with the Paillier scheme. Aside from using other partially homomorphic encryption algorithms, we also plan to look into the use of batching techniques, where multiple plaintexts are packed into the slots of a single ciphertext, so that the sample genotypes need not be encrypted one-by-one, and see if this will improve performance. In order to establish if partial homomorphic encryption schemes can be used as a general tool for GWAS computations, we can explore if we could use it to perform more complex statistical computations that are not just limited to additions.

REFERENCES

Aslett, L. J. M., Esperanca, P. M., & Holmes, C. C. (2015). *A review of homomorphic encryption and software tools for encrypted statistical machine learning.* arXiv:1508.06574.

Ayday, E., Cristofaro, E. D., Hubaux, J. P., & Tsudik, G. (2013). *The chills and thrills of whole genome sequencing*. arXiv:1306.1264.

Ayday, E., Raisaro, J. L., McLaren, P. J., Fellay, J., & Hubaux, J.-P. (2013). Privacy-preserving computation of disease risk by using genomic, clinical, and environmental data. In *Proceedings of the 2013 USENIX conference on safety, security, privacy and interoperability of health information technologies* (pp. 1–1). Berkeley, CA, USA: USENIX Association.

Baldi, P., Baronio, R., De Cristofaro, E., Gasti, P., & Tsudik, G. (2011). Countering GAT-TACA: Efficient and secure testing of fully-sequenced human genomes. In *Proceedings of the 18th ACM conference on computer and communications security* (pp. 691–702). New York, NY, USA: ACM. Retrieved from http://doi.acm.org/10.1145/2046707.2046785 doi: 10.1145/2046707.2046785

Blanton, M., Atallah, M. J., Frikken, K. B., & Malluhi, Q. (2012). Secure and efficient outsourcing of sequence comparisons. In S. Foresti, M. Yung, & F. Martinelli (Eds.), *Computer security – ESORICS 2012* (pp. 505–522). Berlin, Heidelberg: Springer Berlin Heidelberg.

Boneh, D., Goh, E.-J., & Nissim, K. (2005). Evaluating 2-DNF formulas on ciphertexts. In J. Kilian (Ed.), *Theory of cryptography* (pp. 325–341). Berlin, Heidelberg: Springer Berlin Heidelberg.

Brutlag, D. (1998). *Scientific American molecular neurology (scientific American introduction to molecular medicine) 1st edition*. New York, USA: Scientific American Inc.

Cheon, J. H., Kim, M., & Lauter, K. (2015). Homomorphic computation of edit distance. In M. Brenner, N. Christin, B. Johnson, & K. Rohloff (Eds.), *Financial cryptography and data security* (pp. 194–212). Berlin, Heidelberg: Springer Berlin Heidelberg.

Collins, F. S., Green, E. D., Guttmacher, A. E., & Guyer, M. S. (2003). A vision for the future of genomics research. *Nature, 422,* 835–847. Retrieved from https://doi.org/10.1038/nature01626 doi: 10.1038/nature01626

ElGamal, T. (1985). A public-key cryptosystem and a signature scheme based on discrete logarithms. *IEEE Transactions on Information Theory, 31*(4), 469–472. doi: 10.1109/ TIT.1985.1057074

for Biomedical Communications, L. H. N. C. (2018). *What are genome-wide association studies?* https://ghr.nlm.nih.gov/handbook/genomicresearch/gwastudies. (Accessed: 2018-12-08)

Frederick, R. (2015). Core concept: Homomorphic encryption. *Proc Natl Acad Sci USA.*

Genome: Unlocking life's code. (n.d.). http://naturalhistory.si.edu/exhibits/genome/. (Accessed: 2016-03-25)

Genome-wide association studies. (n.d.). http://www.nature.com/nrg/series/gwas/index.html. (Accessed: 2016-03-20)

Genome-wide association studies. (2015). https://www.genome.gov/20019523. (Accessed: 2016-03-20)

Gentry, C. (2009). *A fully homomorphic encryption scheme* (Ph.D. Dissertation). Stanford University, California, USA.

Gentry, C. (2010). Computing arbitrary functions of encrypted data. Commun. ACM, 53(3), 97–105. Retrieved from http://doi.acm.org/10.1145/1666420.1666444 doi: 10.1145/1666420.1666444

Global alliance for genomics and health. (n.d.). https://genomicsandhealth.org/. (Accessed: 2015-04-01)

Guttmacher, A. E., & Collins, F. S. (2003). Welcome to the genomic era. New England Journal of Medicine, 349(10), 996–998. Retrieved from https://doi.org/10.1056/NEJMe038132 doi: 10.1056/NEJMe038132

Gymrek, M., McGuire, A. L., Golan, D., Halperin, E., & Erlich, Y. (2013). Identifying personal genomes by surname inference. Science, 339(6117), 321–324. Retrieved from http://science.sciencemag.org/content/339/6117/321 doi: 10.1126/science.1229566

Hayden, E. C. (2013). Privacy loophole found in genetic databases. Nature. doi: doi:10.1038/nature.2013.12237

The homomorphic encrytion project. (n.d.). https://code.google.com/p/thep/. (Accessed: 2016-01-12)

Karczewski, K. (n.d.). *How to do a genome wide association studies*. http://stanford.edu/class/gene210/files/gwas-howto.pdf. (Accessed: 2016-03-20)

Kim, M., & Lauter, K. (2015). Private genome analysis through homomorphic encryption. *BMC Medical Informatics and Decision Making, 15*(5), S3. Retrieved from https://doi.org/10.1186/1472-6947-15-S5-S3 doi: 10.1186/1472-6947-15-S5-S3

Kumar, R. R., Navya, V., Swetha, M., Sindhusha, V., & Kalyan, T. M. (2012). A cryptographic approach to securely share genomic sequences. *International Journal of Computer Science and Information Technologies, 3*(2).

Kupersmith, J. (2013). *The privacy conundrum and genomic research: Re-identification and other concerns*. http://healthaffairs.org/blog/2013/09/11. (Accessed: 2016-03-25)

Lauter, K., López-Alt, A., & Naehrig, M. (2015). Private computation on encrypted genomic data. In D. F. Aranha & A. Menezes (Eds.), *Progress in Cryptology – LATINCRYPT 2014* (pp. 3–27). New York, USA: Springer Interntional Publishing.

Naveed, M., Ayday, E., Clayton, E., Fellay, J., Gunter, C., Hubaux, J.-P., … Wang, X. (2015). Privacy in the genomic era. *ACM Computing Surveys*, 48(1), 6:1–6:44.

New SNP attribute. (n.d.). http://www.ncbi.nlm.nih.gov/projects/SNP/docs/rs attributes.html. (Accessed: 2016-03-20)

Paillier, P. (1999). Public-key cryptosystems based on composite degree residuosity classes. In J. Stern (Ed.), Advances in cryptology — EUROCRYPT '99 (pp. 223–238). Berlin, Heidelberg: Springer Berlin Heidelberg.

Quality control for genome wide association studies. (n.d.). http://cgondro2.une.edu.au/snpQC/QCtutorial.pdf. (Accessed: 2016-03-20)

Rivest, R. L., Adleman, L., & Dertouzos, M. L. (1978). On data banks and privacy homomorphisms. *Foundations of Secure Computation.*

Rivest, R. L., Shamir, A., & Adleman, L. (1978). A method for obtaining digital signatures and public-key cryptosystems. *Commun. ACM, 21*(2), 120–126.

Smith, J. G., & Newton-Cheh, C. (2009). Genome-wide association study in humans. In K. DiPetrillo (Ed.), Cardiovascular genomics: Methods and protocols (pp. 231–258). Totowa, NJ: Humana Press.

Steen, K. V. (2015). *Genetics and bioinformatics.* http://www.montefiore.ulg.ac.be/~kbessonov/present data/GBIO0002-1 GenAndBioinf2015-16/lectures/L3/GBIO0002_1516_Lecture 3.pdf. (Accessed: 2016-04-08)

Tabangin, M. E., Woo, J. G., & Martin, L. J. (2009). The effect of minor allele frequency on the likelihood of obtaining false positives. *BMC proceedings, 3 Suppl 7(Suppl 7), 3.*

Tanner, A. (2013). *Harvard professor re-identifies anonymous volunteers in DNA study.* http://www.forbes.com/sites/adamtanner/2013/04/25. (Accessed: 2016-03-25)

Tebaa, M., Hajji, S. E., & Ghazi, A. E. (2012, April). Homomorphic encryption method applied to cloud computing. In 2012 *national days of network security and systems* (p. 86–89). doi: 10.1109/JNS2.2012.6249248

Trinidad, S. B., Fullerton, S., Bares, J., Jarvik, G., Larson, E., & Burke, W. (2010). Genomic research and wide data sharing: Views of prospective participants. *Genetics in Medicine: Official Journal of the American College of Medical Genetics*, 12(8).

Yasuda, M., Shimoyama, T., Kogure, J., Yokoyama, K., & Koshiba, T. (2013). Secure pattern matching using somewhat homomorphic encryption. In *Proceedings of the 2013 acm workshop on cloud computing security workshop* (pp. 65–76). New York, NY, USA: ACM. doi: 10.1145/2517488.2517497

Yoshizawa, G., Ho, C. W. L., Zhu, W., Hu, C., Syukriani, Y., Lee, I., Kato, K. (2014). ELSI practices in genomic research in East Asia: implications for research collaboration and public participation. *Genome Medicine*, 6(5), 39. doi: 10.1186/gm556

Zhao, Y., Wang, X., & Tang, H. (2015). Secure genomic computation through site-wise encryption. In *AMIA joint summits on translational science*, 2015 (p. 227–31).

Zheng, G., Yang, Y., Zhu, X., & Elston, R. (2012). *Analysis of genetic association studies.* New York, USA: Springer.

Theory and Practice of Computation – Nishizaki et al. (eds)
© 2019 Taylor & Francis Group, London, ISBN 978-0-367-20417-4

Building RDF models of multidisciplinary data sets under the One Health framework in the Philippine setting

M.L.B. Dela Rosa
Department of Computer Science, University of the Philippines Diliman, Quezon City, Philippines
Headstart Business Solutions, Inc., Quezon City, Philippines

N.V. Tesoro, R.V.L. Canseco & J.D.L. Caro
Department of Computer Science, University of the Philippines Diliman, Quezon City, Philippines

J.A. Malinao & A.R. Codera, Jr.
Headstart Business Solutions, Inc., Quezon City, Philippines

ABSTRACT: The One Health framework realizes the importance of a multidisciplinary approach to health—merging data on humans, animals, and the environment in the analysis of public health events. However, the representation of these multidisciplinary and heterogeneous data sets using a comprehensive and integrated data model is currently lacking in the implementation of One Health in the Philippines. This research introduces the use of the Resource Description Framework (RDF) data model to represent multidisciplinary health data sets under the One Health framework in the Philippine setting. The data sets undergo profiling and conversion to RDF graphs, identifying key points in the data sets called interface nodes that act as unifying variables between the multidisciplinary domains. A unified RDF graph is produced and assessed for known information, facilitated by the interface nodes for examining discoverable structures and relationships which raise potentially novel insights previously unknown to the heterogeneous data sets.

1 INTRODUCTION

1.1 *One Health*

In the One Health approach, the convergence of (1) human, (2) animal, and (3) environmental health and data are evaluated together, making up the One Health framework (American Veterinary Medical Association, 2008). This recognizes that human health and diseases are results of an interplay of humans and their environment including plants and animals. This approach to health is applied in international projects (Kelly et al. 2017) and adapted by countries to solve national problems such as epidemiological outbreaks and environmental problems (Nyatanyi et al. 2017). In the Philippines, the One Health approach has also been quietly implemented through collaborative activities between local sectors and the Philippine Department of Health (DOH) (Interagency Committee on Antimicrobial Resistance, 2015; Amurao et al. 2017) and through an ongoing Commission on Higher Education–Philippine-California Advanced Research Institutes (CHED-PCARI) project on One Health (CHED, 2017).

1.2 *PIDSR*

The Philippine Integrated Disease Surveillance and Response (PIDSR) System (National Epidemiology Center [NEC], 2014a) is the DOH's official disease surveillance system, established to improve the Philippine surveillance systems by integrating all surveillance and response activities such as monitoring and detecting epidemics at all levels, from the lower levels (villages or *barangays*) up to the national level. The PIDSR Manual of Procedures (NEC, 2014) contains information on the multi-level Philippine governmental structure in relation to the flow of health information and reporting, as well as instructions on the specific forms to be used in reporting health cases. These PIDSR forms collect data on Human Health which is part of the One Health framework.

1.3 *Resource Description Framework*

The Resource Description Framework (RDF) is a framework for expressing information about resources such as documents, people, physical objects, and abstract concepts (Cyganiak et al. 2014). It is part of the Semantic Web technologies, introduced as a standard to describe data on the Web, referenced by Uniform Resource Identifiers (URIs). The simplest form of this data model is the RDF Triple, made up of a subject, an object, and a predicate that links them. Together, multiple RDF triples can be imagined as a graph (RDF Graph) with arrows (predicates) pointing from one node (subject) to another (object).

RDF has the ability to represent the interconnection of data, as seen in various researches (Lam et al. 2007; Andersen et al. 2014) that work on integrating heterogeneous data sources such as those involved in the One Health framework.

1.4 *Integration of heterogeneous data*

In a paper by Chen et al. (2009), some applications of Semantic Web technologies in biomedical networks were presented. A type of semantic association, *Transitive Association*, was introduced in the aforementioned paper which is used to check the relation (transitively associated) of one resource to another (Chen et al. 2009). Transitive association can be further used to discover and establish the relationships between multidisciplinary domains, enabled through the connection of resources or nodes shared between them.

2 METHODOLOGY

Data on human health will mainly come from the PIDSR Manual of Procedures (NEC, 2014a) and the PIDSR forms publicly available (NEC, 2014b). This research focuses on health data related to vector-borne diseases (World Health Organization, 2017) closely watched by One Health, specifically on diseases Dengue and Malaria which are commonly present in the Philippines. Documents from the ongoing CHED-PCARI project on One Health will provide additional data on human health, animal health, and the environment. All results, insights, and conclusions are derived solely from the framework incorporating the given data sets.

2.1 *Profiling*

2.1.1 *Predicate construction*
The RDF predicates used in this study are guided by the research of Headstart Business Solutions, Inc.

Table 1 shows the RDF predicates according to Association types, most of which are inspired by UML relationships. In the **Generalization/Specialization** and **Aggregation** association types, the Subject is considered as the child class while the Object is taken as the parent class, e.g. "Epidemic-prone Diseases *is a type of* Disease" for Generalization/Specialization and "Street *is a part of* Address" for Aggregation. Table 1 also shows how to use and interpret the predicates for **Composition**, **Dependency**, and **Equivalence** association types.

Table 2 shows the RDF predicates according to Field types. The predicate *is a type of* for the Generalization/Specialization association type works also as a predicate for the **Category Field** type. The Object works as a common concept or category among the set of terms or Subjects that

Table 1.   RDF predicates according to association types.

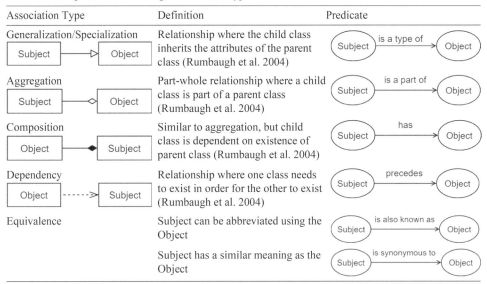

Association Type	Definition	Predicate
Generalization/Specialization	Relationship where the child class inherits the attributes of the parent class (Rumbaugh et al. 2004)	Subject *is a type of* Object
Aggregation	Part-whole relationship where a child class is part of a parent class (Rumbaugh et al. 2004)	Subject *is a part of* Object
Composition	Similar to aggregation, but child class is dependent on existence of parent class (Rumbaugh et al. 2004)	Subject *has* Object
Dependency	Relationship where one class needs to exist in order for the other to exist (Rumbaugh et al. 2004)	Subject *precedes* Object
Equivalence	Subject can be abbreviated using the Object	Subject *is also known as* Object
	Subject has a similar meaning as the Object	Subject *is synonymous to* Object

Table 2.   RDF predicates according to field types.

Field Type	Definition	Predicate
Category	A field (Object) contains a finite set of items (Subjects) related by a common concept	Subject *is a type of* Object
List	A field (Object) contains an enumeration of items (Subjects) with no strict similarity in concept between them	Subject *is a part of* Object
Unitary Value	A field (Subject) that refers to a single item or a literal value (Object)	Subject *is* Object

point to it. The predicate *is a part of* for the Aggregation association type also works as a predicate for the **List Field** type, in which the set of terms or Subjects are part of the Object which it points to. The predicate *is* for the **Unitary Value Field** type refers to a literal value (Object) that describes the Subject. The Subject points to a specific value (Object), which is usually a terminal node in the RDF graph.

Table 3 shows the RDF predicates of **Requirement** types. The *requires* predicate shows a relationship in which the Subject requires or needs the Object, while the *can have* predicate shows a relationship in which the Subject may or may not have the Object. Table 4 shows the RDF predicates used for **Collection** and how they are interpreted, e.g. the predicate *is collected by* represents the relationship of something being collected (Subject) and an entity that collects (Objects).

The data sets used in this study are in PDF format and are unstructured. In the first step of profiling, an unstructured data set undergoes manual analysis. We read through the information in the data set to gain an idea of the relationships contained in the information, then choose a candidate subject and object. From the list of predicates previously enumerated, we then choose the predicate that appropriately captures the relationship between the subject and the object, forming a **triple**. This triple is then recorded in an Excel spreadsheet as a row with the subject, predicate, and object in three different columns in that order. The output is a CSV file of the profiled data set in s, p, o (triples) format.

Table 3. RDF predicates according to requirement types.

Requirement Type	Definition	Predicate
Required	Subject needs the presence of the Object, though they may be disjoint	(Subject) —requires→ (Object)
Not required	Subject may have the Object, though it is optional	(Subject) —can have→ (Object)

Table 4. RDF predicates according to collection.

Collection Predicate	Definition
(Subject) —is collected by→ (Object)	Relationship in which the Object collects the Subject
(Subject) —is collected from→ (Object)	Relationship in which the Object possesses the collected Subject
(Subject) —is collected using→ (Object)	Relationship in which the Subject is collected through a medium or using the Object
(Subject) —is collected on→ (Object)	Relationship in which the Subject is collected during a process, a date value, or frequency of collection (Object)
(Subject) —is collected→ (Object)	Relationship in which the Subject is collected on a date value, within a duration of time, or frequency of collection (Object)

2.1.2 Steps in profiling
1. Manual analysis of unstructured data set
2. While not end of data set:
   - Select candidate *subject* and *object*
   - Choose appropriate predicate to represent the relationship between the candidate subject and object
   - Record the triple as a row in a spreadsheet
3. Export spreadsheet as CSV file

2.1.3 Profiling challenges
The following are the most common challenges encountered and identified during the preprocessing step, as well as the actions taken in order to resolve them.

1. Naming of Terms
   - General & Specific Terms
   Compound the words or add an adjective to a noun or word to be more specific in naming terms, such as when a term should belong to a particular government level or a term is of a particular type. The format is *<name>* + *<attribute>* or vice versa, depending on which is more grammatically correct, and may include the preposition *of* (e.g. *'Name of Disease Reporting Unit'*).
   An example of this is 'Regional feedback' ('Regional' + 'feedback') which is a more specific form of the general term 'feedback'. The predicate *is a type of* may be used to link them together, forming the following triple: "Regional feedback *is a type of* feedback".
   - Aggregation of Terms
   In naming, some terms are made up of other terms or a conjunction of criteria. For example, a term 'Monitoring and Evaluation' is made up of two separate terms 'Monitoring' and 'Evaluation'. Use the predicate *is a part of* to show the relationship between the separate terms

and the term formed using the aggregation of the others' names ("Monitoring *is a part of* Monitoring and Evaluation", "Evaluation *is a part of* Monitoring and Evaluation").

- Consistency of Terms between Data Sets

    Some names may appear on multiple data sets. To ensure consistency of the used names between data sets, we suggest keeping a list of all the terms already in use. Compare the terms to ensure similarity and correctness in spelling and case sensitivity. For example, the term *'Dengue'* is not equal to the term *'dengue'* in an RDF graph and will create two separate nodes.

2. Unknown Values or User-dependent Fields

    These are for situations wherein there are fields in the forms that require user input.

    - *[user specified]:* If the required field is specified by the user or person answering the form (e.g. *'Other Medical Condition is [user specified]'*)
    - *[Unknown ___]:* If the answer to the field is 'Unknown' or if the user does not know; replace the *'___'* with the name of the field being asked (e.g. *[Unknown income]* or may just use *[Unknown]* in general)
    - *[N/A]:* For fields that may not be applicable to other users
    - *[None]:* If answer to a field is 'None'

3. Special Characters

    Some characters in a term's name make invalid URIs when converted. To prevent this, use the word form of the character (e.g. *'greater than'* in place of >) or use a corresponding HTML character entity. For names that make use of slash (/) or 'or': if the separated words are semantically different, separate them into two different terms, e.g. "Heart Attack/Chest Pain *is a type of* Medical Conditions". In this example, 'Heart Attack' and 'Chest Pain' are made into two different terms, but both are related to the Object 'Medical Conditions' through the predicate *is a type of*.

Each data set was profiled using the predicates, although there were some parts left out of the profiling such as tables with relationships that were challenging to model using the predicates.

2.1.4 *Segregation of triples*

The rows of triples listed in the Excel spreadsheets also undergo segregation based on the following categories: Human, Animal, Environment, Government, and Miscellaneous. The categories **Human**, **Animal**, and **Environment** are inspired by the three domains in the One Health framework. The **Government** category is for triples that pertain to governmental structure or process, while the **Miscellaneous** category is for those that do not fall under the other categories. The purpose of segregating the triples into categories is in order to know which domain they belong to. The segregation of the triples is done by labeling each row with the category they belong to, added as a fourth column in the original spreadsheet.

2.1.5 *Conversion of CSV to RDF*

For this step, the conversion of CSV to RDF graph in RDF/XML serialization is done using Python and the RDFLib package.

Taking the CSV file as input, the Subject, Predicate, and Object (s, p, o) in each line are converted into URIs. Whitespaces between words are converted into dashes (–) and special characters are changed into their corresponding HTML character entities. Since the data set is unstructured, a temporary namespace URI may be used for the purpose of this research only, although this could be changed later on if needed. Each s, p, o triple is added into one common RDF graph for a data set. The resulting RDF graph is then serialized to RDF/XML.

The list of all terms used in an RDF graph of a data set are saved in another file. This is manually checked for possible naming or spelling errors that were missed during the preprocessing step in the Excel spreadsheet. If such errors are found, the spreadsheet is corrected and the process of exporting to CSV and converting to RDF in RDF/XML serialization are repeated.

2.2 Integration

To establish the relationship of the multidisciplinary domains for the creation of a **unified RDF graph**, the following is used:

2.2.1 Criteria for connecting RDF_1 and RDF_2

For every $x \in RDF_1$ and $y \in RDF_2$, where $RDF_1 \neq RDF_2$:

1. (Exact Matching) If $x = y$, then $x \xrightarrow{r} y$, $r \in \{\text{"is also known as"}, \text{"is synonymous to"}\}$, and $y = x$.
2. Given $p \in RDF_1$, if there is a transitive association from p to x and $x = y$, then $p \xrightarrow{r'} y$ where $r' = \text{"is related to"}$ and is a special type of predicate used for merging. p is obtained by selecting the vertex with the largest value from the matrix generated using Johnson's algorithm.

We call "$\xrightarrow{r}$" and the "$\xrightarrow{r'}$" newly-added arcs as *interfacing arcs*. Furthermore, for every p and x in the RDF where an interfacing arc is created, we call p and x as *interface nodes*. Similarly, x and y are also called interface nodes.

- Steps in getting interface nodes:
  1. Input two RDF graphs RDF_1 and RDF_2
  2. *Exact Matching:* Get the list of common terms between the two RDF graphs
  3. Generate distance matrix for RDF_1 using Johnson's algorithm
  4. For each common term x:
     - Get list of terms ('dlist') with the largest value connected to x from the distance matrix
     - If dlist is not empty:
       - For each p in dlist, create the triple
         - **Subject:** p
         - **Predicate:** *is related to*
         - **Object:** x
         and export to a new file in CSV format
  5. New file now contains triples with interface nodes of RDF_1
  6. Repeat steps (3) and (4) using RDF_2

This process is repeatedly done between the pairs of RDF graphs of the data sets. Each data set gets an output CSV file containing the interface nodes connected using the special predicate *is related to*. The transitive associations established by the predicate between the interface nodes show the relationship between the multidisciplinary domains and can be used in analyzing the relationships of the domains.

The CSV files containing the interface node triples are also converted into corresponding RDF graphs in RDF/XML serialization. These RDF graphs will be included in the unified RDF graph to show interface nodes and the connections between them.

In the process of integrating the different RDF graphs, the common terms between them will be merged and considered as one term in the unified RDF graph. This merging is guided using the following criterion:

2.2.2 Merging criterion

For every $x \in RDF_1$ and $y \in RDF_2$, where $RDF_1 \neq RDF_2$:

- If $x = y$, then $y' = \{x, y\}$ (Exact Matching)
- Reconnect all edges going to and coming from x to y'
- Reconnect all edges going to and coming from y to y'

The RDF graphs of the data sets are integrated using RDFLib, including the separate RDF graphs containing the interface node triples. The unified RDF graph is also serialized to RDF/XML.

Table 5. Properties of the RDF graphs.

RDF Graph	# of terms	# of triples	# of terms used as subjects	# of terms used as predicates	# of terms used as objects	# of interface node triples
case-inv-form[a]	187	223	143	9	115	73
case-report-form[b]	152	187	97	11	96	112
dengue[c]	161	179	119	10	84	76
malaria[d]	120	146	76	7	87	86
one-health-form[e]	571	789	535	10	199	69
pidsr-1[f]	409	556	306	13	238	221
pidsr-2[f]	404	559	308	14	261	660
pidsr-3[f]	383	552	312	13	223	198
wndr[g]	84	95	64	12	37	49
barangay-workflow[h]	66	84	48	8	38	12

[a] PIDSR Case Investigation Form for Malaria.
[b] PIDSR Case Report Form for Dengue.
[c] Information on Dengue.
[d] Information on Malaria.
[e] One Health Form.
[f] PIDSR Manual of Procedures (divided into three parts).
[g] PIDSR WNDR Summary Page.
[h] Barangay Workflow Documents.

3   RESULTS & DISCUSSION

The profile for the PIDSR Manual of Procedures was divided into three data sets due to constraints in visualization but this also enabled more interface nodes to be discovered between them, increasing the number of their interface node triples as seen in Table 5.

3.1   *Component diagram with summary of statistics*

The following data sets used in this research are forms and records collected and utilized between government levels as well as supporting information on Dengue and Malaria illnesses:

1. PIDSR Manual of Procedures (3rd ed., Vol. 1) (NEC, 2014a)
2. PIDSR Case Investigation Form for Malaria (NEC, 2014b)
3. PIDSR Case Report Form for Dengue (NEC, 2014b)
4. PIDSR WNDR Summary Page (NEC, 2014b)
5. One Health Form (CHED, 2017)
6. Barangay Workflow Documents (CHED, 2017)
7. Information on Dengue (NEC, 2014c)
8. Information on Malaria (NEC, 2014c)

For each form, we count the number of triples belonging to each category during the process of segregation. The categories are abbreviated as follows: **H** for Human, **A** for Animals, **E** for Environment, **G** for Government, and **M** for Miscellaneous.

3.1.1   *Per government level*

The data sets are compiled per government level to get a comparison of the kinds of data belonging to multidisciplinary domains collected and utilized in each level. All five forms are utilized in the community level data collection and as the collected data is submitted to higher government level, additional data such as summary reports and interpretations are also consolidated. An example can be seen in Figure 1, in which reports coming from the Regional level are collected in the National level.

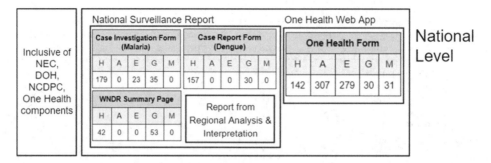

Figure 1. Collected data sets and the sensors/collectors of data in the National level. The number of triples for each category is shown per data set.

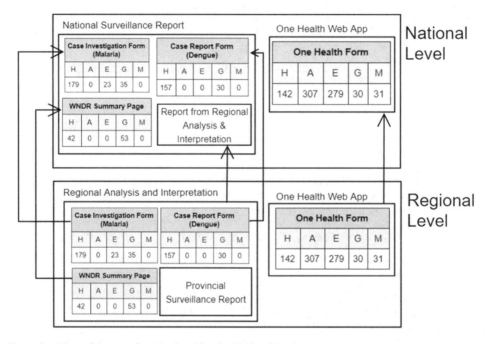

Figure 2. Flow of data sets from Regional level to National level.

In summary, most of the data collected belong to the category of Human health. All five forms have triples under the Government category, which suggest possible significance of government-related data such as government structure and processes in the implementation of One Health in the Philippines. None of the PIDSR Forms have triples under the Animal category, although some contain data under the Environment category. The One Health Form is able to provide the triples under these two categories, supplementing what is lacking in the PIDSR Forms.

3.1.2 *Between government levels*

The interactions between the government levels by looking at the flow of data sets being collected are also compared.

The data sets visible in all government levels are the three PIDSR Forms and the One Health Form. As the data sets reach higher levels, additional information is passed alongside them, as higher levels are also consolidating forms coming from different areas in the lower levels (e.g.

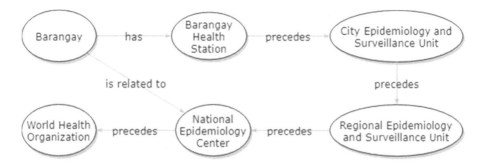

Figure 3.   RDF graph showing path from Barangay to National Epidemiology Center.

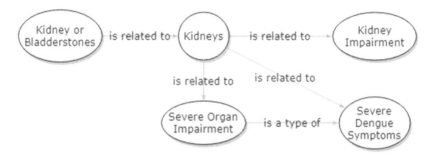

Figure 4.   RDF graph showing path from kidney or bladderstones to severe dengue symptoms.

Figure 2). In some cases, some of the forms may be passed directly to the higher levels, skipping a few levels between them, in order to report health cases that need immediate attention. The existence of accessible One Health mobile tools/Web App (CHED, 2017) in all levels may also provide a faster way of communication and reporting since the data collected can be accessed by all levels.

3.2   Selected RDF models

The files containing the interface nodes are manually analyzed, checking the relationships represented as RDF graphs for well-known facts verifiable through literature, as well as potentially novel insights previously unknown to the separate data sets.

The unified RDF graph can be assessed for the relationships of the governmental structures and processes as well as communication links. Figure 3 shows the path from 'Barangay' to 'National Epidemiology Center' which is also connected to 'World Health Organization'. This path can be verified as the flow of information for Chartered Cities (NEC, 2014a).

Through the unification of different data sets using the RDF model, new connections may possibly appear in the unified RDF graph. Terms from one data set may be related to terms from another data set, such as the relationship of 'Kidney or Bladderstones' to 'Severe Dengue Symptoms' connected through the predicate *is related to* (Figure 4). These potentially novel insights derived from the unification are subject to expert validation.

4   CONCLUSIONS

The Resource Description Framework is used as a model to represent the multidisciplinary data sets involved in the implementation of the One Health framework in the Philippine setting. The unstructured data sets were profiled and converted to their corresponding RDF graphs. The connectivity between the different domains involved is established through interface nodes, and the RDF graphs of the data sets are integrated into a unified RDF graph. The unified RDF graph and the interface nodes are then assessed for known information and potentially novel insights derived from the integration. Furthermore, the segregation of triples into categories provide insights on the organization of the health and medical communities under One Health in the country.

Additionally, this research also provides a framework for building RDF models of unstructured data sets related to One Health, as well as a template for integrating new data sets to the existing model.

REFERENCES

Amurao, S.S.Jr., Lopez, E.L., Lagayan, M.G.O., Calub, N.P. & Jorca, D.L. 2016. One Health Approach: The Philippine Experience. Food and Fertilizer Technology Center for the Asian and the Pacific Region. http://www.fftc.agnet.org/library.php?func=view&style=type&id=20170329160947.

American Veterinary Medical Association 2008. One Health: A New Professional Imperative. *One Health Initiative Task Force: Final Report.* https://www.avma.org/KB/Resources/Reports/Documents/onehealth_final.pdf.

Andersen, A.B., Gür, N., Hose, K., Jakobsen, K.A. & Pedersen, T.B. 2014. Publishing Danish Agricultural Government Data as Semantic Web Data. In Supnithi, T., Yamaguchi, T., Pan, J.Z., Wuwongse , V. & Buranarach, M. (eds.), *Proceedings of the 4th Joint International Conference Semantic Technology, JIST 2014*, Lecture Notes in Computer Science 8943: 178–186.

Chen, H., Ding, L., Wu, Z., Yu, T., Dhanapalan, L. & Chen, J.Y. 2009. Semantic web for integrated network analysis in biomedicine. *Briefings in Bioinformatics* 10(2): 177–192.

Commission on Higher Education (CHED) 2017. Philippine-California Advanced Research Institutes (PCARI) Project Request for Proposals (RFPs). http://ippao.upm.edu.ph/sites/default/files/2017-06/Announcement%20PCARI%20RFP%20for%20Cycle%205%202017.pdf.

Cyganiak, R., Wood, D. & Lanthaler, M. 2014. RDF 1.1 Concepts and Abstract Syntax. https://www.w3.org/TR/rdf11-concepts/.

Interagency Committee on Antimicrobial Resistance (ICAMR) 2015. The Philippine Action Plan to Combat Antimicrobial Resistance: One Health Approach. Department of Health, Philippines. http://icamr.doh.gov.ph/index.php/publications/national-action-plan-to-combat-amr.

Kelly, T.R., Karesh, W.B., Johnson, C.K., Gilardi, K.V., Anthony, S.J., Goldstein, T., Olson, S.H. & Machalaba, C., PREDICT Consortium & Mazet, J.A. 2017. One Health proof of concept: Bringing a transdisciplinary approach to surveillance for zoonotic viruses at the human-wild animal interface. *Preventive Veterinary Medicine* 137: 112–118.

Lam, H.Y., Marenco, L., Clark, T., Gao, Y., Kinoshita, J., Shepherd, G., Miller, P., Wu, E., Wong, G.T., Liu, N., Crasto, C., Morse, T., Stephens, S. & Cheung, K.-H. 2007. AlzPharm: integration of neurodegeneration data using RDF. *BMC Bioinformatics* 8(3): S4.

National Epidemiology Center (NEC) 2014a. *Manual of Procedures for the Philippine Integrated Disease Surveillance and Response (PIDSR) 3rd edn.* Department of Health, Philippines. https://www.doh.gov.ph/sites/default/files/publications/PIDSRMOP3ED_VOL2_pp1-54_2014.pdf.

National Epidemiology Center (NEC) 2014b. PIDSR Forms, http://ro6. doh.gov.ph/index.php/health-statistics/diseasesurveillance/120-pidsr-forms.

National Epidemiology Center (NEC) 2014c. *Section 10: Guidelines for Diseases, Syndromes and Health Events under Surveillance.* Department of Health, Philippines. https://www.doh.gov.ph/sites/default/files/publications/PIDSRMOP3ED_VOL2_pp1- 54_2014.pdf.

Nyatanyi, T., Wilkes, M., McDermott, H., Nzietchueng, S., Gafarasi, I., Mudakikwa, A., Kinani, J.F., Rukelibuga, J., Omolo, J., Mupfasoni, D., Kabeja, A., Nyamusore, J., Nziza, J., Hakizimana, J.L., Kamugisha, J., Nkunda, R., Kibuuka, R., Rugigana, E., Farmer, P., Cotton, P. & Binagwaho, A. 2017. Implementing One Health as an integrated approach to health in Rwanda. *BMJ Global Health* 2: e000121.

Rumbaugh, J., Jacobson, I. & Booch, G. 2004. *Unified Modeling Language Reference Manual, The (2nd Edition).* Pearson Higher Education.

World Health Organization (WHO) 2017. Vector-borne diseases. http://www.who.int/en/news-room/fact-sheets/detail/vector-borne-diseases.

Theory and Practice of Computation – Nishizaki et al. (eds)
© 2019 Taylor & Francis Group, London, ISBN 978-0-367-20417-4

Analyzing the effect of video media on emotion using a VR headset platform and physiological data

Hayato Uraji, Taweesak Emsawas & Juan Lorenzo Hagad
Graduate School of Information Science and Technology, Osaka University, Osaka, Japan

Ken-ichi Fukui & Masayuki Numao
The Institute of Scientific and Industrial Research, Osaka University, Osaka, Japan

ABSTRACT: Assessing the effects of audio-visual media can help content creators learn how audiences regard their creations. However, this process can be challenging, in part because traditional methods involve using self-reported questionnaire data which are subject to different forms of bias (participant bias, experimenter bias, or simply human variability). To address this subjective variability, this work proposes a method to supplement questionnaires with autonomic physiological data readings for assessing affective responses to video content. Specifically, it combines subjective self-report questionnaires with electroencephalograph (EEG) and heart rate readings. The target subjects are viewers of short Japanese video commercials and news programs shown through a VR headset platform. Support vector machines were used to detect different types of affect related to the context of the videos. Finally, an analysis of the versatility of the trained models was done by applying a model trained for short TV commercials to a smaller dataset obtained from viewing news programs. The results show a possible link between positive emotions and clarity of understanding.

1 INTRODUCTION

Traditionally, evaluation of TV commercials and other types of consumed media was carried out using questionnaires administered to subjects. However, in recent years the use of physiological information in media evaluation has been on the rise. One limitation of traditional questionnaires is the constraint of having to express complex emotions and ideas in words. Answers limited to short verbal feedback, or worse still those constrained to selected number of options, may not necessarily be representative of a person's true feelings. On top of this, human beings are social animals so subjects tend to have their responses influenced by what they feel may be the experimenter's expectations. This is called the subject-expectancy effect, and can result in skewed experimental data. It is also often seen that human decision making is not logical enough to express linguistically. Therefore, it is difficult to express human emotions and thoughts only in words, and the accuracy of the words is limited. Therefore, efforts are being made to measure emotions and thoughts based on physiological responses [7].

One way to obtain several affective indicators is through the use of electrocardiographs (ECG) [2]. These indicators feature strong correlations with changes caused by autonomic nervous system and, by extension, human emotions [4]. It is for this reason that EEG and galvanic skin response (GSR) are commonly used in affective analysis.

Ramzan et al. (2016) [3] used electroencephalographs (EEG) as well as ECG to estimate emotions while watching movie video clips. They built machine learning models trained on arousal and valence labels. This is similar to a number of previous works aimed at predicting emotion. The goal of the current work is to analyze the effect of short video commercials, which come with their own challenges. A similar work, Granero et al. (2016) [1] analyzed video commercials in relation to how engaged viewers felt. They used the ACE score index as reference and their work focused on estimating how viewers felt using the same three-point scale, i.e. positive, negative or neutral. Using EEG, ECG and GSR, their work aimed to find the best features for predicting positive effectiveness. Their work found that GSR and HRV provided the best features. However, a major limitation of GSR and HRV is their responsiveness. They usually require observations over a minute long to be considered barely acceptable. Many video commercials occur in the span of a few seconds, and oftentimes this is not long enough to elicit a clear response from these types of physiological channels. To address this limitation, the current work also attempts to use EEG to evaluate responses to commercials that are less than 15 seconds long. This type of data has the advantage of being easier to administer to a large number subjects. As such, this work also attempts to apply models build on larger dataset with shorter videos, to longer videos with fewer samples.

2   METHOD OVERVIEW

In this research, we perform evaluation of videos through physiological signals and questionnaire data. By doing so, we expect to obtain more reliable evaluations from fewer subjects. Two types of audio-visual media are analyzed, news programs and short video commercials.

For the news programs, these were analyzed based on the clarity of the content as affected by the presence of different types of text captions. ECG is used as the primary source of physiological information since it has been found to be one of the most reliable for emotion recognition, however EEG was also recorded. Three versions of the same new programs were compared: no caption (N), detailed captions (A), and simple captions (B). In total, 24 subjects were included in the experiment. After watching the 2minute video clip, subjects answered a questionnaire which, among a large number of other questions, asked how easy it was for them to understand the content. From these questions, a 5-point scale of clarity was obtained. A machine learned model was trained and tested, and useful features for analysis were identified.

The second dataset contained data from TV commercials (TVCM) and was comprised of 3 sets of shorter than 15-second videos. Due to the length limitation, EEG data was primarily used due to its quick response time. We obtained three emotions labels: positive emotion, negative emotion and neutral.

3   VR ON AIR TEST

In this research, data was acquired using VR OAT (VR ON AIR TEST) developed by SOOTH Corp. [9]. This system acquires video viewing behavior under a VR environment. Responses to questionnaires are acquired through a touch interface, and a slew of physiological sensors are included in the platform. VR also carries the advantage of allowing users to focus on specific content. Also, compared to other existing platforms it is easier to use since it only requires a headset and a controller. As such, it is expected to have real use-cases for media evaluations conducted by companies.

4   EXPERIMENT PROTOCOL

The following section explains in detail how the two video viewing experiments were carried out.

4.1   *News video*

Video clips, about 2 minutes in length, from news programs were shown to 24 subjects around 20 years of age. Questionnaires were also administered before and after each viewing session, while EEG and ECG data were recorded throughout. Three versions of videos were used: no caption (N), detailed captions (A), and simple captions (B). All 24 subjects viewed video N, after which they were split into two groups to view either video A or B. All captions featured similar Japanese descriptions of the content of the program.

4.2 TVCM

TV commercials were shown to 213 men and women from 20–50 years of age, with sensor recordings similar to the previous section. Video clips contained 15-second commercials for products from 3 competing brands. Questionnaires were also administered before and after each viewing session.

5 FEATURES

5.1 *News video*

From the questionnaire in the first experiment, we obtained a 5-point measure to describe the clarity of news programs:

1. very hard to understand
2. hard to understand
3. neutral
4. easy to understand
5. very easy to understand

In the case of the videos without captions, we obtained responses from all 5 levels. However, in the case of the videos with captions, almost all responses were from level 4 and above. This could mean that captions were truly effective for improving the clarity of the programs, however we needed additional confirmation. Therefore, we analyzed whether questionnaire responses were consistent with the physiological responses. Since it is hard to distinguish between levels 1 and 2 or between 4 and 5, we merged 1 and 2 into "hard to understand", and 4 and 5 into "easy to understand".

5.2 *TVCM*

From TVCM, we obtained 11 scenes each with affective labels for each scene. These scenes and times are shown in Table 1. The 9 labels are as follows:

1. got pleased
2. was excited
3. calmed down
4. feel relieved
5. There is nothing to apply
6. Was nervous
7. bored
8. got sad
9. felt bad

From these 9 labels, we obtained 3 feeling scores (Positive, Neutral, Negative). To map scene to each second, data is weighted by time.

$$f_t = \sum_i^{N_i} (sf_i \times t_i) \tag{1}$$

where
  f_t is the feeling score at time t
  sf_i is the feeling score at scene i
  t_i is time weight at scene i
  N_t is number of scene which relates to time i
  t is observed timestamp $(1, 2, 3, \ldots 15)$

Table 1.   Scenes and times.

Scenes	Start time	End time	Period time
1st scene	00:00	02:24	02:24
2nd scene	02:24	03:20	00:56
3rd scene	03:20	05:08	01:48
4th scene	05:08	05:23	00:15
5th scene	05:23	07:05	01:42
6th scene	07:05	08:04	00:59
7th scene	08:04	08:28	00:24
8th scene	08:28	10:05	01:37
9th scene	10:05	11:14	01:09
10th scene	11:14	13:18	02:04
11th scene	13:18	15:00	01:42

5.3   *ECG data*

ECG is caused by a change in the distribution of electricity occurring in the heart.

When the heart contracts and is detected as a potential from the body surface. The peaks of electric signals are named like P, Q, R, S, T. R is the highest point of the interval. The RR interval is not always constant but fluctuates. This change also reflects psychological effects with strong ties to emotion.

Here, ECG data was collected using Neurosky [10] and the following features were extracted:

RMSSD   – Root mean square of successive RR interval differences
SDNN   – Standard deviation of RR intervals
NN50   – The total number of consecutive adjacent RR intervals exceeding 50 ms
PNN50   – Percentage of heartbeats in which the difference between consecutive
          adjacent RR intervals exceeds 50 ms
HF   – Absolute power of the high-frequency band (0.15–0.4 Hz)

5.4   *EEG data*

Electroencephalography (EEG) is an electrophysiological monitoring method to record electrical activity of the brain. And it is typically noninvasive, with the electrodes placed along the scalp. The latter analyzes the type of neural oscillations (popularly called "brain waves") that can be observed in EEG signals in the frequency domain. Brainwaves are produced by synchronized electrical pulses from masses of neurons communicating with each other.

EEG data was also collected using Neurosky [10]. Brainwave frequency is measured in Hertz (cycles per second) and they are divided into bands delineating slow, moderate, and fast waves [8].

Delta waves (0.5–3 Hz) – Deepest meditation and dreamless sleep
Theta waves (3–8 Hz) – Deep relaxation and meditation, mental imagery
Alpha waves (8–12 Hz) – Relaxation, relaxed focus, calm, not thinking (resting state for the brain)
Beta waves (12–38 Hz) – Alertness, cognition, consciousness, concentration, arousal
Gamma waves (38–42 Hz) – Hyper brain activity

6   MODELS

Using the data and labels obtained machine learning models were trained using support vector machines (SVM), and the results were tested and analyzed.

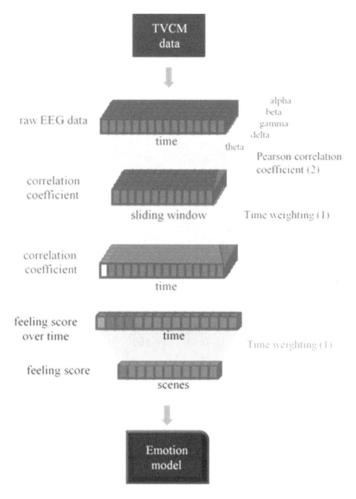

Figure 1. Emotion model in advertisement.

6.1 *News video models*

Learning was carried out using various features obtained from the ECG of the 24 subjects who watched the new program videos. Of the 24 subjects, stable and reliable data was found to only be present in 15 subjects. Therefore, using these 15 samples, 4-fold cross-validation was performed.

6.2 *TVCM model*

Learning was performed using data (alpha, beta, gamma, delta, theta) obtained from EEG. We used a sliding window with a 4-second width. Data from a total of 118 subjects was used, as shown in Figure 1.

In Figure 1, the emotion model was trained from the TVCM dataset, which contains alpha, beta, gamma, delta, and theta brainwave readings, as well as scene feeling scores derived from the questionnaire. First, we calculated correlation coefficients between time and raw EEG data set of advertising data by using Pearson's correlation coefficient. Then, these values were mapped to the corresponding time segment by time weighting. The feeling score of each scene also was mapped to the feeling score over time by time weighting. The yellow blocks and green block represent the training data and label respectively.

155

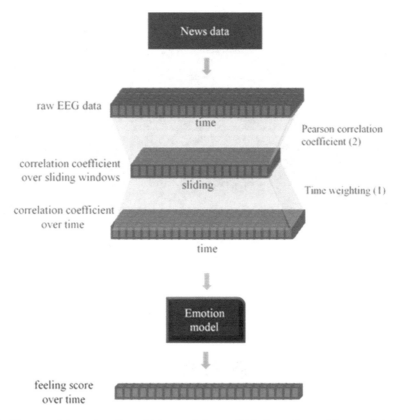

Figure 2. The news data was transformed into correlation coefficient over time and then predicted using the emotion model which was trained from TVCM data.

6.3 *Applying news video*

Next, using the emotion model obtained from TVCM, the emotions of subjects in news videos were estimated. The number of subjects at this time was 24, as shown in Figure 2.

6.4 *Classification algorithm*

A support vector machine (SVM) was used for the identification algorithm. SVM is one of pattern recognition models using supervised learning and in this time can be applied to classification. In 1963, Vladimir N. Vapnik and Alexey Ya. Chervonenkis announced [5] and in 1992 Bernhard E. Boser, Isabelle M. Guyon and Vladimir N. Vapnik expanded to nonlinear.

7 RESULT

7.1 *News video result*

The results for predicting the clarity of news videos using SVM's is shown in Table 2.

Based on these results, we identify nn50 as the best feature for prediction.

Next, we apply the model trained using cross-validation to predict values for the videos with captions. Note that these featured a mono-label of "easy to understand" and were unusable as a lone training set. This set contained a total of 20 samples (11 from A, 9 from B). Classification results are as follows:

Table 2. Prediction result.

model	parameters	feature	training	test	recall	f-value
rbf	c = 2, gamma = 0.15	nn50	100	72.9	66.7	59.4
Poly	c = 2, degree = 1, gamma = 0.0001	Rmssd	84.3	52.1	45.8	42.2
rbf	c = 0.1, gamma = 0.15	Hf	46.6	45.8	33.3	20.8
linear	c = 1	sdnn(std)	97.7	33.3	33.3	23.6
rbf	c = 1000 gamma = 0.3	Pnn50	100	45.8	45.8	36.1

Table 3. Prediction result with captions.

data	model	Parameters	feature	test
A	rbf	c=2, gamma=0.15	nn50	100
B	rbf	c=2, gamma=0.15	nn50	100

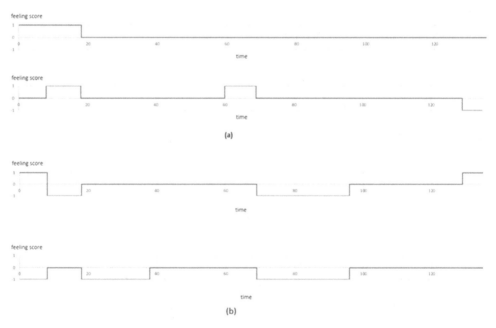

Figure 3. (a) The scene feeling score for "easy to understand" samples show a more stable trend and generally "positive" feelings

(b) The scene feeling score for "hard to understand" samples show a less stable trend and more "negative" feelings.

7.2 Applying TVCM for news video

Finally, since the news video dataset did not have enough samples to train a reliable EEG model, we attempt to use the model trained using the TVCM dataset for evaluation. The results of this test can be observed in Figure 3.

The vertical axis represents feeling score and the horizontal axis represents time. By looking at these graphs, we can obtain the mood of each scene:

1: positive
0: neutral
−1: negative

People who answered that it is easy to understand feel positive about some scenes. But people who answered that it is hard to understand feel negative for the same scenes. In addition, Figure 3(a) is more stable than Figure 3(b).

8 CONCLUSION

In this work, we obtained a machine learner for predicting the clarity of news based on ECG features. In the case where captions were used, subjects rated all videos as at least "easy to understand". In order to verify whether this was accurate or due to the expectancy effect, a model trained on the remaining dataset without captions was used. The results show that clarity detections are consistent with the questionnaire result, with all video rated as "easy to understand". Thus, this work demonstrated how to enhance the credibility of dubious questionnaire labels. Moreover, it also confirms how the presence of captions can make news programs easier to understand. For the final model, among ECG features, nn50 was found to have the strongest correlation to the clarity of news programs.

Secondly, we obtained a model to estimate emotions from TVCM using EEG data. Using three emotion labels: positive emotion, negative emotion and neutral, an emotion model was built and then applied to the dataset featuring news programs. From the results in Figure 3, it seems that videos that were labelled as "easy to understand" also tended to feel "positive", more often than not. On the other hand, videos labelled as "hard to understand" tended to contain "negative" emotions for the same scenes and for longer continuous segments. Based on the results, it may be possible to create easier to understand new programs based on affective positivity models. It may even be possible to combine these automated detections with traditional questionnaire results to obtain a more reliable evaluation.

REFERENCES

[1] Granero, A. C.; Fuentes-Hurtado, F.; Ornedo, V. N.; Provinciale, J. G.; Ausin J. M. and Raya, M. A. Comparison of Physiological Signal Analysis Techniques and Classifiers for Automatic Emotional Evaluation of Audiovisual Contents, Front. Comput. Neurosci., 15 July 2016

[2] Shaffer, F. and Ginsberg, J. P. An Overview of Heart Rate Variability Metrics and Norms, Front. Public Health, 28 September 2017

[3] Ramzan, N.; Palke, S.; Cuntz, T.; Gibson, R. and Amira, A. Emotion Recognition by Physiological Signals, 2016 society for Imaging Science and Technology

[4] Quintana, D. S.; Guastella, A. J.; Outhred, T.; Hickie, I. B.; Kemp, A. H. Heart rate variability is associated with emotion recognition: Direct evidence for a relationship between the autonomic nervous system and social cognition, International Journal of Psychophysiology 86 (2012) 168–172

[5] Vapnik, V. and Lerner, A. Pattern recognition using generalized portrait method. Automation and Remote Control, 24, 1963

[6] Boser, B. E.; Guyon, I. M.; Vapnik, V. N. A Training Algorithm for Optimal Margin Classifiers (1992), Proceedings of the 5th Annual ACM Workshop on Computational Learning Theory

[7] Koyama, S. The limit of conventional investigation method and possibility of public notice investigation by biological reaction (in Japanese), AD STUDIES Vol. 38 Autumn 2011.11.25

[8] https://brainworksneurotherapy.com/what-are-brainwaves

[9] https://www.vr-insight.com/en/oat.html

[10] http://neurosky.com/

Theory and Practice of Computation – Nishizaki et al. (eds)
© 2019 Taylor & Francis Group, London, ISBN 978-0-367-20417-4

Dominating tree problem heuristics for scale-free networks

K.P. Urog & J.Y. Bantang
National Institute of Physics, College of Science, University of the Philippines Diliman, Quezon City, Philippines

H.N. Adorna
Department of Computer Science, University of the Philippines Diliman, Quezon City, Philippines

ABSTRACT: The Dominating Tree Problem (DTP) aims to find a dominating tree $T^* \subset G_0$ of minimum total edge weight on a given undirected connected graph G_0. The most common heuristic approach for this problem considers Kruskal's Algorithm, an ideal choice for minimizing the total edge weights of the generated T^*. In this paper, we focus on a DTP heuristics applied to a special class of graphs called scale-free networks. The proposed algorithm exploits the scale-free property of vertex degree distribution $p(k)$ of G_0 such that a considerable improvement in computational time is achieved.

1 INTRODUCTION

The dominating tree problem (DTP) is a combinatorial optimization problem that is gaining a lot of interest because of its very wide range of applicability to different real world problems; particularly, in the field of wireless sensor networks or WSN (Shin, Shen, & Thai 2010; Thai, Tiwari, & Du 2008; Park, Willson, Wang, Thai, Wu, & Farago 2007).

Moreover, the intensive study of graph theory and networks, leads to the discovery of different properties of graphs and networks that helps us generate better algorithms and solutions to problems involving them. One special class of graphs called scale-free networks became an important concept in network theory because many complex systems that are represented as networks are reported to exhibit this property (Barabási et al. 2016). These scale-free networks are characterized by its degree distribution that follows a power law distribution.

In this paper we present a heuristic algorithm, that solves the dominating tree problem for any network, which effectively works better for scale-free networks. This is due to the major consideration of the properties of a scale free network in the algorithm. We also looked into previous heuristics which are extremely dependent on the idea behind Kruskal's algorithm to minimize the edge weight of the resulting tree. We then compared run time results from one of these heuristics with that of the proposed algorithm.

1.1 *Dominating Tree Problem (DTP)*

A graph $G_0 = (V_0, E_0)$ has the tree $T = (V_T, E_T)$ as subgraph when $V_T \subset V_0$ and $E_T \subset E_0$. A subgraph tree becomes the dominating tree (DT) T^* of G_0 when either: (a) each vertex $\upsilon \in V_0$ is in T^* (*i.e.* $\upsilon \in V_T$); or (b) υ is adjacent to at least one vertex of T^* (*i.e.* $\exists e \in E_0$ that connects υ to T^*). Here, G_0 is an undirected and connected graph with V_0 as the set of vertices and E_0 as its set of edges.

The dominating tree problem (DTP) can now be defined as follows: Consider an undirected connected graph G_0 described above. Further, let each edge $e \in E_0$ be associated with a unique non-negative weight $w(e) \in \Re^+$. The goal of DTP is to find the $T^* \subset G_0$ such that the total edge

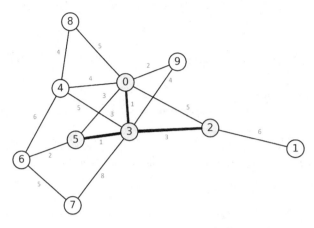

Figure 1.   A graph G and its corresponding DT as highlighted.

weight $\sum_{e \in E_T} w(e)$ is a minimum. The vertices in DT ($\upsilon \in V_T$) are called dominating vertices, otherwise they are non-dominating vertices.

Figure 1 presents a connected, undirected and edge weighted graph G with 10 vertices and 16 edges. Also highlighted in the figure, is the DT of G whose dominating edges involving 4 vertices and 3 edges with a total edge-cost of 5. Note that all nodes in this example is on the DT or is reachable (1 edge) away from the DT. This example lets us a see its practical applicability to different real life networks. The DTP concept is inspired by initial studies on connected dominating sets (Guha & Khuller 1998) which later evolved due to the demands of minimization (Shin, Shen, & Thai 2010; Thai, Tiwari, & Du 2008; Park, Willson, Wang, Thai, Wu, & Farago 2007). This led to the introduction of DTP (Shin, Shen, & Thai 2010; Zhang, Shin, Li, Boyaci, Tiwari, & Thai 2008) on the construction of routing backbones for WSNs. With the generality of network representations, a minimal tree or DT on the graph can serve as a backbone not only for WSNs but also for different networks such as road network, social network or biological networks.

The DT can also be an optimal basis for network improvement; wherein efforts can be focused to dominating nodes and edges rather than allotting on the non-dominating nodes or edges, to significantly improve the network.

From the formal definition, a special case and another related problem can be defined when the weight function is assumed to be uniform. This is known as the Minimum Connected Dominating Set (MCDS) problem (Kutiel 2018).

1.2   *Scale-free network*

The scale-free network is defined as a network whose degree distribution follows a power law distribution such that,

$$p_k \sim k^{-\gamma} \tag{1}$$

where the exponent γ is its degree exponent. A random network can be characterize with a $\gamma > 3$, while a network with exponent value in the range of $2 < \gamma < 3$ is found to be scale-free. Networks of major scientific, technological and societal importance have varying properties that can be approximately generalized of these two types as shown in Fig. 2: a random network (left) or a scale-free network (right). A typical network of interest are random networks and most algorithms are designed based on their properties. Random network especially those planar in nature, represents those network of interest such as wireless sensing routes and road networks. Unlike the heavy-tailed distribution of a scale-free network, the degree distribution of a random network follows an

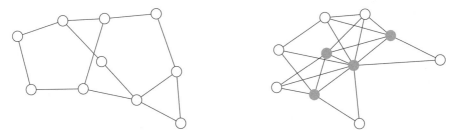

Figure 2. Two types of networks: random (left), and scale-free (right).

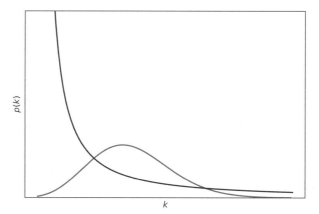

Figure 3. Complex network degree distribution of random and scale-free.

approximately Poisson distribution. This makes the nodes of a random network to be of comparable degrees.

The main difference between a random and a scale-free network can be observed in the tail of the degree distribution (Barabási et al. 2016) shown in Figure 3. Most nodes in a scale-free network are characterized by low degrees. On the other hand, it is consisted by a few number of nodes with a degree that greatly exceeds the average to hold those low degree nodes. In a scale-free network like Figure 2, nodes with higher degree, shown in gray, are called "hubs". One notable example of this network is the World Wide Web network, where nodes are web pages, and the links are urls, to and from that web page. Some other examples are, a biological network (protein interactions), a communication network (emails) and a network characterizing scientific communications (citations). In the recent years, many networks are proven to be of scale-free, thus making them worthy of attention.

2 PRELIMINARIES

Almost all of the heuristic approach for solving DTP does not consider the degree distribution of a graph. Usually the graphs that are considered are a random network and algorithms only consider minimization of edges, by finding the shortest paths.

Moreover, most algorithms for solving DTP of a graph start with the idea behind Kruskal's algorithm, where one computes all shortest paths between nodes before optimizing these shortest path information between nodes. This actually makes sense because of the edge minimization objective of the DTP. Kruskal's algorithm finds an edge of the least possible weight that connects any two trees in the forest to create a minimum-spanning-tree. This ensures that the resulting DT is of the minimum edge-cost.

2.1 Related literatures

As introduced earlier, the DTP has been inspired by the solutions to the dominating set problem (Guha & Khuller 1998; Park, Willson, Wang, Thai, Wu, & Farago 2007) applied to the routing problem of wireless sensor networks (Shin, Shen, & Thai 2010; Thai, Tiwari, & Du 2008; Park, Willson, Wang, Thai, Wu, & Farago 2007; Wan, Alzoubi, & Frieder 2002). Some papers have proposed heuristic algorithms to solve it like the following examples while proving the NP-hardness of this problem as well the inapproximability and proposed approximation algorithm with quasi-polynomial time complexity ($|V|^{O(\log|V|)}$) for the DTP (Singh & Sundar 2017; Shin, Shen, & Thai 2010; Zhang, Shin, Li, Boyaci, Tiwari, & Thai 2008).

2.1.1 Heuristics

Four of the most notable heuristic approach for solving the DTP are briefly summarized by Singh et al. (2017) (Singh & Sundar 2017) on their paper. *Heu_DT*1 (Shin, Shen, & Thai 2010) is done based on active and inactive edge concepts while the more recent heuristics, namely, *Heu_DT*2 (Zhang, Shin, Li, Boyaci, Tiwari, & Thai 2008), *H_DT* (Sundar & Singh 2013), and *M_DT* (Chaurasia & Singh 2016) are tightly based on Kruskal's algorithm. The differences of these heurisitics came from how they utilize the shortest path information computed on each pair of nodes.

On the same paper Singh et al (2017) (Singh & Sundar 2017), introduced a new heuristic *Heu_2C_DTP* (Singh & Sundar 2017) which considers the degree of the nodes. *Heu_2C_DTP* (Singh & Sundar 2017) starts with a similar approach with the Kruskal algorithm; it then considers a minimum edge-weight set and set of vertices covering the given entire graph *G*. Their results showed that this consideration did not degrade the quality of solution.

2.1.2 Other non-heuristics

Other non-heuristic approach has also been studied in solving the DTP. Two swarm intelligence techniques is proposed by Sundar and Singh (Sundar & Singh 2013); by an artificial bee colony algorithm ABC_*DT* and ant colony optimization algorithm ACO_*DT*. Zorica et al. (Dražić, Čangalović, & Kovačević-Vujčić 2017) presented a variable neighborhood search algorithm for the DTP.

Along with the *Heu_2C_DTP* Singh et al. (Singh & Sundar 2017) proposed an artificial bee colony algorithm *ABC_DTP* for the DTP which is different from the existing ABC algorithm in the literature on its two main components: initial solution generation; and determining a neighboring solution. The improvements and differences from the earlier method were observed.

2.2 Proposed algorithm

As introduced earlier, the proposed heuristic algorithm is motivated by the existence of a scale-free network. In this regard, we propose a heuristic approach that is highly dependent with the degree distribution rather than the shortest path. On the other hand, we do not want to compensate that with the the minimization objective of *DTP*.

As such, the idea is to consider shortest path information second, to the degree distribution (first). For a scale-free network, the selection of the highest degree nodes intuitively follows the edge-cost minimization objective as it covers a lot of node that may not be required in the *DT*. Further minimization will be achieved by utilizing the Kruskal's algorithm to the nodes that are proven to be important or "required" to be included in the *DT*, by virtue of its degree information and not solely by shortest distance.

The algorithm is closely related to the *Heu_2C_DTP* algorithm minus the Kruskal's idea as a starting point. The algorithm is expected to behave like *Heu_2C_DTP* for cases that are far from a scale-free network. Since the algorithm is motivated by solving DTP for the specific case of scale-free networks, we would like to call the algorithm as *SF_H_DT*. The pseudocode is as follows:

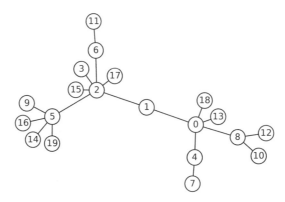

Figure 4. A sample 20-node scale-free network used to illustrate the following phases of the proposed algorithm.

Algorithm 1 Pseudocode for SF_H_DT

    Input: A connected, weighted, and undirected graph, $G(V, E, w)$
    Output: A dominating tree, DT
    $DT \leftarrow \emptyset$, $Required\_Nodes \leftarrow \emptyset$

1: **for** each vertex i in V **do**
2:     $Mark[i] \leftarrow 0$ $\triangleright$ 0 means unmarked, 1 means marked
3:     $degree[i] \leftarrow$ total number of adjacent vertices to i
4:     **if** $degree[i] == 1$ **then**
5:         $u \leftarrow adj[i]$ $\triangleright$ gets node adjacent node to i as u
6:         $Required\_Nodes \leftarrow u$
7: Sort all nodes V in descending order according to degree.
8: Collect top 20% of nodes with the highest degree $\rightarrow$
    $Required\_Nodes$
9: **for** each vertex i in $Required\_Nodes$ **do**
10:     $Mark[i] \leftarrow 1$, $Mark[adj(j)] \leftarrow 1$ $\triangleright$ Mark i, nodes adjacent to i
11: Complete $Required\_Nodes$
12: **while** all vertices in V are not marked **do**
13:     Select a node k that will reach many unmarked nodes
14:     $Required\_Nodes \leftarrow k$, $Mark[k] \leftarrow 1$, $Mark[adj(j)] \leftarrow 1$
15: Do Kruskal's algorithm for U in $Required\_Nodes$
16: **while** all vertices in $Required\_Nodes$ are not marked **do**
17:     Select e_{ij} of minimum cost
18:     Find ST connecting DT and $\{i, j\}$
19:     $DT \leftarrow DT \cup ST \cup \{i, j\}$
20:     **for** each vertex i in ST **do**
21:         $Mark[i] \leftarrow 1$ $\triangleright$ 0 means unmarked, 1 means marked
22:         **for** each vertex v adjacent to i **do**
23:             $Mark[v] \leftarrow 1$
    return DT

2.2.1 *Phase 1*

Determining Required Nodes.

Compute degree of each node v in G. Given the prior knowledge that a node must be at least one node away from the DT, we say that adjacent nodes to nodes with *degree* $== 1$ must be required to be part of the DT.

Sort all nodes V in descending order according to degree. We then collect the top 20% given an assumption that a scale free network will have a degree distribution approximately obeying a Pareto distribution or "80–20" rule. In this case, the Pareto principle states that the connections in

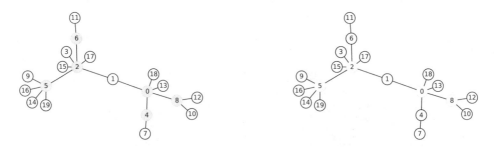

Figure 5.   Three types of required nodes: Blue by having a root node (degree = 1), Yellow by having top-rank degree. Third type (not depicted) is obtained by nodes unreached by this first two types.

the entire network can be attributed to 20% of the nodes. We say that these nodes with ranking at the top of the degree distributions, are required.

All nodes that are required and one node away from this required nodes are marked as "reached".

2.2.2   *Phase 2*
Determining Required Nodes to reach "unreachable" nodes from Phase 1.

All nodes that are not marked as "reached" from Phase 1 will be considered. While all nodes are not reached, we get the set of neighbors of each "unreached" node and select a node that will be able to mark as many "unreached" node as possible. The best node given this criteria is added to the list of required node. If two different node can reach same number of "unreached" node, the choice will be arbitrary. This will iterate until all nodes are reached.

2.2.3   *Phase 3*
Connecting Required nodes by Kruskal's Algorithm.

The results from Phase 2 ensures that all nodes are reachable from the required nodes. We implement a Kruskal's algorithm to those required nodes in G and obtain a DT that will span the whole network.

3   RESULTS AND DISCUSSION

Unlike all the other algorithms that start with the Kruskal's algorithm, the proposed method starts by getting the degree of each nodes. The idea is that because of the definition of a dominating tree, it is actually intuitive to come up with a list of required nodes for the DT, without any prior calculations. These are obtained in Phase 1, just by looking at the degree of each node.

Based on the definition, all nodes must be reachable via the DT at least with one node away from the DT. Given this definition, we can say that all nodes with a degree of 1 actually points us to those nodes that are required to be part of the *DT*. Figure 4 shows a small network with scale-free-like properties.

The first part of the algorithm is quite intuitive. We select those nodes that are adjacent to a node with a degree=1 as a required node in the *DT*. In figure 5, because of the presence of the hubs, and a very small number of nodes. It is easily verifiable that the colored nodes are required to be part of the *DT*. All we have to do is to create the minimum spanning tree that will connect all these required nodes. This verifies that the method can actually solve the *DT* problem logically and with less time than other heuristics, because of minimizing the possible/required nodes to be part of the *DT*. Moreover since the method is closely the same with *HEU_2C_DTP*, we can say that the quality of solution will be around the same quality from this heuristic; which is proven to be better than previous heuristics. Quantitative run time results are shown in Figure 6.

Obviously, this analysis only applies to scale-free networks, and thus we have to discuss its limitation for solving any graph that can possibly be encountered.

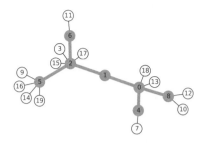 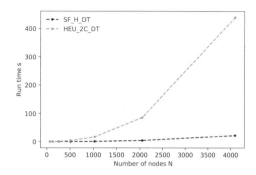

Figure 6.   DTP solution and run time comparison.

3.1   *Limits of Kruskal's Algorithm*

One of the main issues of using Kruskal's Algorithm is its effect on the run time. Obviously, computing the shortest paths for all node combination takes a lot of time and may take a proportional relation to N^2.

Nevertheless, almost all heuristic consider the algorithm for solving the DT. This is quite obvious because it is aligned with the minimization objective of the DT problem. In this regard, it is easy to say that the Kruskal's Algorithm can be the baseline for the quality of our solution.

It is now important to find a way to improve certain use cases of this algorithm. In this paper, it is assumed that for scale-free networks, the properties of the degree distribution is quite helpful to solve such problem.

3.2   *Advantages of SF_H_DT*

The idealization of the SF_H_DT algorithm obviously caters the growing interest in scale-free networks. On the other hand, it is also greatly considered that no loss of generality in the idea of minimizing the total edge weights can be observed with the way the algorithm uses the degree distribution. The minimization of edge weight is assumed to be intrinsic in picking the node with highest number of degree such that, all the edges connected to that node is covered and is surely way of weight minimization. With this in mind, lets look at the two extreme cases of the algorithm.

3.2.1   *Case 1: Scale-free network*
This is the ideal case for the algorithm. We can say that in this specific type of network, the algorithm should work if not better but faster than any other algorithm that has been discussed. One may actually determine a benchmark by characterizing the networks degree distribution. A network with a more prominent scale-free properties should be handled easily by the algorithm.

3.2.2   *Case 2: Random network*
In this case, the differences on the degrees of each node are not really significant. Typically a random network is characterized by an average degree $\langle k \rangle = 2$ to 3 such that, the algorithm converges to almost a random picking of required nodes, since their degrees are almost the same. In Phase 1 it would be most likely that the required nodes to be picked will be almost arbitrary. This will also be the case for the *HEU_2C_DTP* heuristics. The difference will be that *HEU_2C_DTP* has a solid baseline of Kruskal's algorithm that may produce better DT results but will still be obviously slower than our algorithm. Since *SF_H_DT* algorithm also utilizes Kruskal's algorithm for minimization, the quality should not be really that far from the optimal given that the same graph will be used to compute shortest paths. The effects of having to randomly pick the required nodes to the quality of the DT solution is not studied in this paper but should be a good recommendation for a new use case of the Kruskal's algorithm.

4 CONCLUSION

In this paper, we introduce a new heuristic algorithm to solve the dominating tree problem (DTP). Here we consider the idea of scale free network solution such that the algorithm considers the degree distribution of the system rather than only relying on the shortest paths. The algorithm is idealized such that at extreme cases where the network is found out to be scale-free, the algorithm will work better than any other proposed algorithm, and if tested on a random network, which is is the more usual approach, the algorithm converges back to the *HEU_2C_DTP*, which is proven to not degrade the quality of results.

In this paper, we have proposed a new and effective problem-specific heuristic for the DTP, we called SF_H_DT that will produce better results on a set of benchmark instances than existing problem-specific heuristics in the literature, especially for scale-free networks.

4.1 *Recommendation*

One of the limitations of this paper is the assumption of the uniformity of the edge weights $w(e)$ (i.e. length or capacity). An interesting problem which is not really considered even with previous studies of *DT* problem is the effect of the distribution $f(w)$. This is only applicable in this work, as the average and the variance of the edge weights on a hub may have a significant effect on the network. Nonetheless, a better use case of Kruskal's algorithm may be suggested.

ACKNOWLEDGEMENT

H. Adorna is supported by Semirara Mining Corp Professorial Chair for Computer Science and Engineering; the grant from ERDT – DOST project, and an RLC grant from UPD-OVCRD.

The authors also wish to thank Rich Juayong for the stimulating and inspiring discussions.

REFERENCES

Barabási, A.-L. et al. (2016). *Network science*. Cambridge university press.

Chaurasia, S. N. & A. Singh (2016). A hybrid heuristic for dominating tree problem. *Soft Computing 20*(1), 377–397.

Dražić, Z., M. Čangalović, & V. Kovačević-Vujčić (2017). A metaheuristic approach to the dominating tree problem. *Optimization Letters 11*(6), 1155–1167.

Guha, S. & S. Khuller (1998). Approximation algorithms for connected dominating sets. *Algorithmica 20*(4), 374–387.

Kutiel, G. (2018). Hardness results and approximation algorithms for the minimum dominating tree problem. *arXiv preprint arXiv:1802.04498*.

Park, M. A., J. Willson, C. Wang, M. Thai, W. Wu, & A. Farago (2007). A dominating and absorbent set in a wireless ad-hoc network with different transmission ranges. In *Proceedings of the 8th ACM international symposium on Mobile ad hoc networking and computing*, pp. 22–31. ACM.

Shin, I., Y. Shen, & M. T. Thai (2010). On approximation of dominating tree in wireless sensor networks. *Optimization Letters 4*(3), 393–403.

Singh, K. & S. Sundar (2017). Two new heuristics for the dominating tree problem. *Applied Intelligence*, 1–21.

Sundar, S. & A. Singh (2013). New heuristic approaches for the dominating tree problem. *Applied Soft Computing 13*(12), 4695–4703.

Thai, M. T., R. Tiwari, & D.-Z. Du (2008). On construction of virtual backbone in wireless ad hoc networks with unidirectional links. *IEEE Transactions on Mobile Computing 7*(9), 1098–1109.

Wan, P.-J., K. M. Alzoubi, & O. Frieder (2002). Distributed construction of connected dominating set in wireless ad hoc networks. In *INFOCOM 2002. Twenty-First annual joint conference of the IEEE computer and communications societies. Proceedings. IEEE*, Volume 3, pp. 1597–1604. IEEE.

Zhang, N., I. Shin, B. Li, C. Boyaci, R. Tiwari, & M. T. Thai (2008). New approximation for minimum-weight routing backbone in wireless sensor network. In *International Conference on Wireless Algorithms, Systems, and Applications*, pp. 96–108. Springer.

Theory and Practice of Computation – Nishizaki et al. (eds)
© 2019 Taylor & Francis Group, London, ISBN 978-0-367-20417-4

Safe art: A digital artwork plagiarism detector

John Harley C. Bayudan, Felipe Pati Jr., Rowen Edward Slater & Thelma D. Palaoag
University of the Cordilleras, Philippinees

ABSTRACT: The main aim of this research is to study the rise of digital plagiarism, specifically with focus on digital artwork. The problem statement relies on understanding the root cause of this and how this may affect artists in the short term and the long-term. In order to comply with the research objectives, several methods and algorithms were used in creating the application as well as the usage of surveys and tests in order to gauge the usability and accuracy of the application. The challenges faced were met with countermeasures taken from the literature and experience gained by the researchers in creating the proposed system.The application has two main features, of which are a) The applications social media feature, where the user is able to share their digital artwork, send messages to each other and view and follow the art of others, and b) Comparison feature where the user is able to present an image, which the application determines if there is a similar image in the application's database and presenting the user with a percentage of the similarity and highlight of the modifications if a match is found in the database. The algorithms used in the application are a combination of algorithms, namely, HTML Canvas, SSIM index and Hamming Distance to accurately gauge the similarities and differences between two images. Using the application, it was able to accurately determine discrepancies of the two images. Thus, this could be a good way for digital artist to use this application to determine plagiarism on their digital works.

1 INTRODUCTION

The internet had an increase in relevance since its conception, with the internet rapidly making itself a facet of the everyday lives of the public, several different ways of using the internet has been discovered. The internet has opened up communications for the world by giving people the ability to communicate with others anywhere. For an artist, the act of posting and sharing his own art online has become increasingly popular. Online communities on websites such as DeviantArt, Tumblr and Instagram have revitalized the art scene and contributed to the increase of interest in art as a whole. However, the aforementioned positives the web has given to the art community comes with a slew of negatives. A big negative being the prevalence of plagiarism on several works of art being copied, shared online and claimed as created by someone other than the original creator.

Plagiarism is a type of fraud involving the stealing of a person's idea or product, then claiming its contents to be original. Plagiarism is described as the reuse of someone else's previous ideas, work or even words without sufficient attribution to the source (Abdi et al, 2015). To "plagiarize" another person's content is to marginalize the contribution of the original author, disrespecting both the author and the people you are sharing it to, and disrespecting oneself, proving to yourself that you are incapable of creating original content and must then resort to effectively stealing someone else's content.

Plagiarism has become an increasingly serious problem in the academic world. It is aggravated by the easy access to and the ease of cutting and pasting from a wide range of materials available on the internet. It constitutes academic theft – the offender has 'stolen' the work of others and presented the stolen work as if it were his or her own. It goes to the integrity and honesty of a person. It stifles creativity and originality, and defeats the purpose of education. The plagiarism is a widespread and growing problem in the academic process. The traditional manual detection of

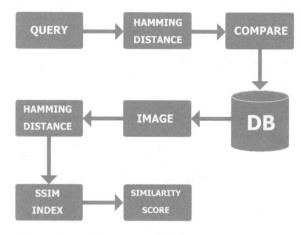

Figure 1.   General architecture of an indexing and retrieval image system.

plagiarism by human is difficult, not accurate, and time consuming process as it is difficult for any person to verify with the existing data. The main purpose of this paper is to present existing tools about in regards with plagiarism detection. Plagiarism detection tools are useful to the academic community to detect plagiarism of others and avoid such unlawful activity (Ramesh et al., 2015).

The researchers have created SafeArt with the objective of providing artists, both professional and amateur, a service tool that would provide the user with a way of finding out or proving that their works have been plagiarized. The researchers also wish to achieve the following objectives: a) to identify the architecture framework needed in the proposed SafeArt: A Digital Artwork Plagiarism Detector Application; b) to identify the features of the proposed SafeArt: A Digital Artwork Plagiarism Detector Application; c) to discuss the process of the algorithm used in the proposed SafeArt: A Digital Artwork Plagiarism Detector Application; and d) to measure the extent of usability of the proposed SafeArt: A Digital Artwork Plagiarism Detector Application.

Figure 1 illustrates the process of the comparison system and the algorithms used during the comparison and in what order.

SafeArt: A Digital Artwork Plagiarism Detector Application; b) to identify the features of the proposed SafeArt: A Digital Artwork Plagiarism Detector Application; c) to discuss the process of the algorithm used in the proposed SafeArt: A Digital Artwork Plagiarism Detector Application; and d) to measure the extent of usability of the proposed SafeArt: A Digital Artwork Plagiarism Detector Application.

2   DISCUSSION OF FINDINGS

2.1   Architecture framework of the proposed application

As a part of the application, the researchers created diagrams for readers to understand the researcher's goals and objectives for the application. The diagrams used to showcase the flow of the processes of the system were efficient and useful in the development of the proposed application.

The researchers implemented the use of two algorithms in determining the factors of comparison between the two images. Hamming distance and SSIM Index.

Hamming distance is a metric expressing the distance between two objects by the number of mismatches among their pairs of variables. The SSIM algorithm is based on the fact that pixels of a natural image demonstrate strong dependencies and these dependencies carry useful information about the structure of a scene. These two algorithms combined results in a comparison system that accurately gauges the differences between two images.

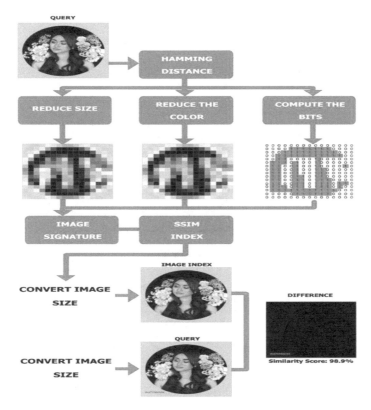

Figure 2.   Illustrates the process in comparing the two image in the comparison system of the application. The picture, once selected is put through the Hamming Distance algorithm, which reduces the size and color and computes the number of pixels in the image. The image signature is then put through the SSIM index which converts the image size to a 16 × 16 format. The image is then compared to an image match found in the database.

Figure 3.   The effect of different filters on SSIM. (a) Original; (b) JPEG compression; (c) Noise; (d) Pixelate; (e) Posterize; (f) Sharpen; (g) Blur.

Distortion	SSIM	Similarity score	Comparison
(a) Original	0.1	100%	Same
(b) JPEG Compression	0.99	99.50%	Same
(c) Noise	0.71	71.10%	Very likely
(d) Pixelate	0.88	88%	Extremely likely
(e) Posterize	0.89	89.20%	Extremely likely
(f) Sharpen	0.91	89.10%	Same
(g) Blur	0.93	93.90%	Same

3 CONCLUSIONS

After answering each objectives of this study, the researchers came up with the following conclusions: a) The diagrams used to showcase the flow of the processes of the system were efficient in the development of the proposed application; b) The features of SafeArt are simple and user-friendly which users who will use the application for the first time will have little difficulty in learning how to use it; c) The algorithms and APIs used in SafeArt are accurate and successful in detecting similarities between two images and; d) The average SUS score of the application is 71.6 with an adjective rating of a good level of extent of usability and is above the average SUS score 68.7.5.

REFERENCES

Ashworth et al., 1997 P. Ashworth, P. Bannister, P. Thorne Guilty in whose eyes? University students' perceptions of cheating and plagiarism in academic work and assessment Studies in Higher Education, 22 (2) (1997), pp. 187–203.

Barrón-Cedeño, A., Vila, M., Martí, M. A., & Rosso, P. (2013). Computational linguistics – association for computational linguistics: Plagiarism meets paraphrasing: Insights for the next generation in automatic plagiarism detection MIT Press.

Gondaliya, T., Tapan P. Gondaliya, Hiren D. Joshi, & Hardik Joshi. (01/01/2014). International journal of computer applications: Source code plagiarism detection 'SCPDet': A review Foundation of Computer Science.

Marsden, R. (2014) The big steal: rise of the plagiarist in the digital age retrieved from https://www.jstor.org/stable/40071543?seq=1#page_scan_tab_contents.

Morago, B., Bui, G., & Duan, Y. (2016). 2D Matching Using Repetitive and Salient Features in Architectural Images. IEEE Transactions on Image Processing, 25(10), 4888–4899. doi:10.1109/tip.2016.2598612

Rani, R., Kumar, R., & Singh, A. P. (2017). An empirical evaluation of translational and rotational invariance of descriptors and the classification of flower dataset. Pattern Analysis and Applications. doi:10.1007/s10044-017-0641-8

Su, S., Ge, H., & Yuan, Y. (09/01/2016). Infrared physics & technology: Kernel-aligned multi-view canonical correlation analysis for image recognition Pergamon. doi:10.1016/j.infrared.2016.08.010

Zanoni, M., Marco Zanoni, Francesca Arcelli Fontana, & Fabio Stella. (05/01/2015). The journal of systems and software: On applying machine learning techniques for design pattern detection Elsevier.

Theory and Practice of Computation – Nishizaki et al. (eds)
© 2019 Taylor & Francis Group, London, ISBN 978-0-367-20417-4

Spatial analysis of voter turnout in Manila

Ma. Christine Camille P. Chua, Ligaya Leah L. Figueroa, Rommel P. Feria,
Ada Angeli D. Cariaga & Ma. Rowena C. Solamo
Department of Computer Science, University of the Philippines, Quezon City, Philippines

ABSTRACT: Political processes, like elections and voting, are inherently spatial by nature. Geography plays a key role in understanding them. This paper employs GIS and spatial statistics to identify and examine the spatial patterns of voter turnout in Manila during the 2013 and 2016 Philippine elections. Choropleth maps, Ripley's k-function, Moran's index and Getis-Ord G_i^* statistic are utilized to analyze the spatial patterns of voter turnout at the barangay level. Initial observations on the turnout data showed that higher turnout rates are found in highly populated areas with a bustling and thriving business sector, while lower turnout rates are found in areas where a lot of government offices, private offices and tourist attractions are located. These observations are found to be consistent with the voter turnout hot spots and cold spots identified by the study. The results show that there are spatial patterns in the voter turnout in Manila, and that these patterns change over time.

Keywords: GIS, spatial autocorrelation, hot spot analysis, Ripley's k-function, Moran's index, Getis-Ord G_i^* statistic, voter turnout, Manila elections

1 INTRODUCTION

The increased availability of data has opened opportunities for detailed spatial analysis of social behavior. The use of geographic information systems (GIS) and spatial analysis tools "has become increasingly common in social science applications" (Ryngnga 2010).

In political science, the potential of GIS is particularly significant. "Politics is, after all, inherently spatial" (Cho and Gimpel 2012). Governing jurisdictions, political institutions, and political representation are defined by "clear geographic boundaries" (Cho and Gimpel 2012) that "individuals [tend to] develop identities based on where they live and the characteristics of these places" (Cho and Gimpel 2012). Incorporating these spatial relationships in the analysis of these institutions and processes provides new insights on why certain behavior and phenomena occur.

In many developed nations like America and Europe, GIS has been used not only as a tool for visualizing data geographically, but as a medium of analysis to produce broader insights about electoral processes and voting behavior. Unfortunately, this has not been the case in many developing countries like the Philippines due to the "lack of accurate and detailed spatial and demographic data" (Mennecke and Jr. 2001). This could be seen in the lack of research regarding the use of GIS as a spatial analysis tool for analyzing voting behavior and turnout.

The objective of this study is to demonstrate how GIS and spatial statistics could be used in determining and analyzing the spatial patterns of voter turnout in the Philippines by using the turnout data from the 2013 and 2016 Manila[1] elections as a case study. The city of Manila was selected for a number of reasons. First is because of the availability and accessibility of spatial

---

[1] Manila is the capital of the Philippines, and its second most populated city.

and non-spatial data. Second is because Manila, as the nation's capital city, is one of the top areas observed during elections due to the large voting population[2] and high turnout rate in the area[3].

2 REVIEW OF RELATED LITERATURE

Elections and voting are an integral part of democracy (Mansley and Demšar 2015). Their study has long been a principal area of interest for researchers and scholars from various disciplines, especially those from the social sciences (Taylor, Combs, and Burger 2016).

Being spatial in nature, elections and voting are "inherently linked to the locations at which they occur" (Mansley and Demšar 2015). Because of this, research on how space affects these social phenomena has continued to grow over the years, with the "rapid development of geographic information systems" (Cho and Gimpel 2012) only bolstering the endeavor.

Among the many topics under study in this growing body of literature is the study of spatial patterns in voting behavior. According to Cutts and Webber (Cutts and Webber 2009), "there is an increasing amount of empirical evidence supporting the proposition that spatial variations in voting patterns exist . . . However, few aggregate analyses that employ regression techniques . . . explicitly take account of spatial effects". They argued that "ignoring spatial effects may well bias results". They demonstrated this in their study of voting patterns and party spending during the 2005 general elections in England and Wales when they found that political party vote shares were spatially autocorrelated, and that regression analysis produced under-predicted or over-predicted results when spatial effects were not accounted for in the analysis, while it improved when they were (Cutts and Webber 2009).

Other studies that examined the spatial autocorrelation of voting patterns include the study conducted by Mcgahee (Jr. 2008) on the Virginia elections from 2003 to 2006, and the study conducted by Eskov (Eskov 2013) on the Canadian general elections from 2006 to 2011. Like Cutts and Webber (Cutts and Webber 2009), Mcgahee (Jr. 2008) and Eskov (Eskov 2013) also investigated spatial patterns in voting behavior using Moran's I statistics, but they did it at different geographic scales. Mcgahee (Jr. 2008) showed that "location and propinquity are key factors which impact voting patterns". On the other hand, Eskov (Eskov 2013) showed that while voting patterns are spatially determined, the level of spatial determinance varies depending on the geographic scale applied.

Besides spatial autocorrelation, research on spatial patterns in voting behavior also involve locating and analyzing areas with high and low clustering (i.e. hot and cold spots). One such study was conducted by Taylor et al. (Taylor, Combs, and Burger 2016) using turnout rates during the 2012 general elections in Omaha, Nebraska. Using the Getis-Ord G_i^* statistic from the hot spot analysis tool in ArcGIS, they were able "to demonstrate statistically significant spatial-clustering of high and low values of voter participation and turnout at the census block-group level . . . in the Omaha metropolitan area" (Taylor, Combs, and Burger 2016).

3 DATA

The study uses two data sets: turnout data from the 2013 and 2016 Manila elections, and spatial data on the 896 barangays in the City of Manila.

---

[2] In 2013, Manila's voting population was 953,382 which was 1.83% of the voting population in the Philippines. In 2016, it's voting population increased to 974,479 and constituted to 1.79% of the voting population in the country.
[3] Manila had a turnout rate of 71.84% in 2013, and 78.46% in 2016.

The turnout data set was obtained from the Philippine Commission on Elections (COMELEC). It contained information on the number of registered voters, number of valid ballots, and voter turnout rates per clustered precinct[4] during the 2013 and 2016 Manila elections.

On the other hand, the spatial data set was obtained from the research conducted by Engr. Ransie Joy A. Apura entitled "Development of a GIS Model for Evaluating Accessibility of Health Care Facilities in the City of Manila". The data set that she provided contained information on the barangay[5], zone and district boundaries of the city.

Initial data processing steps included aggregating the turnout data to barangay level, importing the aggregated turnout data into ArcGIS, joining the aggregated turnout data with the spatial data according to barangay, and exporting the joined data sets as a new layer in ArcGIS.

4 METHODS

To determine the spatial patterns in the turnout data, the study underwent four steps. First, choropleth maps of the 2013 and 2016 turnout rates are created to visualize the spatial distribution of the data. Second, Ripley's k-function is used to determine the threshold distance to be used in the analysis. Third, Moran's index is used to determine whether the data is spatially clustered, random or dispersed. Lastly, Getis-Ord G_i^* statistic is used to determine the areas where high and low clustering are observed.

All four methods are implemented using the spatial statistics tools available in ArcGIS.

4.1 *Choropleth maps*

Choropleth maps are "thematic maps in which areas are distinctly colored or shaded to represent classed values of a particular phenomenon" (Esri 2016). Areal units are colored or shaded in proportion to the values associated to them. This type of map is useful for mapping and visualizing the spatial distribution of a particular phenomenon (Kumar 2003).

4.2 *Ripley's k-function*

Ripley's k-function is "a tool for analyzing completely mapped spatial point process data . . . [It] can be used to summarize a point pattern, test hypotheses about the pattern, estimate parameters and fit models" (Dixon 2002).

Sometimes called the L-function, it is computed using the following equation:

$$L(d) = \sqrt{\frac{A \sum_{i=1}^{n} \sum_{j=1, j \neq i}^{n} k_{i,j}}{\pi n(n-1)}} \tag{1}$$

where d is the distance, n is the total number of features, A is the total area of the features, and $k_{i,j}$ is the weight. The value of the weight depends on whether an edge correction method is applied. Without edge correction, the weight is equal to one when the distance between i and j is less than d, and is equal to zero otherwise (Esri 2017b).

---

[4] According to the COMELEC Resolution No. 10019 promulgated on December 1, 2016, established precincts are to be clustered or grouped to accommodate "the limited number of voting and counting machines, inadequacy/non-availability of public school buildings and other structures which may be used as voting centers, the lack of qualified individuals who shall serve as members of the Special/Board of Election Inspectors (S/BEIs), and the peace and order situation in critical areas identified by the Philippine National Police/ Armed Forces of the Philippines (PNP/AFP)". The clustering or grouping of the precincts shall be "as far as practicable, contiguous and compact and located within the same barangay and voting center".
[5] smallest administrative division in the Philippines.

Its graph shows the range of distances over which "statistically significant clustering or dispersion" (Esri 2017d) could be observed on the values under study.

4.3 Moran's index

Moran's index is "a widely used global index that measures the similarity [of] values in neighboring places from an overall mean value" (Jackson, Huang, Xie, and Tiwari 2010). It is also used for measuring and examining the spatial autocorrelation of a variable (Getis 2008).

Considered as an inferential statistic, its results are "always interpreted within the context of its null hypothesis[6] . . . [which] states that . . . the spatial processes promoting the observed pattern of values is [by] random chance" (Esri 2017c). It is computed using the following equation:

$$I = \frac{n \sum_{i=1}^{n} \sum_{j=1}^{n} w_{i,j} z_i z_j}{S_0 \sum_{i=1}^{n} z_i^2} \tag{2}$$

where z_i is the deviation of an attribute for feature i from its mean ($x_i - \overline{X}$), $w_{i,j}$ is the spatial weight between feature i and j, n is the total number of features, and S_0 is the aggregate of all the spatial weights (where $S_0 = \sum_{i=1}^{n} \sum_{j=1}^{n} w_{i,j}$) (Esri 2017c).

Its significance is then evaluated through its z-score and p-value, which are used to determine the spatial distribution of the observed patterns (Esri 2017c).

Table 1. How to interpret the p-value and z-score of the Moran's Index.

p-value	z-score	Null Hypothesis	Spatial Distribution
not statistically significant	any	accept	random
statistically significant	positive	reject	clustered
statistically significant	negative	reject	dispersed

4.4 Getis-ord G_i^* statistic

Getis-Ord G_i^* statistic is a local spatial autocorrelation index that is commonly used for "discerning cluster structures of high or low concentration" (Manepalli, Bham, and Kandada 2011). It is computed using the following equation:

$$G_i^* = \frac{\sum_{j=1}^{n} w_{i,j} x_j - \overline{X} \sum_{j=1}^{n} w_{i,j}}{S \sqrt{\frac{n \sum_{j=1}^{n} w_{i,j}^2 - (\sum_{j=1}^{n} w_{i,j})^2}{n-1}}} \tag{3}$$

where x_j is the attribute value for feature j, $w_{i,j}$ is the spatial weight between feature i and j, n is the total number of features, $\overline{X}$ is the mean (where $\overline{X} = \frac{\sum_{j=1}^{n} x_j}{n}$), and S is the standard deviation (where $S = \sqrt{\frac{\sum_{j=1}^{n} x_j^2}{n} - \overline{X}^2}$) (Esri 2017a).

The significance of the G_i^* statistic is evaluated through its p-value, since the G_i^* statistic is also considered a z-score. Both values are then used to determine whether a location is a hot spot or a cold spot. This is done for each areal unit in the area under study (Esri 2017a).

---

[6] Complete Spatial Randomness.

Table 2. How to interpret the *p*-value and *z*-score of the Getis-Ord G_i^* statistic.

p-value	*z*-score	Spatial clustering
statistically significant	positive	hot spot
statistically significant	negative	cold spot
not statistically significant	near zero	none

5 RESULTS AND DISCUSSION

5.1 *Spatial distribution of voter turnout*

In order to understand the spatial distribution of voter turnout during the 2013 and 2016 Manila local elections, choropleth maps of the turnout rates during both elections were created.

Both maps show that higher turnout rates during both elections are mostly concentrated at the northwestern and eastern parts of the city, while lower turnout rates are mostly concentrated at the central and southwestern parts of the city.

Although there does not seem to be any significant change in the spatial distribution of the voter turnout from 2013 to 2016, a slight movement of higher turnout rates towards the southeastern part of the city could be observed during the 2016 elections. This is probably because of the new player who took part in the mayoral race during the 2016 elections, but did not take part in it during the 2013 elections. This player is known to have a strong voter base in District 5 and 6, which is located at the southern part of the city.

It should be noted though, that the reasons given above to explain the observed spatial distribution in the data are based on basic knowledge about the area and the major players who took part in the 2013 and 2016 Manila elections. Empirical tests to support these suppositions are beyond the scope of this study, and would need to be further investigated.

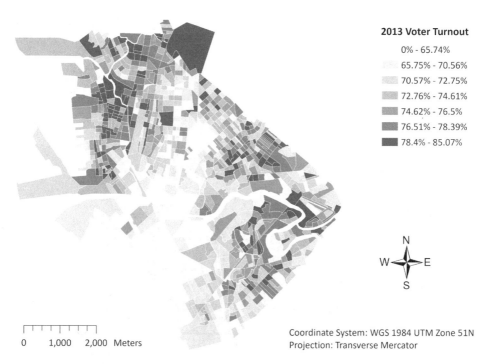

Figure 1. Map of the 2013 voter turnout in Manila.

175

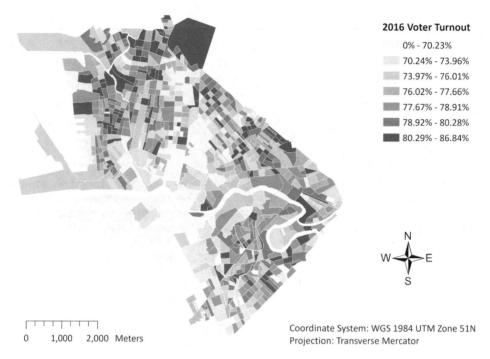

Figure 2.   Map of the 2016 voter turnout in Manila.

5.2 *Spatial clustering pattern of voter turnout*

Using the Ripley's k-function, k-function graphs of the 2013 and 2016 turnout data were created.
Visually, the graphs produced seem almost identical, without much noticeable difference in the shape and position of the k-function. This probably means that there is no significant change in the degree of spatial clustering of voter turnout over a range of distances from 2013 to 2016.

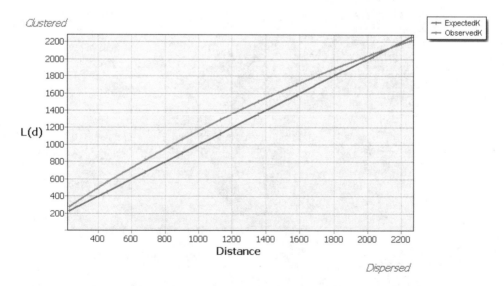

Figure 3. k-function of the 2013 voter turnout in Manila.

176

Figure 4. k-function of the 2016 voter turnout in Manila.

Despite this, the distance where peak clustering is observed, is slightly different for each data set. It is observed to be at 2,060 meters for the 2013 turnout data, and at 2,055 meters for the 2016 turnout data. These distances indicate the threshold over which the spatial clustering observed in the data begins to decrease.

5.3   Spatial autocorrelation of voter turnout

Using the distances where peak clustering was observed as the threshold distance for the analysis, the 2013 and 2016 turnout data were examined for spatial autocorrelation.

Table 3.   Moran's index summary.

Variable	Threshold Distance	Moran's Index	z-score	p-value	Evaluation
2013 Voter Turnout	2,060 m	0.034266	14.715314	0.000000*	clustered
2016 Voter Turnout	2,055 m	0.045010	19.191975	0.000000*	clustered

*p-value is significantly less than 0.01.

The results produced show that the voter turnout during the 2013 and 2016 Manila elections is significantly clustered with less than 1% chance of it being random. This is shown by the statistically significant positive z-score produced by the tool for both turnout data.

Besides this, it could also be observed that the Moran's index and z-score of the 2016 voter turnout is slightly higher than that of the 2013 voter turnout. This means that the voter turnout was more spatially clustered during the 2016 elections compared to the 2013 elections.

5.4   Voter turnout hot spots and cold spots

Applying the same threshold distances that were used in the spatial autocorrelation analysis, hot and cold spot maps of the 2013 and 2016 turnout data were created.

The first map shows that voter turnout hot spots during the 2013 elections are mostly concentrated in the northwestern part of the city, and in a small area northeast of it; while voter turnout cold spots are mostly concentrated in the southwestern part of the city, and in a very small area east of it.

On the other hand, the second map shows that voter turnout hot spots during the 2016 elections are concentrated at the northern and southeastern parts of the city, while voter turnout cold spots are concentrated at the central and southwestern parts of the city.

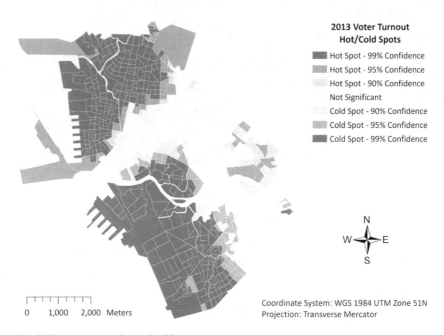

Figure 5.   2013 voter turnout hot and cold spots.

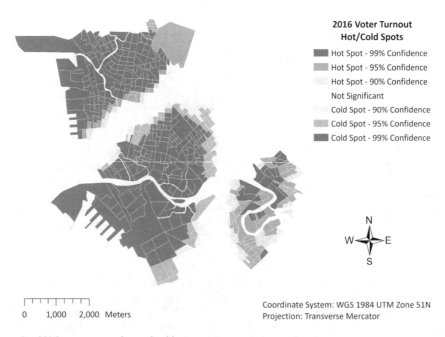

Figure 6.   2016 voter turnout hot and cold spots.

Looking at both maps, a northward and southeastward movement could be observed in the voter turnout hot spots from 2013 to 2016, while a northeastward movement could be observed in the voter turnout cold spots from 2013 to 2016.

The patterns and movement identified above are consistent with the initial observations made on the spatial distribution of the turnout data in Section 5.1. The factors behind them, however, are beyond the scope of this study and would need to be further investigated.

6 CONCLUSION

Building on the methods that were applied in the literature, this study used the spatial statistical tools from ArcGIS to determine and analyze the spatial patterns of voter turnout during the 2013 and 2016 Manila elections.

Initial observation of the spatial distribution of the turnout data from both elections showed that there is no significant change in the spatial distribution of turnout rates from 2013 to 2016, only a slight movement towards the southeast. Similarly, there is not much difference in how spatially clustered the turnout data from both elections were over a range of distances as shown by the shape of their observed k-functions.

Despite these observations, the Moran's indices and z-scores of the turnout data indicate that the voter turnout in Manila was more spatially clustered during the 2016 elections compared to the 2013 elections. Moreover, even though some of the voter turnout hot spots and cold spots are the same for both elections, a significant change or movement could be observed in the pattern and direction of the spatial clustering of high and low turnout rates from 2013 to 2016.

The results show that voter turnout in Manila is indeed spatially determined, and that spatial patterns of voter turnout change over time. However, the results do not explain why voter turnout is more spatially clustered at one area compared to another, or why spatial patterns of voter turnout change over time. To answer these questions, further studies would need to be undertaken. One suggestion is to incorporate demographic and socioeconomic factors along with spatial factors in the analysis, and to use regression techniques to identify the relationship between them. Still, the value of the study lies in its potential utility as the methods demonstrated could be used as a guide or reference for GIS-based analysis of election data at the local and national levels.

Overall, this study showed that GIS and spatial statistics are useful tools in determining and analyzing spatial patterns in voting behavior and turnout. The results produced by these tools provide new insights on the study of these inherently spatial social phenomena.

ACKNOWLEDGEMENTS

The authors would like to thank Engr. Ransie Joy A. Apura for providing the barangay map of the City of Manila, as well as the Philippine Commission on Elections for providing turnout data from the 2013 and 2016 Manila elections.

REFERENCES

Cho, W. K. T. and J. G. Gimpel (2012, March). Geographic information systems and the spatial dimensions of american politics. *Annual Review of Political Science 15*, 443–460.

Cutts, D. and D. J. Webber (2009, September). Voting patterns, party spending and relative location in england and wales. *Regional Studies 44*(6), 735–760.

Dixon, P. M. (2002). Ripley's k function. In A. H. El-Shaarawi and W. W. Piegorsch (Eds.), *Encyclopedia of Environmetrics*, Volume 3, pp. 1796–1803. Chichester: John Wiley & Sons, Ltd.

Eskov, A. (2013, March). Spatial patterns and irregularities of the electoral data: General elections in canada. Master's thesis, NOVA Information Management School, Lisboa, Portugal. Appears in collections: NIMS – MSc Dissertations Geospatial Technologies (Erasmus-Mundus).

Esri (2016). Choropleth map. https://support.esri.com/en/other-resources/gis-dictionary/term/choro pleth%20map.

Esri (2017a). How hot spot analysis (getis-ord gi*) works. http://pro.arcgis.com/en/pro-app/tool-refer ence/spatial-statistics/h-how-hot-spot-analysis-getis-ord-gi-spatial-stati.htm.

Esri (2017b). How multi-distance spatial cluster analysis (ripley's k-function) works. http://pro.arcgis.com/en/ pro-app/tool-reference/spatial-statistics/h-how-multi-distance-spatial-cluster-analysis-ripl.htm.

Esri (2017c). How spatial autocorrelation (global moran's i) works. http://pro.arcgis.com/en/pro-app/tool- reference/spatial-statistics/h-how-spatial-autocorrelation-moran-s-i-spatial-st.htm.

Esri (2017d). Multi-distance spatial cluster analysis (ripley's k function). http://desktop.arcgis.com/en/arcmap/ 10.3/tools/spatial-statistics-toolbox/multi-distance-spatial-cluster-analysis.htm.

Getis, A. (2008, July). A history of the concept of spatial autocorrelation: A geographer's perspective. *Geographical Analysis 40*(3), 297–309.

Jackson, M. C., L. Huang, Q. Xie, and R. C. Tiwari (2010, June). A modified version of moran's i. *International Journal of Health Geographics 9*(1).

Jr., M. T. M. (2008, December). Scale and the interpretation of voting patterns in virginia, 2003-2006. Master's thesis, Virginia Polytechnic Institute and State University, Blacksburg, Virginia.

Kumar, N. (2003, October-December). Mapping spatial and statistical distributions in a choropleth map. *ArcUser*, 48–49.

Manepalli, U. R. R., G. H. Bham, and S. Kandada (2011). Evaluation of hotspots identification using kernel density estimation (k) and getis-ord (g_i^*) on i-630. Submitted to the 3rd International Conference on Road Safety and Simulation at Indianapolis, USA on September 14-16, 2011.

Mansley, E. and U. Demšar (2015, December). Space matters: Geographic variability of electoral turnout determinants in the 2012 london mayoral election. *Electoral Studies 40*, 322–334.

Mennecke, B. E. and L. A. W. Jr. (2001, October). Geographic information systems in developing countries: Issues in data collection, implementation and management. *Journal of Global Information Management 9*(4), 45–55.

Ryngnga, P. (2010). Spatial data analysis: Application of spatial analysis in social sciences and its insinuation. *The International Journal of Interdisciplinary Social Sciences 5*(4), 419–432.

Taylor, K., H. J. Combs, and P. R. Burger (2016, November). A giscience approach to analyzing spatial patterns of voter turnout in omaha, nebraska. *The Geographical Bulletin 57*(2), 99–114.

Theory and Practice of Computation – Nishizaki et al. (eds)
© 2019 Taylor & Francis Group, London, ISBN 978-0-367-20417-4

Performance of serial and parallel processing on online sentiment analysis of fast food restaurants

B. Quijano Jr., M.R. Nabus & L.L. Figueroa
University of the Philippines Diliman, Quezon City, National Capital Region, Republic of the Philippines

ABSTRACT: 'Sentiment analysis has had a rise in popularity as a research field due to social media and the volumes of opinionated data shared through them. Also an emerging trend brought about by big data is the development of database management systems that deviate from the relational DBMS structure, such as the NoSQL DBMSs. This paper investigates the processing of sentiments of opinionated restaurant-related text that are stored in MongoDB, a NoSQL DBMS, and compares them to processing text on OS-managed text files. In connection with this, the paper also discusses the construction of a user interface that displays sentiment analysis in real-time. Results shown by the finished software highlight the faster performance of processing data in MongoDB over text files in searching restaurant-related tweets, especially when querying for multiple restaurants is done in parallel.

1 INTRODUCTION

The opinions of other people are important aspects of human behavior due to the fact that humans tend to consult one another before making decisions. The rise of social media has highlighted the study of opinions like never before, allowing people to consult not only their family and peers but also strangers from public forums and blogs when looking for sentiments on a specific service or topic. This made sentiment analysis more crucial than ever, as public opinion can make or break businesses, industries, and other institutions. Examples of sentiment analysis studies done in the past are on predicting sales performance via blogs (Liu et al. 2007), election prediction using political sentiments (Tumasjan et al. 2010), and using public opinion to forecast box office revenue of movies (Asur & Huberman, 2010). Sentiment analysis was also applied to restaurant reviews, as shown by the studies of Lee & Grafe (2010), Kang et al. (2012), and Govindarajan (2014). These studies attempted to improve the quality of sentiment analysis by introducing sentiment lexicons and/or proposing a different classifier for sentiment analysis.

However, this project aims to study sentiment analysis in connection to the storage system used by the data. After all, another notable trend that emerged due to the advent of social media alongside sentiment analysis is the research of database models that are more suitable to handle huge amounts of data, as exemplified by Google's introduction of Bigtable, a NoSQL DBMS, in 2006 (Chang, 2006). To achieve this, we create a sentiment analysis program that scores restaurant-related tweets on a tweet corpus stored on a NoSQL DBMS, MongoDB to be exact. Inspired by the work of Hellerstein et al. (1997) on a user interface for online aggregation in databases, we also let the program also displays the average sentiment score of tweets in real-time as each tweet is read and scored (if tweet is relevant to the restaurant/s of interest). Then, we compare the classification speed of tweets in MongoDB to the classification speed of tweets in text files.

2 REVIEW OF RELATED LITERATURE

2.1 *Sentiment analysis*

Analysis of people's sentiments and opinions was not an active area of research until the early 2000s. The surge of active research on sentiment analysis (Nasukawa & Yi, 2003), also known as opinion mining (Dave et al. 2003), was due to the massive increase of opinionated data coming from the World Wide Web in particular; examples of these opinionated data are online user reviews of service institutions such as hotels, restaurants, and travel agencies (Pang & Lee, 2008). While processing natural language has extensively made use of non-probabilistic models such as Chomsky Normal Form (Chomsky, 1959) in the past, statistical and probabilistic models such as the bag-of-words model have made a resurgence due to the increased processing power of computers that can be used to handle huge amounts of data (Lee, 2016). The bag-of-words model is the representation of words in a text document as a set of words and their frequencies, regardless of the ordering of the words in that document (Brownlee, 2017). Document classification methods such as the Naive Bayes classification makes use of this model for applications such as spam filtering (Sahami et al. 1998).

Sentiment analysis can make use of the bag-of-words model to analyze the overall sentiment of a document. For example, each word in a document can be given an emotional rating based on a library of words with corresponding emotional ratings; the document's overall sentiment is then based on the sum or average of the ratings of all words in the document. An example of a library that can be used for sentiment analysis is the Affective Norms for English Words (Bradley & Lang, 1999), a set of more than 1000 words with corresponding scores such as valence scores i.e. scores pertaining to how pleasant (or unpleasant) a word is. Using the aforementioned concept, Finn Årup Nielsen analyzed the sentiments of microblogs such as Twitter tweets with a modified ANEW that accounts for Internet slang and acronyms, which he then called AFINN (Nielsen, 2011).

2.2 *MongoDB*

Due to the advent of cloud computing, a movement in database management systems arose, which involved a surge of non-relational DBMSs that focused on availability, horizontal scalability and distribution among remote servers. This group of DBMSs were referred to in 2009 as "NoSQL" (Evans, 2009). NoSQL DBMSs follow the BASE properties, wherein BASE is an acronym for **B**asically **A**vailable (all requests are responded to, but responses may contain inconsistent data), **S**oft state (system may change over time due to system updates for "eventual consistency"), and **E**ventually consistent (data eventually becomes consistent if system is given time to propagate to servers without receiving input) (Meir-Huber, 2011). Examples of NoSQL DBMSs are column-store systems such as Hadoop and Cassandra, document-store systems such as CouchDB and MongoDB, key-value or tuple-store systems such as Amazon's DynamoDB and Redis, and graph DBMSs such as Neo4j.

MongoDB is a document-oriented DBMS that manages "documents" i.e. a set of key-value or key-array pairs that can be semi-structured, unlike records in relational DBMSs. Its documents are stored in a Binary JavaScript Object Notation (BSON) format (MongoDB Inc., 2017), which allows it to store data that make use of the JSON format as is, such as raw data streams provided by Twitter APIs (Twitter Inc., 2017). Previous research studies such as the ones done by Oliveira et al. (2013) and Bing et al. (2014) have used MongoDB to store Twitter data for their sentiment analysis studies on Twitter sentiments and stock price correlation.

3 METHODOLOGY

All of the following steps discussed in the methodology are implemented using the programming language Python and tweets from Stanford's SNAP datasets (Leskovec & Krevl, 2014).

3.1 *Sentiment analysis*

By utilizing the AFINN-111 which contains 2,477 words and phrases as labeled by Finn Årup Nielsen, the sentiment of each tweet is derived. Each word of a given tweet is being checked whether it has a corresponding rate from the AFINN-111 or none. Words that are not found on the list were not considered and not given a score. After getting all the scores of the words in a tweet, we sum them up and divide by their number which yields the mean or the overall sentiment score. All throughout the processing of the data, this computation is performed in every iteration.

3.1.1 Porter stemmer

To maximize the scoring of a tweet, we convert all the letters into lower cases and apply the Porter Stemming algorithm (Porter, 2006) by using the Python package named Natural Language Toolkit or nltk. This strategy basically reduces the inflected words to their word stem or root form. As a result, it can make the scoring more plausible especially since it only depends on the string comparison. For example, if the word "love" has a score 3 from the AFINN-111 and we encounter words such as "loves", "loving" and "loves", the same score will also be assigned. Both words and phrases of AFINN-111 and of each tweet are subjected to this process. The result reduces the AFINN-111 into a smaller amount of words, roughly 60% of the original number.

3.1.2 Randomization of the data

The random retrieval of the tweets is the primary requirement to our assumption for modeling the data as a normal distribution. This would make the computed running average and confidence interval free from bias. As we have two ways of implementation for accessing the data, text file and NoSQL database, we implement the randomization in both ways. In the text file, we randomize the order of the data using Python's library random while in MongoDB, we use the new built-in $sample, a MongoDB aggregation operation for randomly sampling data from the database.

3.1.3 Running mean and confidence interval

At one instance of the process, we retrieve an n number of the tweets. When n is divisible by the user-specified step size, s, it is only when we compute the running average and its confidence interval, and show the results to the user. By default, the step size is 10,000. We use the formula for the running confidence interval from Hellerstein et al. (1997), that is:

$$\epsilon_n = \left(\frac{z_p^2 T_{n,2}(v)}{n} \right)^{\frac{1}{2}}$$

where z_p^2 is the $(p+1)/2$ quantile of distribution, so that the cumulative distribution function $\Phi(z_p) = (p+1)/2$ and $T_{n,2}(\varphi) = (n-1)^{-1} \sum_{i=1}^{n} (\varphi(L_i) - Y_n)^2$ is an estimator of variance σ^2.

We assume the data to be of normal distribution. Consequently, to compute for the inverse cumulative distribution function, the inverse of the normal cumulative distribution or the quantile function is applied. In the implementation, we use the function ppf() from the package scipy.stats to handle this computation.

3.2 System architectures

To make a comparison on the speed of data retrieval, we implement the system into two ways: serial and parallel.

3.2.1 Serial and parallel processes

In a serial process, the fast food restaurant names are run in queue based on the order given by the user. The process for the first fast food restaurant needs to finish before the next one can start. As an option, the user can terminate the process of the current one to proceed to the next one. In a parallel process, the restaurant names are run independently using threads supported by a Python library. This enables the computation of the running average of the sentiments for each restaurant in a parallel way.

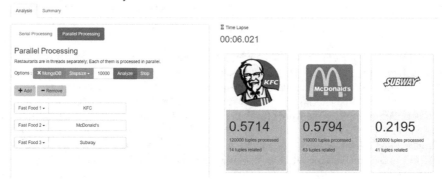

Figure 1.   Average sentiment scores and processing configurations interface.

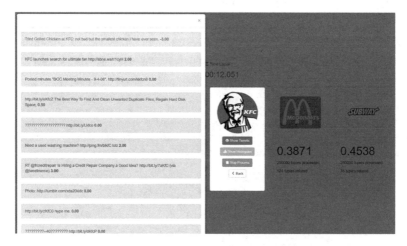

Figure 2.   Tweets mentioning KFC with sentiment scores and color-code, updated in real-time.

3.2.2 *User interface*

The main concept of online aggregation is the ability of the system to show an estimate value without having processed the whole data. This implies that the user needs not to wait for a long time to get a computed value that may serve his purpose. Additionally, the system should be able to allow the user to control the process such as the frequency of update and a way to terminate a process especially in a parallel processing wherein threads are sharing resources. While the process is computing the sentiment of each tweet, we aim to update the user on the value derived from data currently on hand. In this part of the system, we employ Django, a Python web framework that follows MVC model. The user only needs a browser to query the data and see the computed results on the fly. JavaScript plays an important role to send a request from the browser to the server and receive the response the other way. Since the traditional way of requesting data from a server does not suffice for our own purposes because we need a continuous process from the backend side, we employ the use of websocket. Channels allows Django to communicate to the server incessantly. While the backend is still computing the sentiments from a huge amount of data, the communication line with the frontend side remains open to receive any update. Thus, the user gets the online results every time the backend is ready to update.

4 RESULTS AND DISCUSSION

Figure 1 shows sample screenshots of the user interface for the sentiment analysis program. For this project, the browser used for the user interface is Google Chrome.

The performances of serial and parallel processes have been tested with the data both coming from a plain text file and from the MongoDB. We run the experiment of retrieving the data and computing the sentiments many times with the different number of restaurants (which are KFC, McDonald's, Wendy's, Subway, Pizza Hut, and Starbucks); one being the minimum and six being the maximum. To come up with unbiased figures, we took the mean of the time for all the results with respect to the type of architecture and the number of restaurants.

Figure 2 shows a graph comparing the completion times of processes with respect to number of restaurants whose names are searched in the tweets. The graph shows that the serial processes using a text file or MongoDB have a linearly increasing time consumption, because the more restaurants in queue entails the more time is required to process them completely. In contrast, the parallel process shows excellent results both in text file and in MongoDB. For any number of restaurants

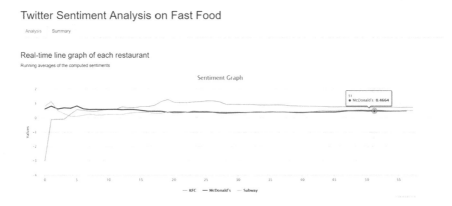

Figure 3. Graphs of sentiment scores over time.

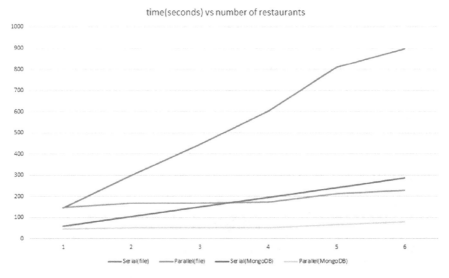

Figure 4. Performances of serial and parallel processing threads.

to be processed, the differences in terms time consumption seem to be negligible as they are being handled independently at the same time.

In both cases, it is worthy to note that the utilization of MongoDB over a plain text file evidently shows an advantage in terms of processing speed.

5 CONCLUSIONS

In this study, we were able to design a program that performs sentiment analysis on restaurant-related tweets and online reporting of average sentiment scores in a user interface. Based from the results of the study, we conclude that:

– Sentiment analysis performed via parallel processing can be done at a near-constant runtime with respect to the number of threads
– Sentiment analysis on data stored in MongoDB is faster than sentiment analysis on data in text files

Should people wish to do more performance tests related to this type of study, we recommend the following:

– Experiment with other types of NoSQL DBMSs, or other types of DBMSs
– Implement additional code within the DBMS to allow it to perform sentiment analysis on its own, instead of relying of a general-purpose programming language to do computations

REFERENCES

Asur, S. & Huberman, B. 2010. Predicting the Future with Social Media. *In Proceedings of the 2010 IEEE/WIC/ACM International Conference on Web Intelligence and Intelligent Agent Technology – Volume 01*. Washington D.C.: IEEE Computer Society

Bing, L. et al. 2014. Public sentiment analysis in Twitter data for prediction of a company's stock price movements. In *2014 IEEE 11th International Conference on e-Business Engineering, pages 232–239.*

Bradley, M. & Lang, P 1999. *Affective norms for English words (ANEW): Instruction manual and affective ratings.*

Brownlee, J. 2017. *A gentle introduction to the bag-of-words model.* https://machinelearningmastery.com/gentle-introduction-bag-words-model/

Chang, F. et al 2006. Bigtable: A Distributed Storage System for Structured Data. In *Proceedings of the 7th USENIX Symposium on Operating Systems Design and Implementation - Volume 7.* Seattle, Washington

Chomsky, N. 1959. On certain formal properties of grammars. *Information and Control, 2(2):137–167.*

Dave, K. 2003. Mining the peanut gallery: opinion extraction and semantic classification of product reviews. In *WWW, pages 519–528.*

Evans, E. 2009. *NoSQL: What's in a name?* http://blog.sym-link.com/2009/10/30/nosql_whats_in_a_name.html

Govindarajan, M. 2014. Sentiment Analysis of Restaurant Reviews using Hybrid Classification Method. In *Proceedings of 2nd IRF International Conference.* Chennai, India

Hellerstein, J. et al. 1997. Online Aggregation, *SIGMOD Rec. 26, 171–182*

Kang, H. et al. 2012. Senti-lexicon and Improved Naive Bayes Algorithms for Sentiment Analysis of Restaurant Reviews. *Expert Syst. Appl. 39, 6000–6010*

Lee, L. 2016. *I'm sorry, Dave. I'm afraid I can't do that: Linguistics, statistics, and artificial intelligence in the big data era.* https://www.youtube.com/watch?v=x7oXHLAE3nc

Lee, M. and Grafe, P. 2010. *Multiclass Sentiment Analysis with Restaurant Reviews.*

Leskovec, J. & Krevl, A. 2014, *SNAP Datasets: Stanford Large Network Dataset Collection.*

Liu, Y. et al. 2007. A Sentiment-aware Model for Predicting Sales Performance Using Blogs. In *Proceedings of the 30th Annual International ACM SIGIR Conference on Research and Development in Information Retrieval,* New York: ACM

Meir-Huber M. 2011. *NoSQL - the trend for databases in the cloud?* http://soa.sys-con.com/node/1615716

MongoDB Inc. 2017. *JSON and BSON.* https://www.mongodb.com/json-and-bson

Nasukawa T. & Yi, J. 2003. Sentiment analysis: Capturing favorability using natural language processing. In *Proceedings of the 2nd International Conference on Knowledge Capture, K-CAP '03, pages 70–77*. New York: ACM

Nielsen, F. 2011. A new ANEW: evaluation of a word list for sentiment analysis in microblogs. *CoRR, abs/1103.2903*.

Oliveira, N. et al. 2013. Some experiments on modeling stock market behavior using investor sentiment analysis and posting volume from Twitter. In *Proceedings of the 3rd International Conference on Web Intelligence, Mining and Semantics, WIMS '13, pages 31:1–31:8*. New York: ACM.

Pang, B. & Lee, L. 2008. Opinion mining and sentiment analysis. *Found. Trends Inf. Retr., 2(1-2):1–135*.

Porter, M. 2006. *The Porter Stemming algorithm*. https://tartarus.org/martin/PorterStemmer/

Sahami, M. et al. 1998. A Bayesian approach to filtering junk E-mail. In *Learning for Text Categorization: Papers from the 1998 Workshop*. Madison, Wisconsin: AAAI Press

Tumasjan, A. et al. 2010. Predicting Elections with Twitter: What 140 Characters Reveal about Political Sentiment. In *The Fourth International AAAI Conference on Weblogs and Social Media*. Washington D.C.: AAAI Press

Twitter Inc. 2017. *Introduction to tweet JSON*. https://developer.twitter.com/en/docs/tweets/data-dictionary/overview/intro-to-tweet-json

Theory and Practice of Computation – Nishizaki et al. (eds)
© 2019 Taylor & Francis Group, London, ISBN 978-0-367-20417-4

Assessing the quantitative description of the accessibility of buildings in the University of the Philippines Diliman (UPD)

J.M. Choa, P.G. Santiago, A.A. Cariaga, R.P. Feria, L.L. Figueroa & R.C. Solamo
Department of Computer Science, University of the Philippines Diliman,
Quezon City, Philippines

ABSTRACT: In this paper, the accuracy of a proposed mathematical function to describe the accessibility of buildings in the University of the Philippines Diliman (UPD) is assessed. A mobile application for indoor building navigation was developed to focus on the independent travel of a physically-impaired user. The application was used to test the results of machine-decided building accessibility classifications against the perceptions of both physically-able and physically-impaired students while navigating academic buildings in UPD. Results indicate that independent travel had to be available for physically-impaired students to consider a nearby building as accessible. The proposed mathematical function had an accuracy of 78.38%. Automated building accessibility evaluations indicate that the buildings of the College of Social Welfare and Development (CSWCD), Institute of Biology, and Institute of Civil Engineering (ICE) have the highest accessibility ratings and are suitable as a venue for the university's annual admission exam.

1 INTRODUCTION

First time visitors of the University of the Philippines Diliman (UPD) experience difficulties navigating through the 21-hectare campus core which contains over 100 academic buildings. Indoor navigation is also difficult because floor maps are not readily available and building entrances or exits are not noticeable. Furthermore, a cursory inspection of most of the older buildings on campus reveal the lack of features to accommodate for the mobility of the physically disabled entering and moving about the buildings. Buildings without these accessibility features restrict the physically impaired from having access to all facilities and utilities within the building, unless they ask for assistance. Though many tools exist to help facilitate mobility and navigate outdoor environments like roads and urban environments, there are few tools to help the physically disabled to move about indoor environments. Recent publications regarding indoor pathfinding have illustrated simple yet effective instruction-based solutions for the elderly and the visually impaired. This paper attempts to compare the classifications of a quantitative definition of accessibility (Choa et al. 2018) against the qualitative observations of physically impaired visitors while navigating through the buildings of UPD. Additionally, the usefulness of the criteria considered in the accessibility function is also assessed.

2 REVIEW OF RELATED LITERATURE

Transport planning, urban planning, and geography have pioneered the term "accessibility," which is defined according to the field of study where it is mentioned (Montague 2010). Past studies and works that attempted to define accessibility did so with regard to distance, but a study in 2003 in Belgium noted the inadequacy of such a criterion and suggested that a more current measure of "mobility and behavior" be used to evaluate the accessibility of outdoor facilities (Chittaro & Burigat 2012). We note that all such definitions are relevant to outdoor open spaces, and it is unclear to what extent this would apply to indoor spaces, although common sense may dictate that it does apply fully.

In the university setting, accessibility is defined as the "ability of persons with disabilities to access fundamental services and benefits from the university system, from admission to graduation, including environment and other benefits of being enrolled in a higher education institution" (Herzele and Wiedemann 2003). This includes the ability to get to the next class on time (Enano 2015). When taken into the context of transportation, accessibility is the degree of available options to reach a certain place (Kim & Ko 2017). In more general settings, both indoors, and outdoors, architects Raymond Lifchez & Cheryl Davis (1987), professors of the University of California, add a dual definition for accessibility: the ability of a person to reach their destination easily and make full use of the establishment's services and resources. Other than a measure of distance and travel, accessibility also encompasses the experience of the traveler making the trip.

The experiences of the people involved in the traveling is tied with the definition of accessibility. The experience of a physically, or even visually, impaired student (henceforth referred to as "impaired students") has little documentation other than the needs that common sense would dictate they would have. While many technologies and techniques have been developed to aid the disabled in navigating their environment, there is not many documentations of the actual experiences and needs of impaired students (Vu 2006). Stefano Burigat & Luca Chittaro (2012) of the University of Udine conducted their own needs assessment investigation on this matter, and found four factors that affected the accessibility of a university building: navigation barriers, navigation knowledge gathering, access to physical and information resources, and specific habits with mobile devices.

In particular, navigation barriers were noted to be architectural features of a building, like stairs, wide open spaces, and lighting. Figuring out an accessible or any route at all is also a problem, as without a neatly made map or people with accurate directions, getting to the next room requires significant effort on the part of the impaired students (Vu 2006). These maps were often packed with information to the detriment of its readability (Vu 2006) or showed only aerial representations and symbols of routes and entrances to the point of being too abstract (Enano 2015). Jessica Vu (2016) of the University of Washington cites the university's efforts to involve impaired students in the creation of building maps, clarifying the physical barriers and all the accessibility information relevant to them. Their unique perspective is required in order to "include the physical geographies of people with disabilities" (Enano 2015).

When speaking of navigation, it is important to realize that path finding, as it applies to outdoor environments, still apply to indoor buildings as well. But multilevel buildings are not the same as the simple planar representation of an outdoor location, as there are now very arbitrary and very necessary separation of different floors (Santana et al. 2014), which, when coupled with navigation barriers, would certainly require the perspective Vu (2006) wrote about in order to properly represent them in visual form or even in audio. This perspective can be further extended to include not just the visual cues, but also the contextual cues of the situation (Jones 1981). Even without an available visual map, verbal instructions can be used as an alternative as long as elements of the situation can be identified, with the added benefit of assisting the visually impaired.

Beyond accessibility features, distance still plays a key factor in determining accessibility in our chosen context. A study done in Portugal found that hospital emergency rooms receive less visits from areas farther away than the urban centers they were placed in (Kapunan et al. 2017). Despite the full range of medical help available at an emergency room, residents would rather visit a smaller or less adequate facility that was closer. In order to accurately assess accessibility for the sake of impaired students, a balance between both architectural features and travel distance needs to be struck.

3 METHODOLOGY

3.1 *Survey on academic buildings*

Physical building features and facilities within each floor were considered in evaluating the buildings' accessibility (Choa et al. 2018). The following building features were selected for the mathematical function: the number of accessible entrances, number of elevators present in the

Figure 1.   A mezzanine in the 2nd floor of Palma Hall.

building, the average accessibility of all floors of that building. While the mathematical function for evaluating the average accessibility of a floor used the following physical features: the presence of stairs on the floor itself (henceforth referred to as a mezzanine), the number of ramps on the floor, the accessibility of all rooms on the floor (determined by the layout and size of the classroom).

Both functions were derived by using matrix algebra, where the measured features were either converted to boolean values of 0 or 1, or simply converted into a count of the number of the specific feature.

Four experiments were conducted on the building floor features, with the final experiment using over 10 combinations of 5 equally and randomly divided partitions of 108 building floors across 37 buildings. Then, using the resulting coefficients of the final experiment, one experiment was conducted on the considered building features on a single, randomly sampled selection of buildings.

The results of these experiments may be found in Tables 1 and 2, respectively. The greater the magnitude of the coefficient, the greater effect it has on the machine's definition of accessibility. Positive values point toward accessibility, and negative values point toward inaccessibility.

Experiment 1 (Building Exp-1) was the initial training function. It was discarded due to its small sample size (37 buildings). It had produced strange implications, such as accessible entrances being a marker for inaccessible buildings.

Experiment 2 (Floor Exp-1) was the initial experiment that used the individual classroom floors (floors that are likeliest to have students all the time) of only some buildings. This function was discarded as it included elevators in the parameters. In retrospect, elevators did not necessarily help with traveling through a single floor.

Experiment 3 (Floor Exp-2) was a refinement of Experiment 2. The elevator parameter was removed and more classroom floor samples were included.

Experiment 4 (Floor Exp-3) included all classroom floors on all buildings.

Experiment 5 (Building Exp-2) was a refinement of Experiment 1, with the results of Experiment 4 used to generate values for the average floor accessibility of each building. Ramps, average room accessibility, and outdoor curb cuts were removed from the training parameters.

A final experiment, Experiment 6, was carried out as an improvement of Experiment 5, adding number of floors and number of ramps connecting floors to the training parameters.

A summary of the results may be found in Tables 1 and 2.

3.2   *Preparation for user testing*

A simple Android application was developed for the use of UPD students, in particular for physically-impaired students. This Android application contains a map viewer built on the OSMAndroid library, where map markers were added to indicate the location of 37 student academic buildings. (OSM stands for OpenStreetMap, a free, editable online world map akin to Google Maps in both function and features.) These markers contain further information about the accessibility of the building, such as a user-readable rating of the classifications produced by the previous

Table 1. Results of Building Experiments – Coefficients.

Parameters	Experiment 1	Experiment 5	Experiment 6
Training acc., err.	1, 0	0.82, 0.18	0.95, 0.05
Testing acc., err.	1, 0	0.67, 0.33	0.93, 0.06
No. of accessible entrances	−0.32	−0.12	−0.05
No. of ramps	−0.09	not used	not used
No. of ramps between floors	not used	not used	0.65
No. of elevators	−0.32	1.87	1.96
Accessibility, each floor	1.12	0.48	0.01
Accessibility, each room	1.05	not used	not used
No. of curb cuts	0.15	not used	not used
No. of floors	not used	not used	−0.08
Linear regression bias	−0.99	−0.89	−0.55

Table 2. Results of Floor Experiments – Coefficients.

Parameters	Experiment 2	Experiment 3	Experiment 4
Training accuracy and error	0.93, 0.70	0.93, 0.07	0.95, 0.05
Testing accuracy and error	0.92, 0.08	0.92, 0.08	0.96, 0.04
Presence of mezzanine	−0.64	−0.53	−0.48
No. of ramps	0.28	0.28	0.07
Accessibility, each room	0.59	0.67	0.85
Linear regression bias	0.27	0.22	0.12

machine learning experiments, as well as physical descriptions of accessibility features available or lacking in the building.

It also contains a path-finding feature for use within one building or between two buildings. As seen in Figure 2, the user must first input four parameters: the origin building and room, and the destination building and room. The application would then return a path from the origin room to an accessible entrance of the origin building, a path from that entrance to the destination room, and a pedestrian route through the streets of the campus. As seen in Figure 3, the latter is a linear path overlaid on the map using GraphHopper Directions API, a reliable and fast web services routing 6, for routing and OSMBonusPack to interact with OSM, while the two former routes are accessed through opening map pointers above the two buildings. These pointers contain user-readable instructions on how to navigate to the destination according to the building selected, as seen in Figure 4.

Since there are no available or obtainable resources regarding the layout of each building to be included in the application, building rooms were surveyed manually. Graph representations of the buildings to be used were constructed in the particular Java implementation of the A* algorithm. Each room, staircase, and notable landmark was represented as a node in the graph, with appropriate adjacency taken as if the node were the origin of a path-finding run. Dijkstra's algorithm, a variant of the A* algorithm, was selected as a balance between optimal path-finding and optimal running time.

The modified A* algorithm behind this feature is the focus of the developed Android application, as finding an appropriate heuristic that will reflect the results of 3 is aimed for. Time was chosen as a heuristic, as this corresponded closely to distance, the usual heuristic of the A* function. Flat surfaces or otherwise accessible features would have a heuristic distance of 1, and staircases would measure 1000 units of time, to force the algorithm to prefer avoiding them. The algorithm does not estimate the remaining distance to destination, as this would not make sense in a 3-D space represented by blocks of rooms separated by the time it takes to travel through them. Again, the goal was not to test the usability of the application, but the path it would return using its path-finding algorithm.

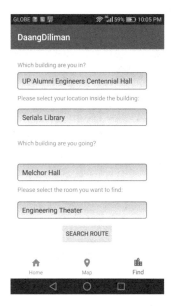

Figure 2.   The Find Route screen, where user selects origin and destination.

Figure 3.   The first result, a map with the recommended walking path overlaid.

3.3   *Testing sessions*

Live testing was conducted with both physically-able and physically-impaired students. Physically-able students were included as a control group, as a reference was needed to compare the answers and

Figure 4. The second result, a set of instructions to follow while inside the (first) building.

comments of the experiment group. After inviting the testers to participate in the testing sessions, the tool was introduced to the testers and a brief description of its purpose and its features were given. During the testing, they were informed of the route that was calculated by the application. After walking the full path, they were asked to fill out a questionnaire, followed by a free-form interview to gather additional comments.

The respondents were asked to rate the following criteria from 1 to 3, with 1 being of the worst quality, 2 being sub-optimal, and 3 being of the best quality:

- Familiarity of route
- Distance traveled
- Convenience of route
- Clarity of route details

The following questions were also asked:

- Do you have any other preferred route other than [the one you just walked]? (Y/N)
- Do you know of any other routes aside from [this one]? (Y/N)
- Were any inconvenience in the route [you just walked] tolerable? (Y/N)
- Do you prefer distance over comfort? (Distance/Comfort)

4 EVALUATION OF SURVEY

4.1 Evaluating the machine training

As seen in Table 3, of 37 accessibility classifications of buildings, 32 were guessed correctly, and 5, incorrectly, giving the matrix algebra function an accuracy of 86.49%.

Table 3. Accessibility ratings made by machine function.

Academic Buildings	Accessibility		Classification by machine	
IEEE	Not accessible	−1.07	Not accessible	Correct
Palma Hall	Not accessible	−1.00	Not accessible	Correct
DMMME	Not accessible	−1.00	Not accessible	Correct
Malcolm Hall	Not accessible	−0.94	Not accessible	Correct
School of Statistics	Not accessible	−0.94	Not accessible	Correct
Department of Computer Science	Not accessible	−0.94	Not accessible	Correct
Institute of Math	Not accessible	−0.93	Not accessible	Correct
Department of Chemical Engineering	Not accessible	−0.93	Not accessible	Correct
National Institute of Physics	Not accessible	−0.89	Not accessible	Correct
Virata Hall	Not accessible	−0.89	Not accessible	Correct
CAL	Not accessible	−0.89	Not accessible	Correct
Gonzalez Hall	Not accessible	−0.88	Not accessible	Correct
SURP	Not accessible	−0.86	Not accessible	Correct
Benitez Hall	Not accessible	−0.86	Not accessible	Correct
NCPAG	Not accessible	−0.85	Not accessible	Correct
School of Economics	Accessible	−0.85	Not accessible	Incorrect
Lagmay Hall	Not accessible	−0.83	Not accessible	Correct
CHK Gym	Not accessible	−0.81	Not accessible	Correct
UP Vanguard	Not accessible	−0.81	Not accessible	Correct
Plaridel Hall	Not accessible	−0.80	Not accessible	Correct
College of Science Library	Not accessible	−0.78	Not accessible	Correct
Abelardo Hall	Not accessible	−0.78	Not accessible	Correct
UP Film Institute	Not accessible	−0.76	Not accessible	Correct
NIMBB	Not accessible	−0.76	Not accessible	Correct
Alonso Hall	Not accessible	−0.69	Not accessible	Correct
Alonso Hall Annex	Accessible	−0.69	Not accessible	Incorrect
College of Fine Arts	Accessible	−0.67	Not accessible	Incorrect
College of Architecture (bldg. 2)	Accessible	−0.08	Not accessible	Incorrect
College of Architecture (bldg. 1)	Accessible	−0.04	Not accessible	Incorrect
SOLAIR	Accessible	0.55	Accessible	Correct
Institute of Biology	Accessible	0.55	Accessible	Correct
Melchor Hall	Accessible	0.93	Accessible	Correct
Law Center	Accessible	1.03	Accessible	Correct
Institute of Civil Engineering	Accessible	1.03	Accessible	Correct
CSWCD	Accessible	1.04	Accessible	Correct
Institute of Chemistry	Accessible	1.12	Accessible	Correct
NIGS	Accessible	1.18	Accessible	Correct

*Buildings whose names were too long were abbreviated.

4.2 Testing

Tests were conducted with 28 physically-able students and 2 wheelchair users. The results of the survey as recorded in the questionnaires can be found in Tables 4–6.

Additionally, the respondents were asked for further comments on their trip. The physically-able students, having done the test as a group, observed that weather conditions affected their comfort in walking outside the buildings. The test was conducted during the summer, so the sun was out, and the summer heat was amplified by it.

12 out of the 28 (43%) physically-able testers had no problem understanding the instructions, while the other 16 (57%) found some problems with the directions they were being led to. This was an error in the relative positioning of the object-oriented representations of the building rooms. However, it is worth noting that the buildings lacked signs that would allow visitors to verify the direction of rooms of interest. The testers would rely on either the application or the directions of

Table 4. Testing survey results of physically-able students, part 1.

Criteria	Worst (1)	Sub-optimal (2)	Best (3)
Familiarity	4	9	15
Distance	4	16	8
Comfort	4	14	10
Clarity	3	13	12

Table 5. Testing survey results of physically-able students, part 2.

Criteria	Yes	No
Other preferences	19	9
Other alternatives	18	10
Tolerable	25	3
Distance or comfort*	19 (Distance)	8 (Comfort)

*1 respondent abstained from choosing an option.

Table 6. Testing survey results of physically-impaired students.

Criteria	Worst (1)	Sub-optimal (2)	Best (3)
Familiarity	0	1	1
Distance	0	0	2
Comfort	0	2	0
Clarity	0	0	2
Other preferences	0	2 no	
Other alternatives	0	2 no	
Tolerable	1 yes	1 no	
Distance or comfort	1 (Distance)	1 (Comfort)	

nearby college staff. They also would rather use Google Maps in navigating through the campus roads.

It was expected that a majority of the respondents would find the PWD-oriented route to be less than optimal, as they were intended to be a control group who could climb stairs. 20 (71%) respondents finding it longer than normal, and 18 (64%) respondents finding it uncomfortable. However, it was not expected that only 4 responded that the quality was the worst. The rest responded that distance (57%) and comfort (50%) were not the worst but still had room for improvement. Perceptions of comfort may have something to do with distance, considering their correlation. Considering the relatively steeper stairs and the fact that 25 (89%) of respondents could tolerate the trip through the route, they may find a more level walk to be more comfortable, regardless of distance.

The 2 wheelchair users noted that UPD, as a whole, is not accessible. Any accessibility features not already built inside buildings was donated by students, rather than provided by the administration; Palma Hall's lobby ramp was paid for by one of the wheelchair user respondents. The lack of accommodation, according to her, for physically-impaired students contributes to the very low PWD population within the student body.

4.3 Analysis and recommendations

The final machine training experiment had an accuracy of 86.49%, predicting 32 of 37 buildings' accessibility ratings correctly. While this would be a good accuracy rate for machine learning techniques, the size of the building samples would be further reduced if further classified according to accessibility. This would have implications for the logistics of assigning venues for the UP College

Admissions Test (UPCAT), since otherwise inconvenient buildings could be chosen as venues, and otherwise convenient buildings will be ignored.

Even though accessibility features exist within and between buildings, the quality of their construction can render them useless. Entrances with ramps may still be inconvenient if they are not level with each other and the road. Curb cuts suffer from the same problem. During his test, one of the two wheelchair respondents, who we shall name as Alex, still had to be assisted in using these accessibility features. This compounded the problem of his wheelchair traveling at slow speeds. Time is still an important factor to consider when traveling in a wheelchair, since these are slower than walking. With the 15 minute grace period in getting to the next class, as mandated by the UPD Student Charter, this may not be as problematic as it should be, but students who have classes in opposite sides of UPD may never arrive to class on time without being driven by car there. Having a car available would require a designated parking slot for physically-impaired students, but none exist in the campus. Even with a car and someone's assistance, there is no guarantee that they would not be marked as late. Unless the university administration allows renovations in the immediate future, the designation of parking slots for physically-impaired students is recommended to ensure that those students can get to faraway classes as fast as possible. With regards to the characteristics used in the experiments, only those that affect the physically impaired are used. How- ever, the route's distance should also be taken into account. This was not considered in the application as it was assumed that only the comfort and independence of the traveler was important in determining a path to take. Weather conditions were also a factor in determining comfort but was not considered when the algorithm was drafted in a time of calm climate conditions.

It is recommended that renovations and additions take place for UPD buildings to include properly constructed accessibility features. For example, Palma Hall has a student-donated ramp for wheelchair users in the main lobby of the building. Plaridel Hall's latest renovation added a proper ramp that is comfortable for wheelchair users to use. However, this does reveal a disconnect in communication between the physically-impaired students and the administration, as these sorts of changes were not even considered initially. Therefore, a heightened priority for the mobility of these students should be insisted upon.

Because few characteristics were used in the experiments, accessibility was accounted for by a single characteristic: average room accessibility and elevators; but this may be too simplistic to serve as a criterion for accessibility. In this case, the inclusion of a statistical study of average proximity of each building to the others is recommended. A suitable measure from that experiment should then be included in the machine training of a matrix-based function.

Upon surveying the 37 academic buildings, a list of buildings recommended for UPCAT examinations is given in Table 3. With over 8000 students taking the exam in UPD, they deserve to be able to access buildings regardless of their physical capabilities. It is apparent that most buildings in the campus are not accessible to PWD so the following buildings are recommended for future UPCAT examinations: the College of Social Work and Community Development (CSWCD), Institute of Biology, and Institute of Civil Engineering. CSWCD proved one of the most accessible building in UPD. It has multiple ramps from its entrance and parking lots. The building is quite spacious that would cater all students well during long lines. Inside, floors can be accessed by ramps and elevator. It is also well ventilated and spacious. The next one is Institute of Biology. It has an accessible entrance and classrooms, which could be used for UPCAT examination, are close to the entrance. The building is well ventilated covered with plants and trees. All floors are connected by a ramp which makes it accessible for PWD students. Finally, the Institute of Civil Engineering is one of the newer buildings in the engineering complex and is quite accessible. On its main entrance, it has a ramp and a spacious walkway. Inside the building is a well ventilated and spacious lobby that is very close to one of the auditoriums. The building also has an elevator. On its back, it has a canteen that would be a great spot for all waiting students and parents/guardians.

According to the Accessibility Law, Educational institutions shall have structural features that would enhance the mobility of disabled persons such as sidewalks, ramps, and railings (Accessibility 1982). On UP System's Master Development Plan (MDP) draft, it was stated that main entrance doorway of buildings should be recessed into the facade and/or located under an arcade or canopy (UP MDP 2014). This feature would provide shelter from rain or excessive sunlight. All the recommended buildings supported these features, following the necessary rules and law.

5 CONCLUSION

After assessing the machine-trained matrix-based function, it was evident that even with a high success rate, the result was not as accurate because proximity to other buildings were not considered. The experiments only ran on physical characteristics of buildings and their floors, but the quality of construction of these building features cannot be disregarded (e.g. accessibility features on the roads, and clear signs and directions for buildings and rooms).

ACKNOWLEDGEMENTS

The authors would like to thank the respondents who took part in their surveys and testing sessions, and for braving the summer heat during the tests.

REFERENCES

Accessibility Law, Batas Pambansa 344. 1982.
Chittaro, L. & Burigat, S. 2012. *Mobile navigation and information services for disabled students in university buildings: A needs assessment investigation.* In MobileHCI '12: Proceedings of the 14th international conference on Human-computer interaction with mobile devices and services. New York: ACM Press.
Choa, J., Santiago, P., Figueroa, L., Feria, R., Solamo, R., & Cariaga, A. 2018. *Quantitative description of the accessibility of buildings in UPD.* Manuscript submitted for publication. University of the Philippines Diliman.
Davis, C. and Lifchez, R. 1987, *Rethinking architecture.* Berkeley: UC Press.
Enano, J.T. 2015. *Padayon U.P. para sa P.W.D.: An investigative study on the admission and accessibility of the University of the Philippines Diliman for persons with disabilities.* Quezon City, National Capital Region (NCR), Philippines: University of the Philippines Diliman.
GraphHopper Directions API Documentation. https://graphhopper.com/api/1/docs/. Accessed 2018-05-23.
Herzele, A.V. & Wiedemann, T. 2003. *A monitoring tool for the provision of accessible and attractive urban green spaces.* Landscape and Urban Planning 63(2): 109-126.
Jones, S.R. 1981. *Accessibility measures: A literature review.* Berkshire, England: Transport and Road Research Laboratory.
Kapunan, J.M., Bunag, M.J., Figueroa, L., Feria, R. & Solamo, R. 2017. *Software architecture of a campus street safety web application.* Unpublished paper. Quezon City, National Capital Region (NCR), Philippines: University of the Philippines Diliman.
Kim, E.Y. & Ko E. 2017. *A vision-based wayfinding system for visually impaired people using situation awareness and activity-based instructions.* Sensors 17(8): 34 pages.
Magna Carta for Persons with Disabilities, Republic Act 7277. 1991.
Montague, K. 2010. *Accessible indoor navigation.* In ASSETS '10: Proceedings of the 12th international ACM SIGACCESS conference on Computers and accessibility. New York: ACM Press. 305-306.
Santana, P., Ramos, P. & Vaz, S. 2014. *Distance effects on the accessibility to emergency departments in Portugal.* SaÃºde e Sociedade 23(4): 1154-1161.
University of the Philippines Charter of 2008, Republic Act No. 9500. 2008.
UP Master Development Plan (MDP) Development Principles and Design Guidelines DRAFT. 2014.
Vu, J. 2006. *A more mobile campus: A proposal for a new mobility map at the University of Washington.* Seattle: University of Washington.

Author index